ISBN: 81-7541-170-8

First Published in India in 2004

Gender Issues—A Road Map to Empowerment

Published by:
SHIPRA PUBLICATIONS
115-A, Vikas Marg, Shakarpur
Delhi-110092, INDIA
Phone: 22458662, 22500954
Fax: 91-11-22458662
E-mail: siprapub@satyam.net.in
www.shiprapublications.com

Laser typesetting by:
Kumar DTP Systems
Delhi-110091

Printed at:
Choudhary Offset Process
Delhi-110051

Dedication

To the woman who thinks
She is and she can

To those men who think
She is and she can

Preface

This is not by any means the first book on empowerment of women. During the last three decades during which the focus of women's development in the third world shifted from welfare to empowerment, there has been considerable literature on the subject. Much of this work concerns policy issues related to gender equality and empowerment, on-going state programmes for empowerment and their evaluation, and those of the non-Government organizations concerned with grass-root level initiatives. Empowerment of women is often considered synonymous with enactment of protective legislative measures to safeguard the interests of women within and outside the household and enactments to enhance opportunities for women to participate in political process, a gender perspective in development thereby providing opportunities for improved access to various social services and expanding non-governmental initiatives to organize women to project their requirements and supporting them with necessary inputs. The implied assumption is that such measures, to use economic jargon, from the supply side automatically lead to social and political empowerment. This book is based on the view, for which there is ample supporting evidence, that this need not always be so in a tradition-bound society, and that it is essential to develop a sense of self-belief and self-confidence among women in general to enable them to seize and benefit from the opportunities provided by the above measures. In a way, organization in groups helps in instilling a sense of confidence even among the individual members of the group and the success of such organization-based initiatives in recent years is a further justification of the view of the authors of this book. The book, therefore, looks at empowerment as a process of self-development instead of mere acquisition of power on transfer by outside forces and initiatives.

The authors wish to express their deep gratitude to various organizations and institutions and individual researchers whose data have been used in the preparation of this book and whose views have been cited in the book at various places. We received valuable assistance from the staff of the Libraries at the Central Secretariat, the

Institute of Applied Manpower Research and the Indian Institute of Public Administration and are grateful to them. We will be remiss in our duty if we do not acknowledge the valuable contribution of Mr. N.K.Chowdhary, educationist and himself author of several books, and who has been a source of strength at all times, for patiently going through the manuscript and offering valuable suggestions which have certainly improved the content of this book.

Thanks are also due to M/s Shipra Publications for providing an excellent get-up and bringing out the book in a short time. It is hoped that the views expressed in this book will make some contribution to the acceleration of the process of empowerment of women.

I Profess...

It is very nice of Shri Rao to have joined me in working on this book and gracious of him to allow me to be the *first author* even though he has all along been my professional senior and mentor for over a decade. I am grateful to him for this gesture of affection for me and his faith in women's empowerment. I also take this opportunity to thank his wife, Mrs. Bharathi, who has had to sacrifice several precious hours of her time with Mr. Rao and cooperate with him in this venture.

At this moment, I fondly remember my late father, Shri B.N.Agrawal, who, as early as in 1930s when women's advancement was rarely, if at all, heard of in ordinary middle class circles, encouraged my mother to develop her talents in diverse fields and become fully educated. I thank all such men who on their own go an additional step forward to facilitate women's development. My mother has several accomplishments to her credit—as a poet, author and as an exponent of classical music, and has always been a source of inspiration to me in my occasional ventures into these fields. At the age of eighty four, she still feels that 'she can' and I believe she is a truly empowered person.

A significant part of this book has been the outcome of my work on women managers under the inspiring guidance of Prof. (Mrs.) Neelima Mishra, Head, Department of Psychology, University of Lucknow. I am grateful to her for her valuable suggestions and helpful supervision that has led to the successful completion of the study.

This work of ours could easily have been a violet that "is born to blush unseen" if our publisher had not willingly come forward and offered to bring out this book. I am thankful to M/s Shipra Publications, Delhi, for lending their usual cooperative hand in bringing out this book in a very short time in spite of their otherwise tight publishing schedule. Their technical staff have, as usual, done an excellent job in producing a book with high quality get-up. I appreciate their excellent effort.

Rashmi Agrawal

How often sitting beside a gurgling stream
I have heard it say
"The mountains were tough and the stones were hard
But I made my way
Down to the planes where parched lands and thirsty throats
Awaited my arrival
I gave them bountiful crops
Running through the turbines
I moved the giant wheels
That gave millions a new life"
Rivers they say are feminine
And so are women
Give them a chance
Let them flow unhindered
A bright new future awaits humanity

Contents

Introduction

"Woman is the companion of the man gifted with equal mental capacities. She has the right to participate in the minutest details of the activities of man, and she has the same right of freedom and liberty as he... By sheer force of vicious custom, eve the most ignorant and worthless men have been enjoying a superiority over women which they do not deserve and ought not to have."

Gandhiji, Young India, 1918

A remarkable feature of the second half of the twentieth century is mankind's effort to atone for the injustice done to one half of its members over centuries. At the beginning of this period, women in most developing countries, and to some extent in some developed countries too, had little say in either the household or in matters relating to the society, enjoyed no freedoms and rights as they are understood now, spent unending hours in hard domestic work which hardly found any recognition, and were generally subservient to men and accepted their lot. There were, however, some undercurrents of dissatisfaction with the prevailing situation leading to movements whose focus varied from time to time emphasizing different aspects of the claims to gender equality. Access to the civil rights of citizenship, especially the rights of married women to civil and economic autonomy, and political rights, especially the right to vote, received attention in the first phase of this struggle in the early decades of the twentieth century, while full and equal access to the labour force was one of the primary claims in the second phase that appeared in the mid-sixties of that century in many countries (Jenson, 2000). This did not, however, mean that by then the objectives of first phase had been achieved in full measure. The struggle for political and civil rights continued in many countries and is still continuing side by side with the struggle for economic independence (Annexures 1 and 2). Many third world countries went through struggles for their independence from colonial rule in the decades that immediately preceded the attainment of freedom around the middle of the century. The leadership of these movements, under the influence of the ideals of equality and human rights, began to involve and organize women as partners in the freedom struggles. The seeds, thus sown, have developed over the second half of the century into a national and international movement of massive proportions for improvement in women's status in all walks of life. Beginning as a benevolent concern of the predominantly male leadership of the world for the extension of the basic human rights enunciated in the Universal Declaration of Human Rights, 1948, to women who were sympathized as the victims of neglect and perhaps abuse, international action transformed itself over the past fifty years into a movement for the empowerment and mainstreaming of women as a necessary pre-requisite for the process of sustainable development itself and as matter of right of the women.

This transformation passed through a series of stages in which different approaches to women's social and economic development, not necessarily at different times, were adopted in the third world countries across the globe. Moser (1989) distinguished between five such approaches: (a) the welfare approach, (b) the equity approach, (c) the anti-poverty approach, (d) the efficiency or instrumental approach, and (e) the empowerment or autonomy approach. The welfare approach prevalent during the fifties and early sixties considered advancement of women as a mere byproduct of general development, in which women remained passive recipients of the benefits of development, an element of welfare assistance thrown in here and there to help those in dire need to survive. In the equity approach, women were considered as active partners in the development process but lagged behind men in having a fair share of the fruits of development, a situation that could be remedied by appropriate measures to provide educational, health and other basic services. During the later seventies, consequent upon the failure of the growth-oriented policies to have trickle-down effects and address the re-distributive aspects, there was a fundamental change in approach to development and a direct attack on poverty was considered essential. This change percolated to strategies for the development of women also. The anti-poverty approach targeted the poorest of the poor women and considered that increasing their access to income generating activities as essential to develop their potential as income earners. In the efficiency approach, women were seen to be under utilized as human resource and the primary concern was to develop their potential by improving access to education, skill and managerial training and integrate them in the development process. The approach, "disregarding the existing role pattern in the society, is based on the premise that women could, without difficulty, perform extra work, and that women's labour has not so far been of benefit to national development"(ILO, 1994). Finally, the empowerment approach that emerged in the seventies takes into account, unlike the other four approaches, the gender gaps in the existing power structure and views enhancement of women's role in decision-making in political, economic, social spheres at various levels as crucial for improving the status of women in the society.

The concept of empowerment itself, though essentially implying the process of enabling sections of people deprived of their rights in some way or another to have a level playing ground with the privileged, is capable of varying interpretations depending on the approach adopted. While it can be considered in a narrow sense taking one aspect at a time, such as economic empowerment, political empowerment or legal empowerment, one can also take a holistic view involving economic, social, cultural, educational and psychological aspects simultaneously. Empowerment in a single area by itself is not likely to lead to true empowerment, which logically requires a holistic approach. Several examples can be cited. A number of middle class women in India have access to higher education but their access to pursuit of gainful activities depends on the whims and fancies of their husbands and elders of their families. Constitutional amendments have reserved decision-making positions in local bodies to women. Nonetheless, they are not always allowed to be effectively in the driving seats and are remote-controlled by men-folk. Access to education and training, employment, role in decision making at home, in the society and in the national affairs at large, etc. are all no doubt important means of achieving empowerment but do not signify empowerment in a real sense. True empowerment comes only when the affected people themselves feel empowered. Development of a positive attitude towards self, higher levels of self-esteem and self-confidence among women is, therefore, the essential ingredient in the process of empowerment. The National Policy on Education (1986 and 1992) has, accordingly, included enhancement of self-esteem and self-confidence of women as an important parameter of empowerment of women. It is this key aspect of empowerment that will be the focal point of the empowerment paradigm proposed in this book.

The struggle for the emancipation initially and empowerment eventually is not confined to one nation or continent. It is a universal movement among all countries cutting across national borders, each country drawing inspiration from the others and benefiting from their experiences. The United Nations system has been and is at the forefront of this movement catalyzing and facilitating its spread through the entire globe through a process of setting international standards to be achieved, and providing technical and other assistance. Chapter 1 outlines this international action in a historical perspective, the goals the international community has set for itself and the extent of progress towards these objectives.

India has a long history, much longer than that of many countries, during which the society's attitudes towards women have fluctuated from admiration and adoration to scorn and ill-treatment. It is believed that in the Vedic times, women were accorded high esteem and had access to knowledge on equal terms with men. Societal values in respect of women degenerated in the subsequent millennia leading to a fairly unacceptable situation by the beginning of the twentieth century. Fired by the zeal of the Independence movement and the dedicated efforts of social reformers, the last hundred years have seen a resurgent India striving for a rectification of the wrongs committed against women over the past several centuries. A survey of the vicissitudes in the status of women over centuries and corrective action initiated in recent times through a series of legislative measures and developmental policies forms the subject of Chapter 2.

The advent of the twenty first century has marked the close of half a century of planned development in the country. Even though the first half of this period witnessed only a couple of women-specific schemes, there has been a greater seriousness with which issues relating to women's development were tackled in the next quarter of a century. In the last two decades, and particularly in the Ninth and the Tenth Five Year Plans, efforts have been intensified and empowerment of women has been enshrined as a specific goal to be pursued in the advancement of the nation. Apart from schemes for education of girl children, health and nutrition schemes, schemes for providing vocational training and employment to women in difficult circumstances and wage and self-employment assistance schemes, large scale programmes for groups of poor women pursuing economic activities and provision of essential inputs like micro-credit to make these activities more productive have been taken up. The latest paradigm of women's development through empowerment is anchored on this process of organizing women. Social mobilization of the unorganized women is considered a pre-requisite as well as complement of economic and political empowerment. It is the women's organizations that, through the activities undertaken and pressures exerted by them, have not only reaped benefits economically and socially for their own members but contributed to shaping national legislations and policies aimed at bettering the lot of women and progressing towards gender equality and empowerment for women at large. Such organisations are of various hues—state-sponsored women's groups for the purpose of implementing poverty alleviation schemes, trade unions of women workers in the organized sector of economic activities, organisations of women pursuing self-employment activities of similar nature, workers' cooperatives, groups initiated by voluntary agencies pushing for advancement of women in various spheres, etc. The objectives of such association could be economic (thrift and credit, marketing, etc.), employment-related (collective bargaining), social (welfare, cultural activities, etc.) and occasionally political. Chapter 3 reviews various on-going schemes for development of women and various models of empowerment through organisation.

What has been the impact of this developmental effort in so far as the situation of women is concerned? Where do Indian women stand today by themselves, in relation to men in the country, and in relation to women elsewhere in the world in matters of enjoyment of social and political rights, in education and health, in employment, in political participation and in decision-making in various spheres of life? Chapter 4 evaluates the available statistical and other evidence in this respect and provides a profile of the current status of women in India and the recent trends.

Chapters 5 and 6 look at the aspects of social orientation and psychological endowments of women in relation to work and, thus, prepare ground for the paradigm of empowerment through self-development delineated in the concluding Chapter of the book. One of the theses often put forward in the context of gender equality in matters of employment and justifying the occupational clustering of women in jobs involving lower levels of skills and responsibility than men is that women are psychologically differently equipped and socially differently oriented, which makes it difficult for the latter to handle occupations involving a high level of stress. Chapter 5 provides a survey of various theories in this regard and brings in additional evidence in the form of the results of a field survey undertaken by the authors, which calls for a change in the process of social orientation of women. Chapter 6 evaluates the results of a study on women in decision-making positions specially conducted by the author on a sample of educated employed women. The study reveals that women are not deficient in characteristics that are necessary in decision-making.

Chapter 7 looks at the concept of empowerment and its diverse aspects—social, economic and political—and suggests a suitable model of empowerment with self development at the centre of the process. As mentioned earlier, a holistic approach towards empowerment is required with over-riding importance attached to development of self-belief. The book concludes with a presentation of a programme for giving a practical shape to and operationalising this model in the Indian context.

I

Towards Empowerment of Women

The Global March

The phenomenon of discrimination against women, overt or covert, intended or otherwise, cuts across geographical boundaries or levels of development. It varies, however, in degree and areas of operation. While the gender bias in the South Asian countries is often deliberately practiced and offends all canons of human rights and dignity, even in highly developed countries gender-based discrimination, perhaps unintended and probably a relic of the past, exists in some areas. Over the last half a century or so, there has been significant concerted global action to promote realization of the principle of equal rights for men and women. The main thrust in this regard has been provided by the United Nations (UN), which, ever since its inception, has spearheaded international action to right the wrongs perpetrated on women over centuries. The Organisation's Charter of 1945 was the first international instrument adopting the principle of equal rights for women as for men. In 1946, The United Nations Commission on the Status of Women was established to promote women's political, economic and social rights. The United Nations Universal Declaration of Human Rights, 1948, spelt out the guidelines of equality and forbids discrimination "of any kind, such as race, sex, colour, language, religion, political and other opinion, national or social origin, property, birth and other status". In 1975, the World Conference of the International Women's Year held in Mexico City adopted the first World Plan of Action and proclaimed 1976 – 85 as the First Decade for Women-Equality, Development and Peace. Marking the beginning of the First Decade, a Voluntary Fund for the UN Decade on Women and the International Research and Training Institute for the Advancement of Women (INSTRAW) were established by the General Assembly in 1976. The progress achieved in the first half of the Decade was reviewed in the World Conference on the UN Decade for Women: Programme of Action for the Second Half of the

UN Decade for Women held in 1980 at Copenhagen. The Voluntary Fund for Women was converted in 1985 as UN Development Fund for Women (UNIFEM), as autonomous organization within United Nations Development Programme (UNDP).

In 1985, the Third UN Conference on Women held at Nairobi adopted the Nairobi Forward-looking Strategies for the Advancement of Women to the Year 2000. The Conference called for equality, women's autonomy and power, recognition of women's unpaid work, improvement in women's paid work, health services and family planning, better educational opportunities and promotion of peace. It set enforcement of laws guaranteeing implementation of women's equality, increase in the expectancy of life of women to at least 65 years in all countries, reduction in maternal mortality, elimination of female illiteracy and expansion of women's employment opportunities as the minimum goals to be achieved by the year 2000. The 1992 UN Conference on Environment and Development held at Rio de Janeiro recognized the key role of women in sustainable development, and in 1994 the International Conference on Population and Development at Cairo visualized empowerment of women an essential and integral part of the development process. The World Summit for Social Development held in Denmark in March 1995 addressed the issues of social integration of women, particularly from the disadvantaged sections of the society, poverty reduction and enhancement of productive employment.

The most recent and important milestone in the international efforts to achieve women's rights is the Fourth World Conference on Women held at Beijing in September1995. The outcome of this Conference, which was attended by 189 countries, was the Beijing Declaration which, *inter alia*, reaffirmed the commitment of the international community to ensure the full implementation of the human rights of women and of the girl child as an inalienable, integral and indivisible part of all human rights and fundamental freedoms; to achieve the full and effective implementation of the Nairobi Forward-looking Strategies; and to further accelerate the process of empowerment and advancement of women. The Declaration emphasized that " women's empowerment and their full participation on the basis of equality in all spheres of society, including participation in the decision-making process and access to power, are fundamental for the advancement of equality, development and peace", and that " equal rights, opportunities and access to resources, equal sharing of responsibilities for the family by men and women, and a harmonious partnership between them are critical to their well-being and that of their families as well as to the consolidation of democracy". The Declaration expressed determination to "ensure women's equal access to economic resources, including land, credit, science and technology, vocational training, information, communication and markets, as a means to further the advancement and empowerment of women and girls".

The Beijing Conference also adopted a Platform for Action as an agenda for women's empowerment aiming at "accelerating the implementation of the Nairobi Forward-looking Strategies for the Advancement of Women, and at removing all the obstacles to women's participation in all spheres of public and private life through a full and equal share in economic, social, cultural and political decision-making. The Platform for Action identified poverty, education and training, health, violence, armed conflict, economy, decision making, institutional mechanisms, human rights, media, environment and the girl-child as the 12 critical areas of concern for women's advancement and empowerment. It considered female education as a priority area and set the target of eliminating gender gaps in primary and secondary education by the year 2005, reducing the female illiteracy through universal access to primary education by the year 2000 and eliminating gender disparities in access to higher education. It placed emphasis on achieving a decline on early marriages and maternal mortality, which have an adverse impact on education and employment of women. The Platform for Action also recognized the importance of the involvement and active participation of women in decision-making at all levels. The Platform for Action outlined the action to be taken by the international community, the national governments, non-government organizations and the private sector to accelerate the achievement of various strategic objectives defined by it.

In June 2000, the United Nations General Assembly convened a Special Session at New York entitled Beijing +5 "Women 2000: Gender Equality, Development and Peace" to review the progress achieved in the implementation of the Beijing Platform for Action adopted five years earlier. Noting the substantial progress made, the Outcome Document of this Special Session Beijing + 5 set new targets which are:

- Closure of the gender gap in primary and secondary education by 2005, and ensuring free, compulsory and universal primary education for both girls and boys by 2015
- Achievement of a 50 per cent improvement in the levels of adult literacy by 2015
- Review of legislation with a view to removing the discriminatory provisions as soon as possible, preferably by 2005

- Universal access to high quality primary health care throughout the life cycle, including sexual and reproductive health care, not later than 2015
- The goal of 50/50 gender balance in all posts in the organizations of the United Nations system, including at the Professional level and above.

Apart from promoting international consensus on the approaches and strategies for advancement of women through conferences, the UN has also adopted a number of Conventions setting standards for action by the national governments to improve the status of women. Some of the important UN Conventions are: (a) Convention for Suppression of the Traffic in Persons and the Exploitation of the Prostitution of Others (1946), (b) Convention on Political Rights of Women (1952), (c) Convention on Nationality of Married Women (1957), (d) Convention Concerning Discrimination in Respect of Employment and Occupation (1960), (e) Convention on Consent to Marriage, Minimum Age for Marriage and Registration of Marriages (1962), and (f) Convention on the Elimination of All Forms of Discrimination against Women (1979) (CEDAW). CEDAW was the culmination of about three and half decades of work by the UN Commission on the Status of Women and is regarded as a 'bill of rights' for women. It is a landmark international instrument drawing world attention to the importance of ensuring for women:

- The right to work being an unalienable fundamental right
- Equal employment opportunities
- The rights to promotion, job security and vocational training and retraining
- Right to equal pay for equal work

The Convention has special provisions for the uplift of rural women, participation in development planning at all levels, access to extension services, organization of self-help groups and cooperation, access to credit and loans, marketing facilities, appropriate technology and equal access to land and other property. About 170 countries (including India) have ratified this Convention. Full text of the Convention is given in Annexure 3.

Over the years, International Labour Organisation (ILO) too has contributed substantially in promoting the rights of women in so far as they fall within the purview of its field of activity. ILO's policies have always had a gender parity perspective on the issue of rights. Inaugurating the International Women's Day on 8 March 1999, the Director General ILO focused on an integrated gender policy that includes appreciation of the "economic and social roles of both men and women and to identify the forces which lead to inequality in different domains. It will involve broadening the focus of attention from the *de jure* achievement of equality of women to the *de facto* results of economic policies, legislative measures and labour market outcomes for different groups of women and men." ILO's integrated approach is based on actions relating to political mainstreaming of women with greater representation in decision-making, technical mainstreaming and institutional mainstreaming. Institutional mainstreaming involves gender sensitive programmes and monitoring systems to enhance employment opportunities for women and technical mainstreaming is weaving gender considerations into ILO's programmes and technical cooperation efforts. ILO included non-discrimination at work place as one of the four Fundamental Rights and Principles at Work along with right to organize and collective bargaining, social security and occupational health and safety.

In so far as women workers are concerned, ILO, through its standard-setting efforts has been striving over the years (a) to guarantee equality of opportunity and treatment in access to training, employment, promotion, organization and decision-making, as well as securing equal conditions of remuneration, benefits, social security and welfare services provided in connection with employment, and (b) to protect women workers especially in relation to conditions of work which may entail risks for maternity. The main Conventions adopted in pursuance of the first of these objectives are: (a) The Convention on Equal Remuneration (No. 100, 1951) and the accompanying Recommendation (No. 90, 1951), (b) The Convention on Discrimination (Employment and Occupation) (No. 111, 1958) and the accompanying Recommendation (No. 111, 1958) and (c) The Convention on Workers with Family Responsibilities (No. 156, 1981) and the accompanying Recommendation (No. 165, 1981). The Equal Remuneration Convention attempts to promote the principle of equal pay (including all payments, in cash and kind) for work of equal value. In particular, the Convention requires that there should be no direct or indirect reference to gender in wage rates, job classifications in collective agreements, payment system, etc. The Convention on Discrimination (Employment and Occupation) calls for elimination of all discrimination, *inter alia*, based on sex, in areas like vocational training, access to employment and terms and conditions of employment. The Convention on Workers with Family Responsibilities is intended to ensure equal opportunities for workers with family responsibilities and others on the one hand and male and female workers with family responsibilities on the other. In pursuance of its second objective of protecting women workers in relation to conditions of work, the ILO has adopted Conventions like: (a) The Maternity Protection Convention (No. 3, 1919) and The Maternity Protection Convention (Revised) (No. 103, 1952), (b) The Underground Work (Women) Convention (No. 45, 1935), and (c) The Night Work (Women) (Revised) Convention (No. 89, 1948). The Maternity Protection Convention requires provision of twelve weeks of maternity leave with financial benefits and medical care through a system of social insurance, no dismissal during the maternity leave, and entitlement to nursing breaks during the working day. The Underground Work (Women) Convention prohibits the employment of women underground in mines. The Night Work (Women) Convention seeks to prohibit the employment of women in industrial undertakings at night. The Night Work Convention (No.171, 1990) considers the issue of working at night without regard to gender. The Maternity Protection Convention (Convention No. 183 of 2000) is the latest adopted by ILO on the subject of maternal safety. Apart from these instruments that specifically benefit women, most ILO standards apply equally to men and women workers. These relate to freedom of association (Conventions No. 87 of 1948 and Convention No. 98 of 1949), employment policy (Convention No. 122, 1964), human resource development (Convention No. 142, 1975), social security (Convention No. 102, 1952) and employment promotion and protection against unemployment (Convention No. 168, 1988). The Home Work Convention (No. 177, 1996), which has special relevance to women, recognizes the rights of home-based workers to treatment equal to that of other workers and sets standards for minimum pay and work conditions for the home-based workers.

What has been the impact of these efforts of the international community on the improvement in the status and the process of empowerment of women? They certainly helped to bring into sharp focus the deplorable situation in many countries as regards the status of women, women's access to rights in various areas like education, health, employment, decision-making in family, society, public and private governance, etc, spurring the national governments into remedial action. They also helped in exchange of country experiences and evolving common strategies to achieve economic and social empowerment of women. Pursuit of gender equality in various spheres of life is now firmly set as one of the goals of the development process in most countries. As summarized by King (2000) " The special session *(Beijing + 5, June 2000)* confirmed that at the global level, Governments, the United Nations system and civil society in the follow up to the Fourth World Conference on Women have achieved much. Governments have taken steps to ensure that the realities of women's lives are more explicitly addressed in planning and policy-making to eradicate poverty. Member States have enacted legislation to comply with human rights and international labour conventions that promote women's economic rights, equal access to economic resources and equality in employment. Significant steps have been taken to achieve progress in girls' education and training at all levels, especially where there was sufficient political commitment and resource allocation. Steps have been taken to improve women's access to health care, including reduction in maternal mortality and introduction of a gender perspective into health care, prevention and treatment of sexually transmitted diseases and greater attention to mental health, occupational hazards and environmental health. Most States emphasized eradication of violence, particularly domestic violence as a national priority area in national crime prevention strategies. Significant efforts to address acts of violence against women during armed conflicts have been made. The statutes and rules of the International Tribunals on the Former Yugoslavia, on Rwanda and on Sierra Leone, and of the Statute of the International Criminal Court reflect this effort, and the first perpetrators have been brought to justice. Provisions guaranteeing the enjoyment of human rights without discrimination on the basis of sex have been included in many Constitutions. Steps have been taken to enact and revise national legislation, including on sexual assault, stalking (UK), harassment and trafficking (EU) to bring it in line with the CEDAW Convention, other international instruments and demands of the Beijing Platform for Action. Women's access to legal remedies often through legal clinics organized by NGOs, such as in India, improved at the national and international levels. A number of countries including those of the Commonwealth have also increased the use of targets and indicators and of special strategies including quotas to increase the participation of women in decision-making until parity is achieved at national, local and community levels."

In spite of these positive gains, however, the situation is nowhere near what is required in several countries. Still a lot needs to be done to come anywhere near the ideal where all women enjoy equal rights and participate equally in the development process as men. The Beijing Conference of 1995 itself highlighted several areas of concern like the persistent and increasing poverty of women (acerbated by the process of globalisation and shrinking employment opportunities during the nineties); gender-based inequalities in access to education and health care; violence against women in the family and society; gender-based inequalities in the economic policies and in all forms of productive activities and in access to resources; inequalities in sharing of power and decision-making at all levels; stereotyping of women and inequalities in access to and participation in all communication media; and persistent discrimination against and isolation of the rights of the girl child. The United Nations (2002) observed that in the seven years since the Beijing Conference:

- The gender gap in enrolment in primary and secondary levels of schooling has been closing. Enrolment has improved more for girls than for boys in regions where girls' enrolment is significantly lower than that of boys. However, it is unlikely that the gap will be fully closed by the year 2005. Even now, nearly two-thirds of the world's illiterates are women. Projections of UNESCO for the year 2025 indicate no decline in gender gap in adult literacy (literacy among those aged 15+);
- While there has been some decline in the incidence of early marriages and early child-bearing in most regions of the world, there have also been exceptions. In 3 out of 5 countries in Southern Asia and 11 out of 30 countries in sub-Saharan Africa for which data are available, at least 30 per cent of young women aged 15 to 19 have been married. While births to young women have declined in some regions, the rates decreased only slowly or remained more or less the same in Southern Asia, sub-Saharan Africa and the developed regions outside Europe. Though there is some decline in the fertility levels in sub-Saharan Africa, the region still has high fertility rates of around 5.4 births per woman;
- Access to reproductive health care is not there for many women. According to estimates made by WHO and UNICEF, women's life-time risk of dying from maternity-related causes is 1 in 16 in Africa against the risk of 1 in 1400 in Europe. WHO also estimated that more than a quarter of all adult women in developing regions of the world have pregnancy-related heart problems;
- Women's participation in the process of governance and leadership has not shown any significant increase since the Beijing Conference. During the first part of the year 2000, only 9 women were heads of state or government. In 1998, only 8 per cent of the world's cabinet ministers were women, compared to 6 per cent in 1994. Sweden is the only country where a majority (55%) of the ministers are women. Women represented only 11 per cent of parliamentarians in the world, slightly higher than the 9 per cent in 1987. Only the Nordic countries and Netherlands are countries in which at least one-third of the parliamentarians are women. In

1999, only 11 to 12 per cent of the corporate officers in the 500 largest corporations in the United States of America were women. In Germany only 1 to 3 per cent of the executive and board directors in the 70,000 largest enterprises were women. Between 1980 and early 1990's women's share in administrative and managerial positions increased in every region of the world (except Southern Asia) but their proportion is still low (14 per cent in sub-Saharan Africa and 9 per cent in Western Asia and 35 per cent in the developed regions outside Europe);

- While the Beijing Platform for Action highlights the potential of the new communication technologies to empower women and to advance their concerns, it has been found that girls are less likely than boys to enroll in mathematics and computer science courses and according to a survey, three men planned careers in computer and information sciences against each woman;
- Although, work participation rates of women have been increasing in the past two decades, and the gender gaps in these rates have been narrowing, the nature of participation continues to be different for men and women. Women have dual roles to perform and they work in occupations and jobs lower in status and less formal than men. Often, women work as unpaid helpers in the family enterprises. Their wages also continue to be lower than those of men. Though there is some evidence to suggest that the gender gap in wages narrowed during the nineties, women's wages in manufacturing industries were 20 to 50 per cent less than those of men in 27 of the 39 countries for which data were available. It is also observed that women are increasingly taking up self-employment activities in non-agricultural micro-enterprises. They also predominate in home-based production activities. However, time-use studies conducted in 7 countries (mainly in the developed countries) between 1995 and 1999 showed that women continue to spend substantially more time on unpaid work than men.

This assessment by the United Nations presents a mixed picture of the achievements and indicates that the road to reach the cherished ideal would be long and arduous. One of the eight Millennium Development Goals set at the UN General Assembly in 2000 (which all the 189 member-states of the UN pledged themselves to achieve by 2015) was to "promote gender equality and empower women". One of the specific targets of this Goal is to "eliminate gender disparities in primary and secondary education, preferably by 2005, and in all levels of education by 2015." In relation to the prospects of achievement of this target, the UN Human Development Report 2002 observes that while in many developing countries, mainly in Latin America, girls have no disadvantage, substantial gender disparities in enrolment exist in South Asia and West, Central and North Africa. In India, for instance, the enrolment ratio in the age group 6 to 14 is 17 percentage points higher for boys than for girls. In 43 countries, including India, male literacy rates are higher than the female rates by at least 15 percentage points. Such disparities lead to situations where 544 million of the world's estimated 854 million illiterate adults are women and 60 per cent of the estimated 113 million children not in school are girls. Recent world trends are, however, encouraging, with 90 countries (accounting for 60 per cent of the world population) having either achieved or on track of achieving gender equality in primary education and more than 80 countries in secondary education by 2015. Apart from gender gaps in education, the Human Development Report 2002 points out that women still earned only around three-fourths as much as men and that domestic violence against women was common in many societies. " And around the world there are an estimated 100 million "missing women" – 50 million in India alone – who would be alive but for infanticide, neglect or sex-selective abortions. A recent survey in India found 10,000 cases of female infanticide a year, and a study of a clinic in Bombay found that 7,999 of the 8,000 aborted foetuses were female" (UNDP, 2002). Another Millennium Goal relating to women calls for "Improving Maternal Health" with a target to reduce maternal mortality rates by three-quarters by 2015. According to Human Development Report, 2002, half a million women die every year as a result of pregnancy and childbirth. While the lifetime chance of dying in pregnancy or child birth is only one in 4,085 in the OECD countries, it is over one in 1000 in all regions of the rest of the world, with sub-Saharan Africa having the highest incidence of one in 13 and South Asia and Middle, East and North Africa following closely with an incidence of 1 in 55. Only 29 per cent of the births in South Asia and 37 per cent in Sub-Saharan Africa are attended by skilled personnel. As regards political participation of women, while in 10 countries (Sweden, Denmark, Finland, Norway, Iceland, Netherlands, Argentina, Germany, Mozambique and South Africa) more than 30 per cent of the parliamentarians are women, the world percentage is only 14 and in 10 countries none of the parliamentarians is a woman. This balance sheet points to the need for further sustained action, the world over, to accelerate the process of empowerment of women and remove the anomalies of the statement that "Women account for more than one half of humanity and they work for nearly two-thirds of the work hours; but they receive only some one-tenth of the world income, and own less than a bare 1 per cent of the world's productive assets" (Ahuja-Patel, 1993).

Assessments of achievements in the area of advancement of women within the countries and international comparisons are based on several indicators. These indicators can broadly be classified as: (a) demographic (sex ratio, life expectancy at birth and child mortality rate), (b) educational (adult literacy and enrolment in primary, secondary and tertiary education, drop out rates), (c) economic activity related (work participation rate, income earned, work time in market and non-market activities), and (d) decision-making (seats held in parliament, number as ministers, legislators, senior officials and managers and professional and technical workers). Apart from these variables which can be measured for both men and women and hence permit direct comparison and yield an easily understood measure of discrimination, there are others which are not so direct but nevertheless have an important bearing on the lives of women such as high levels of fertility and maternal mortality, prevalence of sexually transmitted diseases like AIDS, lack of or inadequate access to sanitation, health services and to safe drinking water and violence (domestic and otherwise). Women bear the brunt, in most cases exclusively, of the ill effects of these phenomena and are, to that extent, deprived of the opportunities for greater participation in activities in other walks of life. One could, therefore, argue that any measurement of gender-related development should include, in addition to indicators of direct discrimination, measures of fertility, maternal mortality, crimes in which women are the victims including domestic violence, prevalence of sexually transmitted diseases and other relevant variables. Data availability constraints would no doubt inhibit such exercises particularly when one attempts international comparisons, but some attempts have indeed been made to broaden the base of relative evaluation of gender development among countries. For instance, Ahooja Patel (1993) constructed an 'Index of Women's Advancement' based on seven gender relevant variables, viz., real GDP per capita adjusted for purchasing power parity, maternal mortality rate, infant mortality rate, female life expectancy at birth, female enrolment in post secondary education, share of females in labour force and share of females in parliament and made a comparison of the situation in 108 developing countries. Another example of attempts to develop measures of gender-related development is that of Patel (1999), which took into account 18 gender relevant indicators (life expectancy, under-5 mortality rate, adult literacy rate, enrolment in primary, secondary and tertiary education, representation in parliament, access to safe water, access to sanitation, access to health services, maternal mortality rate, percentage of births attended by trained personnel, pregnant women immunized for tetanus, prevalence of contraception and women exposed to FGM). As mentioned earlier non-availability of comparable statistics would be a major obstacle to these exercises apart from methodological issues. It may be mentioned in this connection that one of the aspects emphasized at the Beijing Conference was the importance of generating gender specific statistics on various variables.

The most-often cited combined indicators providing an absolute and relative measure of advancement of women in different countries are the Gender-related Development Index (GDI) and the Gender Empowerment Measure (GEM) developed and released for some years now by the United Nations Development Programme (UNDP) along with its Human Development Index (HDI). The GDI combines the achievements of each country in the areas of life expectancy, literacy and gross enrolment, and per capita income adjusted for Purchasing Power Parity (PPP), the same variables as are included in the HDI, but taking into account the disparity in achievement between men and women. The GEM also measures gender inequality, but in economic and political decision-making areas, measured by the percentage of female administrators and managers and professional and technical workers and the percentage of seats in parliament held by women respectively. Data constraints allowed UNDP to compute GDI for146 countries and GEM for 66 countries out of the 173 countries for which HDI 2000 was computed. As per the Human Development Report 2002, out of the 146 countries for which GDI could be presented, 21 countries had a GDI of 0.900 or more, 43 countries with GDI of 0.750 to 0.899, 51 with GDI of 0.500 to 0.749 and 31 with GDI of less than 0.500. In the year 2000, about one fifth of the world population (restricted to the 146 countries covered in the GDI) is in countries of the first category and over two-thirds in the last two categories.

Percentage of World Population by GDI, 2000

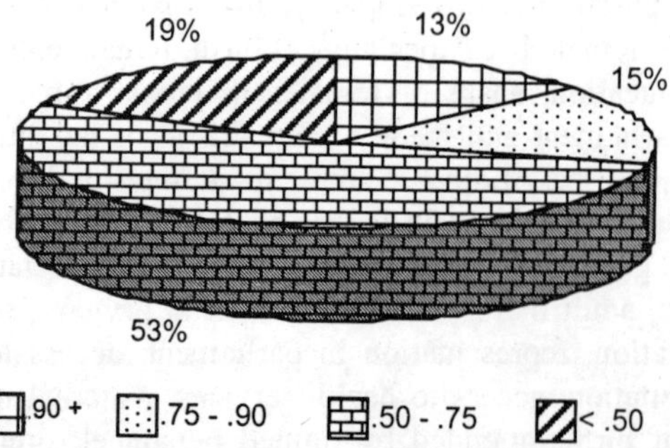

We may now look at the position of gender differentials in some of the relatively large and populous countries of the world. Tables 1.1 to 1.7 provide relevant indicators for 23 countries with an estimated population of 50 million or more in the year 2002 listed in the order of their HDI for 2000 in the Human Development Report, 2002. Of the 23 countries listed in the Tables 1.1 to 1.7, GDI is available for all the 23 while GEM is available only for 12, a notable exception being France. Some inferences that emerge out of these tables are:

- GDI ranking of countries (and for that matter HDI ranking) has very strong correlation with GDP per capita PPP but there are exceptions. Vietnam with a GDP per capita lower than India, Indonesia and Egypt has a higher GDI ranking (and HDI);
- GDI ranking of countries is generally in line with HDI ranking (Table 1.1). While this is logical, it is not an absolute certainty. It is theoretically possible that a country's high human development level may be so high as could hide the relatively lower achievement on the gender front;
- GEM ranking does exhibit some interesting features (Table 1.1). For example, Philippines, ranked lower than Mexico, Russian Federation and Thailand in HDI and GDI, has a higher GEM than these countries, obviously due to the substantially higher level of representation of women in parliament and among legislators, senior officials and managers as well as professional workers in Philippines (Table 1.7);
- All the developed countries and some not so developed (Vietnam, Democratic Republic of Congo and Ethiopia) have a sex ratio (number of females per 1000 males) of over 1000, with the Russian Federation topping the list with a ratio of 1139 (Table 1.2). In China and the South Asian countries, the ratio is less than 950;
- Expectation of life at birth for females varies substantially across countries from over 80 years in USA to 44 in Ethiopia (Table 1.2). However, there is near parity today between the two sexes in so far as this variable is concerned. In most countries, developed as well as developing, female expectation of life at birth is now higher than that for males, with China topping the list;
- Very high total fertility rates (over 3) still prevail in Pakistan, Bangladesh, Nigeria, Democratic Republic of Congo and Ethiopia as well as Philippines (Table 1.2). In Pakistan, Nigeria, Democratic Republic of Congo and Ethiopia the rate is in excess of 5. While the developed countries have very low maternal mortality rates of 10 to 20 per 100,000 live births and some developing countries like Mexico, Thailand, Turkey, China and Vietnam have

rates less than 100, some of the African countries like Nigeria, Democratic Republic of Congo and Ethiopia have shockingly high rates of around or over 1,000 maternal deaths per 100,000 live births (Table 1.3). The rates are also relatively high (ranging from 200 in Pakistan to 600 in Bangladesh) in the South Asian region as well as Philippines and Brazil;

- Countries in South Asia also have high child mortality rates (Table 1.3). What is shocking in so far as gender parity is concerned is the fact that 42 female children in the age group 1 to 4 years die every year per 1,000 population in India[1], while the corresponding number for male children is 29. The rates are high in Bangladesh also at around 15 but there is practically no gender difference;
- As in the case health related indicators, South Asian countries fare very poorly in relation to adult (15+) literacy rates (Table 1.4). The absolute rates for females vary from less than 30 in Pakistan and Bangladesh to 45 in India. Moreover, the rates for females in these countries are one half to two-thirds of the rates for males. In contrast, countries like Thailand, Vietnam and Philippines have near total adult literacy levels both for males and females;
- While there is near gender parity in net primary school enrolment in most countries for which data are available, countries in Africa are exceptions, female enrolment rate being only one third of the rate for males in Democratic Republic of Congo and two-fifths of it in Ethiopia (Table 1.5). At the secondary level, the situation is different and, even in the developed world (except USA), the net enrolment rate for females is about 90 per cent of the rate for males. In most of the less developed countries the rate for females is only one half of that for males;
- Female economic activity participation rates range between 35 to 60 per cent in most countries (Table 1.6). Thailand, China and Vietnam have exceptionally high female participation rates in excess of 70 per cent. The rates have generally been increasing during the nineties. Females constitute the majority of the unpaid workers contributing to household economic activities, in the developed as well as the developing countries (82 per cent in Japan, 75 per cent in Germany, 66 per cent in Thailand and 74 per cent in Bangladesh);
- The estimated income of females workers is around 40 to 60 per cent of the income of male workers (Table 1.6);
- Among the 23 countries listed in these tables, Germany has the highest (31 per cent) female representation in Parliament, followed by China (22 per cent) (Table 1.7). Even in the USA, only 14 per

cent of the parliamentarians are females, less than in UK, Mexico and Philippines. The percentage of females among the legislators, senior officials and managers is in most cases less than or around one-third and is as low than 10 per cent or low in Pakistan, Bangladesh, India and surprisingly Japan as well.

Table 1.1: Per Capita Income and Human Development, Gender Development and Gender Empowerment Indices for Selected Countries

Country	*GDP per Capita PPP (US$) in 2000*	*HDI Rank 2000*	*GDI Rank 2000*	*GEM Rank 2000*
1. USA	34,142	6	6	11
2. Japan	26,755	9	11	12
3. France	24,223	12	12	—
4. United Kingdom	23,509	13	10	16
5. Germany	25,103	17	16	8
6. Italy	23,626	20	20	31
7. Mexico	9,023	54	49	38
8. Russian Federation	8,377	60	52	53
9. Thailand	6,402	70	60	50
10. Brazil	7,625	73	64	—
11. Philippines	3,971	77	63	35
12. Turkey	6,974	85	71	63
13. China	3,976	96	77	—
14. Iran	5,884	98	83	—
15. Vietnam	1,996	109	89	—
16. Indonesia	3,043	110	91	—
17. Egypt	3,635	115	99	65
18. India	2,358	124	105	—*
19. Pakistan	1,928	138	120	—
20. Bangladesh	1,602	145	121	66
21. Nigeria	896	148	124	—
22. Congo (Dem. Rep. of)	765	155	131	—
23. Ethiopia	668	168	142	—

Source: UNDP Human Development Report 2002

Notes: GDP per Capita PPP is GDP per Capita adjusted for purchasing power

HDI is Human Development Index calculated for 173 countries

GDI is Gender Development Index calculated for 146 countries

GEM is Gender Empowerment Measure calculated for 66 countries

* India ranked 95 according to Human Development Report, 1998

Table 1.2: Gender Parity—Demographic and Health Indicators for Selected Countries

Country	Estimated population (millions) in 2002	Sex-Ratio (No. of females per1000 males) in 2002	Expectation of Life at Birth (years) (2000-05)		Total Fertility Rate 2000-05
			Female	% of females' to males' life expectancy	
1. USA	288.5	1,028	80.4	107.8	1.93
2. Japan	127.5	1,045	85.0	109.2	1.33
3. France	59.7	1,053	82.0	109.0	1.80
4. United Kingdom	59.7	1,029	80.7	106.6	1.61
5. Germany	82.0	1,039	81.1	108.1	1.29
6. Italy	57.5	1,062	81.0	108.5	1.20
7. Mexico	101.8	1,022	76.4	108.5	2.49
8. Russian Federation	143.8	1,139	72.5	120.8	1.14
9. Thailand	64.3	1,022	73.8	108.7	2.00
10. Brazil	174.7	1,027	72.6	112.2	2.15
11. Philippines	78.6	986	72.0	105.9	3.24
12. Turkey	68.6	981	73.2	107.6	2.30
13. China	1,294.4	946	73.5	122.3	1.80
14. Iran	72.4	956	70.8	102.9	2.76
15. Vietnam	80.2	1,007	71.6	107.0	2.25
16. Indonesia	217.5	994	69.3	106.1	2.27
17. Egypt	70.3	976	69.9	104.8	2.88
18. India	1,041.1	940	64.9	102.0	2.97
19. Pakistan	148.7	948	60.9	99.5	5.08
20. Bangladesh	143.4	941	60.8	100.3	3.56
21. Nigeria	120.0	983	52.2	100.5	5.42
22. Congo (Dem. Rep. of)	54.3	1,016	53.5	104.9	6.70
23. Ethiopia	66.0	1,010	43.6	102.3	6.75

Source: Based on data from U.N. Population Division, World Population Prospects, The 2002 Revision, Volume I: Comprehensive Tables.

Table 1.3: Demographic and Health Indicators for Selected Countries

Country	Estimated Maternal Mortality Ratio@ around 1995	Child Mortality Rate*		
		Year	Male	Female
(1)	(2)	(3)	(4)	(5)
1. USA	12	1998	0.4	0.3
2. Japan	12	1998	0.4	0.3

Contd.

(1)	*(2)*	*(3)*	*(4)*	*(5)*
3. France	20	1993	0.4	0.3
4. United Kingdom	10	1997	0.3	0.2
5. Germany	12	1996	0.3	0.3
6. Italy	11	1994	0.3	0.3
7. Mexico	65	—	—	—
8. Russian Federation	75	1995	1.2	0.9
9. Thailand	44	—	—	—
10. Brazil	250	1995	1.2	1.0
11. Philippines	240	1991	2.8	2.5
12. Turkey	55	—	—	—
13. China	60	—	—	—
14. Iran	130	1991	5.1	3.9
15. Vietnam	95	—	—	—
16. Indonesia	470	—	—	—
17. Egypt	170	1995	2.8	3.0
18. India	440	1992-93	29.4	42.0
19. Pakistan	200	—	—	—
20. Bangladesh	600	1990	14.2	15.7
21. Nigeria	1100	—	—	—
22. Congo (Dem. Rep. of)	940	—	—	—
23. Ethiopia	1800	—	—	—

Source: Maternal Mortality Ratios are the estimates developed by WHO, UNICEF and UNFPA, reproduced by United Nations Statistics Division, Demographic, Social and Housing Statistics.

@ Number of maternal deaths per 100,000 live births.

* Annual number of deaths in the age group 1 to 4 years per 1000 population.

Table 1. 4 Gender Parity—Educational Indicators for Selected Countries

Country	*Adult (15+) Literacy Rate (2000)*			*Combined primary, secondary and tertiary education Gross Enrolment Ratio (1999)*		
	Male	*Female*	*% of female rate to male rate*	*Male*	*Female*	*% of female rate to male rate*
(1)	*(2)*	*(3)*	*(4)*	*(5)*	*(6)*	*(7)*
1. USA*	99.9	99.9	100.0	91	99	108.8
2. Japan*	99.9	99.9	100.0	83	81	97.6
3. France*	99.9	99.9	100.0	93	96	103.2
4. United Kingdom*	99.9	99.9	100.0	100	112	112.1
5. Germany*	99.9	99.9	100.0	95	93	97.9

Contd.

(1)	(2)	(3)	(4)	(5)	(6)	(7)
6. Italy	98.9	98.0	99.1	81	87	107.4
7. Mexico	93.4	89.5	95.8	71	70	98.6
8. Russian Federation	99.7	99.4	99.7	75	82	109.3
9. Thailand	97.1	93.9	96.7	60	61	101.7
10. Brazil	85.1	85.4	100.4	79	80	101.3
11. Philippines	95.5	95.1	99.6	80	84	105.0
12. Turkey	93.5	76.5	81.8	68	55	80.9
13. China	91.7	76.3	83.2	73	73	100.0
14. Iran	83.2	69.3	83.3	76	69	90.8
15. Vietnam	95.5	91.4	95.7	69	64	92.8
16. Indonesia	91.8	82.0	89.3	68	61	89.7
17. Egypt	66.6	43.8	65.8	80	72	90.0
18. India	68.4	45.4	66.4	62	49	79.0
19. Pakistan	57.5	27.9	48.5	51	28	54.9
20. Bangladesh	52.3	29.9	57.2	41	33	80.5
21. Nigeria	72.4	55.7	76.9	49	41	83.7
22. Congo (Dem. Rep. of)	73.1	50.2	68.7	37	26	70.3
23. Ethiopia	47.2	30.9	65.5	34	19	55.9

Source: Human Development Report, 2002, UNDP

* Rates taken as 99.9 for both males and females by UNDP for HDI and GDI

Table 1.5: Gender Parity - Educational Indicators for Selected Countries

Country	*Net Primary Enrolment (percentage) (2000)*			*Net Secondary Enrolment (percentage) (2000)*		
	Male	*Female*	*% of female rate to male rate*	*Male*	*Female*	*% of female rate to male rate*
(1)	*(2)*	*(3)*	*(4)*	*(5)*	*(6)*	*(7)*
1. USA	100	95	95	73	76	104
2. Japan	100	100	100	—	—	—
3. France	100	100	100	102	95	93
4. United Kingdom	101	100	99	103	95	92
5. Germany	102	88	86	101	88	87
6. Italy	100	100	100	102	89	87
7. Mexico	101	100	99	100	96	96
8. Russian Federation	90	69	77	—	—	—
9. Thailand	97	76	78	105	57	54
10. Brazil	95	96	101	—	—	—
11. Philippines	—	—	—	—	—	—

Contd.

(1)	(2)	(3)	(4)	(5)	(6)	(7)
12. Turkey	92	96	104	—	—	—
13. China	102	92	90	92	48	52
14. Iran	—	—	—	—	—	—
15. Vietnam	95	95	100	104	50	48
16. Indonesia	—	—	—	—	—	—
17. Egypt	94	89	95	—	—	—
18. India	—	—	—	68	31	46
19. Pakistan	—	—	—	—	—	—
20. Bangladesh	96	100	96	—	—	—
21. Nigeria	—	—	—	—	—	—
22. Congo (Dem. Rep. of)	95	31	33	58	9	16
23. Ethiopia	73	30	41	63	12	19

Source: Human Development Report, 2002, UNDP

Table 1.6: Gender Parity - Economic Activity Indicators for Selected Countries

Country	*Economic Activity Rate (2000)*			*Percentage of Contributing Workers (1991-2000)**			*Ratio of estimated female to male income@*
	Female Rate	*Index (1990 =100)*	*% of female rate to male rate*	*Males*	*Females*	*Total*	
(1)	*(2)*	*(3)*	*(4)*	*(5)*	*(6)*	*(7)*	*(8)*
1. USA	58.8	106	81	41	59	100	0.62
2. Japan	50.8	103	67	19	82	100	0.44
3. France	48.5	106	76	—	—	—	—
4. United Kingdom	52.8	105	74	35	65	100	0.61
5. Germany	47.9	100	69	25	75	100	0.50
6. Italy	38.3	106	58	45	55	100	0.44
7. Mexico	39.4	116	47	51	49	100	0.38
8. Russian Federation	59.3	99	82	58	41	100	0.64
9. Thailand	73.3	98	85	34	66	100	0.62
10. Brazil	43.8	98	52	—	—	—	—
11. Philippines	49.5	106	61	—	—	—	0.59
12. Turkey	49.9	114	61	—	—	—	0.46
13. China	72.7	99	86	—	—	—	—
14. Iran	29.0	134	37	—	—	—	—
15. Vietnam	73.8	97	91	—	—	—	—
16. Indonesia	55.2	110	67	—	—	—	—

Contd.

(1)	*(2)*	*(3)*	*(4)*	*(5)*	*(6)*	*(7)*	*(8)*
17. Egypt	35.0	115	44	64	36	100	0.38
18. India	42.1	104	50	—	—	—	—
19. Pakistan	35.3	124	42	61	39	100	—
20. Bangladesh	66.3	101	76	26	74	100	0.57
21. Nigeria	47.6	102	56	—	—	—	—
22. Congo (Dem. Rep.)	60.6	98	72	—	—	—	—
23. Ethiopia	57.3	99	67	—	—	—	—

Source: Human Development Report, 2002, UNDP
*un-paid workers in household economic activities

@ estimated on the basis of ratio of female non-agricultural wage to male wage, female and male shares of economically active population, total male-female population ratio and GDP adjusted for purchasing power per capita (see source).

Table 1.7: Gender Empowerment Indicators for Selected Countries

Country	*% of seats in parliament occupied by females* (2002)*	*% of female legislators, senior officials and managers (1991-2000)@*	*% of females among professional workers*
1. USA	13.8	45	54
2. Japan	10.0	9	45
3. France	10.9	—	—
4. United Kingdom	17.1	33	45
5. Germany	31.0	27	50
6. Italy	9.1	19	44
7. Mexico	15.9	24	41
8. Russian Federation	6.4	37	64
9. Thailand	9.6	27	55
10. Brazil	6.7	—	—
11. Philippines	17.2	35	66
12. Turkey	4.2	9	36
13. China	21.8	—	—
14. Iran	3.4	—	—
15. Vietnam	10.4	—	—
16. Indonesia	8.0	—	—
17. Egypt	2.4	10	31
18. India	8.9	—	—
19. Pakistan	—	9	26
20. Bangladesh	2.0	5	35
21. Nigeria	3.3	—	—
22. Congo (Dem. Rep. of)	—	—	—
23. Ethiopia	7.8	—	—

Source: Human Development Report, 2002, UNDP.
*Weighted average of seats in upper and lower houses if there are two houses
@ Latest year for which data are available.

To sum up what has been said in this Chapter, international efforts during the past fifty years in eliminating gender gap in different fields and accelerating the process of empowerment of women have helped in evolving a global consensus on the subject and target-oriented action to achieve these well-defined goals in the areas of education, nutrition and health, employment and representation in political and managerial decision making activities. As a result, substantial progress has been made in closing the gender gaps on several parameters. However, certain regions of the world continue to cause concern. In South Asia and Saharan Africa, there is still a considerable leeway to be made in all aspects of development of women. The reason for South Asia's lagging behind in this sphere is not to be sought exclusively in its economic poverty. Poverty, measured through Gross Domestic Product, as it is or after adjustment for purchasing power parity, does not appear to be the sole cause for sex-related differences in education, health and other constituents of empowerment of women. Traditions and societal attitudes that solidified over ages also constitute a determining factor, perhaps a more influential factor.

Notes

1 Data for the subsequent years indicate a significant fall in the child mortality rate as well as the gender gap in it. In 1997, according to data from Registrar General of India's Sample Registration System, mortality rate in the age group 0 – 4 was 25 for male children and 22 for female children

II

Evolution of Gender Policy in India

Hard facts about social practices that throw light on the status of women in India in the hoary Vedic ages are hard to come by. Evidence from Vedic literature, however, suggests that women had been treated better and had enjoyed more rights than in later times. That they had full access to education is established by the references to extraordinarily talented women like Aditi, Lopamudra, Gargi, Maitreyi, Ghosha and Apaala whose level of scholarship matched that of the most learned men of that age and who made significant contributions to *Rigveda*. The precepts of the sage Yagnyavalkya allowed adult women freedom to choose their own life partners. It is said that the *rishika* Gargi chose another sage as her husband at a late stage in her life and on her own conditions. The situation seems to have changed for the worse in the Puranic and later times when the status of women was made inferior to that of men, a situation which survived more than two millennia of evolution of human history. No doubt women were worshipped in the form of goddesses. The Hindu deities bringing scholarship and wealth, *Saraswati* and *Lakshmi* respectively, are women. Sankaracharya, in his work *Soundaryalahari*, extols *Shakti* saying that without her association gods are not capable of doing anything. The great epics placed motherhood on a high pedestal. As pointed out by Seth (2001), even Manu[1], considered by many as responsible for several of the social ills in India, exhorted that "where women are respected, Gods reside and where they are insulted, all endeavour is useless". But that is about all that is positive about the society's attitude towards women in the post Vedic period. Except in the form of deities or mothers, women were seldom seen as equals to men. Religious prescriptions and social practices combined and buttressed each other to relegate women to secondary status. *Bhagavadgita* (Chapter 9, Verse 32) equated uneducated women with persons from the lower social strata. Sankaracharya, in another of his works, *Vivekachudamani*, opined that while birth as a human being was difficult to attain, it was even more difficult to attain birth as a man. The birth of a son was considered essential to maintain and perpetuate one's lineage and to achieve salvation after death. There are hardly any instances of female students in the *gurukulas*. Females were not allowed to learn Vedas or chant *mantras*. The role of a married woman was confined to her home and was to serve her husband faithfully and attain her own salvation through self-less service of the husband taking care of his daily needs so that he can conveniently continue his quest for salvation through meditation and Vedic rites. In general, society viewed woman as a weak (*Abala*) person needing protection, an undesirable distraction in one's progress towards salvation, a faithful servant at home to cater to the mundane needs of the man and bear children for him, an unpaid helper in raising income for the family through a variety of chores and, an inauspicious person to come across if widowed. In due course social evils like neglect of the girl child, deprivation of opportunities to women to pursue education, child marriages, the practice of *sati,* barring widows from remarriage and subjecting them to various types of rigors in food, dress, appearance and social conduct, and the dowry system surfaced and took firm roots in the society.

While the status of the woman in the predominant Hindu society thus became deplorable, it was not very much different in respect of other religions in spite of some more liberal features in those religions. Arya (2000) identifies the positive and negative features of Islam, Christianity, Buddhism and Jainism in so far as the treatment of women is concerned. For instance, she points out that while "The *Quran* is replete with injunctions aimed at bettering the lot of women who in the pre-islamic societies had held a very inferior and servile position" ...... "the Muslim *Shariat* Law as it developed over the centuries, places women in a disadvantageous or an inferior position in many respects." In relation to Christianity, Arya observes that while the "*Bible* lays great emphasis on the image of woman as a strong and steady influence for the good" and the religion provides equal access to education and participation in religious activities, the myth of creation "accords a secondary place to woman in domestic and social life" and has also "put a permanent stamp over women as tempters and seducers and has given the husband the right to control the wife." Moreover, it is important to realize that apart from the social customs and religious injunctions inimical to gender equality inherent in the other religions, it would hardly be possible for people professing these faiths, most of them having been converted from Hinduism in one generation or the other, not to be influenced to some extent by the social customs of the dominant Hindu society.

The general image of Indian woman that had evolved over centuries of the past and continued almost to be so till the present times is, by and large, dual –one eliciting respect and affection when mothers and sisters are involved and the other, the predominant image, of a secondary citizen, much discriminated against in all aspects of life. A female child is unwanted, does not deserve the same parental attention as the male child as it grows up, does not need to be educated, is inferior physically and intellectually to a male child, has to assist in family chores, is a burden on the family to be married off at the earliest opportunity without herself having any say in the choice of the partner, is not welcome in the husband's family without bringing in the expected dowry, is an unpaid servant to the husband's family for life and has to suffer widowhood in pain and silence. There are no doubt oases in this vast dark desert but even such instances of equality of treatment of women and mutual affection is often based on the tacit acceptance of the male supremacy. What is worse, women have themselves become so attuned and conditioned to this state of affairs that many of them believe in the correctness of the situation, accept their lot without any reservations and even help men unwittingly to heap inequities on other women. All this has led over time to a lowering of self-esteem, diffidence and inability to break free from the established societal norms among women, particularly in the middle classes, notwithstanding a few notable examples to the contrary. It is only in the last century or two that there have been some social movements, led by reformers like Raja Ram Mohun Roy, to remedy the situation, with limited success.

The freedom struggle was refreshingly gender-neutral with several highly talented as well as hosts of ordinary women coming to the forefront of the movement. The experience of this phase of Indian history, increasing exposure to western education and liberal ideas, international attention to the need to eliminate all forms of discrimination against women summarised in the previous Chapter and some stirring of social conscience within the country has accelerated, over the past half a century or so, these attempts to eliminate the skewed perception of the society about women. In the post-independence India, these attempts have taken the form of Constitutional Rights, legislative action to protect women's interests, gender focus in development activities, institution building and, more importantly, non-Governmental action spearheaded by women's organizations at various levels. As a result, there is today a greater degree of awareness of the inequities perpetrated on women and of their constitutional and other rights, an institutional framework to seek remedies, a greater degree of participation in personal, social and economic development and political decision-making, and narrowing down gender differences in many fields. However, these forays of women into what had hitherto been regarded as the bastion of men has given rise to newer forms of problems like eve-teasing, sexual and other harassment at work places, occupational discrimination and discrimination in work allotment, crimes against women like dowry killings, molestation and rape, etc.

Constitutional Rights

The makers of Indian Constitution, strongly influenced by the Universal Declaration of Human Rights adopted at about that time, were aware of the inequalities and gender-based discriminatory practices against women and, therefore, made specific provisions in the Constitution to enforce equality between men and women. The Preamble of the Constitution specifies the basic philosophy and direction underlying the document, providing for social, economic and political justice to all citizens of the country. Liberty of thought, expression, belief, faith and worship and equality of status and opportunity are the cornerstones on which the Constitution is built and the principle of gender equality is firmly established in it. The Fundamental Rights enshrined in it provide for equality before law and equal protection by the law (Article 14), prohibition of discrimination on the grounds of religion, race, sex or place of birth (Article 15(1)), and equality of opportunity in matter of public employment (Article 16). The Indian Constitution further provides for affirmative action and for positive discrimination by empowering the state to make special provisions for women (Article 15(2)). Protection of life and personal liberty is guaranteed through Article 21. In addition to these justiciable Fundamental Rights, the Constitution also contains provisions, called Directive Principles, which enjoin upon the State, *inter alia*, to secure the right to adequate means of livelihood, equal pay for equal work, the health and strength of workers and ensuring that the citizens are not forced by economic necessity to enter vocations unsuited to their age and strength, irrespective of gender. Further, a duty is cast on every citizen of India to renounce practices derogatory to the dignity of women. Even though the Directive Principles are in general non-justiciable, the Supreme Court of India has issued directives to the State from time to time to implement the Directive Principles and held that the State or any of its organs could not do anything that violates these principles. Some of the principles have already become law as, for example, The Maternity Benefits Act and the reservations for women in institutions of local governance, and the enshrinement of education as a Fundamental Right. There have also been pronouncements of the Supreme Court on such matters as the need for a Uniform Civil Code for all women irrespective of religion, the need for equal property rights for women particularly in case of inheritance, pronouncements on child labour, child prostitution, sexual harassment at place of work, rape cases etc. Article 326 of the Constitution guarantees political equality to women. The elections are held on the basis of universal adult franchise. Article 325 prohibits exclusion from electoral rolls on the basis of sex.

Legislative Support

Apart from the Fundamental and other rights guaranteed under the Constitution, there has been, over the years, substantial legislative action for promoting the interests of women in India. Such legislation has been in the areas of: (i) personal laws governing marriage, divorce, adoption and property rights, etc., and laws relating to marital health such as age at marriage and medical termination of pregnancies, (ii) crimes against women like sex-determination of unborn children, dowry, rape, harassment at work place, etc., (iii) employment, such as equal opportunity and remuneration, social security, occupational health, welfare, etc., and (iv) political empowerment.

Personal Laws

Personal laws for various religions are governed by different Acts. The Hindu Marriage Act, 1955, applies to the Hindus, The Indian Christian Marriage Act, 1862, and the Indian Divorce Act of 1869 to the Christians, The Muslim Women's Protection Act to the Muslims, and the Parsi Marriage and Divorce Act of 1936 to Parsis. Some of the other important legislations enacted in the pre-Independence India were the Child Marriage Restraint Act, 1933, popularly known as Sarada Act prohibiting marriage of girls below the age of 14 years, The Hindu Inheritance (Amendment) Act, 1929 and The Hindu Women's Right to Property Act, 1937, recognizing women's right to property in joint family property. The large participation of women in India's freedom struggle and the progressive ideas pushed forward by social reformist men and women led to a flurry of legislative activity during the fifties benefiting in particular the Hindu women. These include The Hindu Marriage Act, 1955, The Hindu Succession Act, 1956 and The Hindu Adoption and Maintenance Act, 1956, making monogamy mandatory, granting equal property rights for men and women, giving women the right to adopt a child and making the consent of wife compulsory for the adoption of a child by a married man. The Hindu Law guaranteed the right of divorce (for specified reasons, which include husband having more that one wife living or his having been guilty of rape, sodomy or bestiality). The Parsee Marriage and Divorce Act of 1936 as amended in 1987 provides for minimum age for marriage and grants equal rights to men and women to divorce and for reasons as in the Hindu Marriages Act. Under The Indian Divorce Act, 1869, applicable to Indian Christians, both husband and wife can obtain a divorce but the scope of circumstances under which divorce can be obtained is different for the two sexes. The wife has to prove two offenses by the husband before she can obtain a divorce. Steps are afoot to amend this and other discriminatory archaic Christian laws. Under Muslim law, while a husband can divorce the wife unilaterally and unconditionally without the intervention of the Court, the wife does not have any such right to obtain divorce without the intervention of the Court except for reasons covered under The Dissolution of Muslim Marriage Act, 1939. The Termination of Pregnancy Act was enacted as a measure to help promote family planning as well as safeguard the health of the mother. The Child Marriage Restraint Act, 1976 raised the minimum age at marriage of girls to 18 years from 15 years and for boys to 21 years to prevent child marriages, early marriage of girls and consequently early pregnancies and birth of premature babies. In response to the representations of social activists on the lengthy involved procedures and the consequent delays in settling matters, The Family Courts Act was passed in 1984 with jurisdiction to deal with all family law matters such as marriage, matrimonial causes, maintenance and alimony, custody, education and support of children and settlement of property. The Act opts for a less formal procedure and a number of experts like judges, social workers, welfare officers and psychiatrists are engaged in counselling services.

Laws against Social Evils

Evils against women like demand for dowry, domestic and other forms of violence, sex-determination of unborn children, rape, etc. have been the issues of agitation by social activists and Government responded by enacting new laws or amending the existing ones providing for stringent punishments. In the matter of advertisements, the Indecent Representation of Women (Prohibition) Act, 1986, prohibits the indecent representation of women through advertisements, books, pamphlets etc. Rape laws were amended in 1983 (shifting the burden of proof to the accused person if sexual assault is established) as the result of a sustained campaign against the provisions of the Indian Penal Code. There were also important amendments made in the Indian Evidence Act and the Criminal Procedure Code (Cr.P.C). The Criminal Law (Second Amendment) Act, 1983 made significant changes in the Cr.P.C in the interests of women. To deal with cases of domestic violence, the Indian Penal Code has been amended to provide a new offence called cruelty to wife by her husband or his relatives (defined as any willful conduct which is likely to drive the woman to commit suicide or to cause grave injury or damage to the life, limb or health (whether mental or physical) of the woman or harassment of a woman with a view to coercing her or her relatives to meet any unlawful demand for property or valuable security), which has been made punishable with imprisonment up to three years and fine. Provision has also been made for compulsory postmortem in all cases where a woman has, within seven years of her marriage, committed suicide or died in circumstances raising a reasonable suspicion that some other person has committed the offence, and in all cases where a married woman has died within seven years of her marriage and a relative of such a woman has made a request on her behalf. Recently, a new legislation titled Domestic Violence (Prevention) Bill has been introduced in Parliament to curb domestic violence against women. The Dowry (Prohibition) Act, 1961 made demanding and accepting dowry from the bride's family a criminal offence. Later amendments to the Act made punishment for offenses more stringent and shifted the burden of proof that there was no demand for dowry to the person who is alleged to have taken or abetted the taking of dowry. Any advertisement that relates to the offering of any share of property in consideration of marriage has also been made punishable. One of the worst crimes against women emanating out of misuse of the advances in science and technology in modern times has been the increasing use of technology to determine the sex of foetus with a view to abort the pregnancy if the foetus is feminine. This crime against the unborn girl child is sought to be tackled through banning sex selection under The Pre-Natal Diagnostic Techniques (Regulation and Prevention of Misuse) Act 1994. Foeticide is an offence under the Indian Penal Code and Infanticide is tantamount to murder. The Suppression of Immoral Traffic in Women and Girls Act was enacted in 1956 in pursuance of the International Convention for the Suppression of Traffic in Persons and of the Exploitation of the Prostitution of Others and the Indian Constitutional provision banning traffic in human beings. The Act was renamed in 1986 as The Immoral Traffic (Prevention) Act and the scope of the Act was enlarged to cover all persons, male or female, who are exploited sexually for commercial purposes. Further, crimes involving children and minors were made more stringent by enhancing the period of imprisonment and a certain minimum standard of correctional treatment was introduced.

Labour Laws

Although there are a number of labour laws[2] in operation in the country governing employment, wages, working conditions, injury compensation, health, social security, welfare and other aspects of labour, very few relate exclusively to women. Moreover, most of the labour laws generally apply to the workers in the organized sector, which covers only about 8 per cent of the total work force in the country. Almost the entire labour in the unorganised sector, where women find employment more often than men, remains outside the purview of the existing laws and is left without any protective legislative cover. Some of the existing labour laws that specifically cover women workers and other laws with special provisions for women are summarized below.

The Equal Remuneration Act, 1976 was enacted to give effect to the ratification of the ILO Convention (No. 100) by the Indian Government in 1958. The Act prescribes payment of equal remuneration to men and women workers for same or similar nature of work protected under the Act. The Act defines 'same work or similar nature of work' as work in respect of which skill, efforts and responsibility required are same, when performed under similar working conditions by a man or a woman and the differences, if any, between the skill, effort and responsibility required of a man and those required of a women are not of practical importance in relation to the terms and conditions of employment. No discrimination is permissible in recruitment and service conditions except where employment of women is prohibited or restricted by any law. The Act covers all workers employed in any establishment or employment irrespective of its size or nature. In order to ensure that the guarantee of equal remuneration does not result in the general lowering of the wages for the male and female employees, it has been provided in the Act that the employer cannot reduce the rate of remuneration of any worker to ensure compliance with the legal provisions regarding equal remuneration. To ensure that guarantee of equal remuneration may not lead to a policy of refusing employment to women or affecting their further promotions and other conditions of service, the Act prohibits discrimination against women in matters of employment. This prohibition is not restricted to initial recruitment, but also extends to any condition of service subsequent to recruitment or transfer except in places where the employment of women in such work is prohibited or restricted by any other law in force. Heavy penalties have been prescribed in the Act for its violation. In spite all these provisions, it is observed that in practice, wage disparities between men and women do exist. This is in particular so in the informal sector or in contractual form of employment where direct employer-employee relationship is missing. One of the methods of paying differential rates of wages is through the system of piece-rate payment. The Report of the National Commission on Self-employed Women (GOI, 1987) observed that "piece-rate was an institutional mechanism to fix lower wages for women." During the interactions with women workers in *Beedi* and *Agarbati* industries in Ahmedabad it was reported that the items manufactured by them were rejected on the plea that they were not of good quality, often without justification, and the piece-rate wages for these rejected pieces were deducted from the amounts due to them.

The Maternity Benefits Act, 1961 extends to factories, mines, plantations and such establishments where persons are employed for the exhibition of equestrian, acrobatic and other performances. Its provisions have now been extended to shops and commercial establishments where ten or more persons are employed. Under this Act a woman, who has worked in an establishment, directly or through a contractor, for 80 days in the 12 months immediately preceding the date of her delivery, excepting when she is covered by the Employees' State Insurance Act, 1948, is entitled to avail maternity benefits for a maximum period of twelve weeks, of which not more than six weeks can precede the date of her expected delivery. The maternity benefit consists of payment at the rate of average daily wage for the period of actual absence. In addition, a woman is entitled to the prescribed medical bonus if no free pre-natal/post-natal care is provided by the employer. The Act makes a provision for providing two nursing breaks of prescribed duration to women in addition to the intervals of rest provided to her till the child attains the age of 15 months. No deduction in the wages can be made for the reason that a woman is allowed breaks for nursing the child. A woman suffering from any illness arising out of pregnancy, delivery, and premature birth of child is entitled to additional leave for a maximum period of one month.

Apart from payment of monetary maternity benefits in accordance with the law, The Maternity Benefits Act also imposes on the employers the obligation:

- Not to engage pregnant women in work of arduous nature, long hours of standing likely to interfere with pregnancy/normal development of foetus; or in work which may cause miscarriage or is likely to affect health for a period of one month immediately preceding the period of six weeks before delivery.
- Not to dismiss or discharge a pregnant women employee during the period of maternity leave

- Not to vary conditions of service of such women to their disadvantage
- To allow advance benefits on production of medical certificate
- To exhibit the provisions of the Act and the Rules made thereunder in the local language at a conspicuous place in every part of the establishment where women are employed

Penalties in the form of fine and imprisonment are provided in case of violation of the provisions of the Act. Nevertheless some employers appear to circumvent these provisions by not employing married women at all in the first place or discharging such employees on the first signs of pregnancy. A study by Chadha shows that while 94 percent of the women employees are entitled to maternity benefits, only 0.25 percent avail them. In order to provide maternity benefits to the large mass of unorganized and self-employed women workers, certain schemes have been introduced at the Central, State and local levels. Under the Bidi and Cigar Workers Act, 1966 maternity benefits are available to home-based workers also. Some schemes of maternity benefit to women agricultural workers are being implemented by States like Andhra Pradesh, Karnataka, Kerala and Gujarat. The National Social Assistance Programme of the Central Government also has a component under which all poor women can claim maternity benefits for the first two live births.

The Employees State Insurance Act, 1948 confers certain benefits to employees in industrial establishments and other employments to which the Act has been made applicable. Under this Act, the employers and the employees are required to make a prescribed nominal weekly contribution, in return for which the employees become entitled to the sickness benefits, disablement benefits, medical benefits, dependent's benefits and maternity benefits. The maternity benefits include medical care, pre-natal and post-natal care and medical care during confinement and during sickness due to pregnancy and confinement. However, unlike under The Maternity Benefits Act where the benefits are the employers' obligation, benefits are provided under the ESI Act through a system of social insurance.

The Minimum Wages Act, 1948 empowers the Government, Central as well as the State, to fix and revise from time to time the minimum rates of wages for different categories of employment scheduled in the Act. The Act applies to both men and women. However, several employments in the unorganized segment of the economy in which women workers are engaged in large numbers, such as the home-based workers, are not covered by the Act.

The Inter State Migrants (Regulation of Employment and Conditions of Service) Act, 1979 regulates the employment of inter-State migrant workers and provides for their service conditions. Establishments or contractors employing five or more such migrant workers on any day of the preceding twelve months are covered under the Act. In so far as women workers are concerned, the Act requires that where 20 or more migrant women are engaged and the employment is likely to continue for three months or more, crèches should be provided by the employer/contractor. Separate toilets and washing facilities are also required to be provided for women. Unfortunately, the Act does not cover workers who migrate for employment on their own. The threshold of five workers for the provisions of the Act to take effect also limits the applicability of the Act.

Other Acts: There are a number of other Acts containing specific provisions for the benefit of women. The Contract Labour (Regulation and Abolition) Act, 1970 stipulates that women workers, with the exception of midwives and nurses in plantations, are not to be required to work beyond 9 hours between 6 AM and 7 PM. The Mines Act, 1952 prohibits employment of women below ground. The Factories Act, 1948 provides that women are not to be engaged for cleaning, lubricating or adjusting any part of prime or transmission machinery. It also stipulates that maternity leave up to 12 weeks with wages are to be provided. Both the Factories Act and the Mines Act authorize the appropriate Government to fix the maximum load that can be lifted, carried or, moved by women. The State Governments may also prohibit or restrict women's employment in any other operation that exposes them to a serious risk of bodily injury or disease. The Central Government is authorized to prohibit, restrict or regulate the employment of women in any class of mines or particular kinds of labour which may result in danger to the life, safety or health of women workers. Like the Contract Labour Act, The Factories Act, The Plantations Labour Act, The Mines Act and The Bidi and Cigar Workers (Conditions of Employment) Act 1966 also prohibit employment of women between 7 p.m. and 6 a.m., though this can be relaxed to some extent by the appropriate government. The Plantation Labour Act, 1951 requires that women workers should be provided time off for feeding children. The Beedi & Cigar Workers (Condition of Employment) Act, 1966 provides for crèches for women workers. There is a provision for appointment of a woman member in the Advisory Committees under The Beedi Workers Welfare Fund Act, 1976, The Iron Ore Mines, Manganese Ore Mines and Chrome Ore Mines Labour Welfare Fund Act, 1976 and The Mica Mines Labour Welfare Fund Act, 1976. The Industrial Employment (Standing Orders) Act, 1976 safeguards women workers against sexual harassment at work places. The social security provisions contained in The Employees' Provident Fund and Miscellaneous Provisions Act, 1952, and The Payment of Gratuity Act 1972 and the Employees Pension Scheme 1995 and the work-related injury compensation benefits under the Workmen's Compensation Act, 1923 apply equally to male and female workers.

While there is, thus, a plethora of labour laws and some provisions to protect women workers, application of these laws and provisions is grossly unsatisfactory. The reasons are the restricted scope of most of the laws due to the prescribed minimum number of workers for the law to be applicable, lack of awareness of the laws and organization among the women workers, insincere enforcement of the law often through the collusion between the employers and the enforcement machinery, lengthy procedures, etc.

Laws on Political Rights

As already mentioned, the Indian Constitution guarantees political equality to women through Article 326 and prohibits exclusion from electoral rolls on the basis of sex through Article 325. In fact, the freedom struggle threw up a number of highly talented women leaders who had taken active part in the post-Independence politics. There had been a woman Prime Minister at the helm guiding nation's destiny for a decade and a half and others who had been Chief Ministers of the States in the last half a century (thrice in Uttar Pradesh, twice in Tamilnadu, and once each in Orissa, Delhi and Bihar). Even though this is a record for a developing country, which can be compared favourably with that of advanced countries like the United States and United Kingdom, the involvement of women in the political mainstream of the country is far too inadequate. A legislative measure of far-reaching importance in the process of political empowerment of women was the enactment of 73rd and 74th Constitutional Amendments reserving one-third of the seats for women in elected local government bodies, viz. Panchayats and municipalities. To take the process to its logical conclusion, it would be necessary to make similar reservations in the national Parliament and the Legislative Assemblies of the States. Even though most national political parties in the country make a pretence of agreeing in principle to the proposal, a bill to give effect to this is yet to be passed. The male sections of the parties appear to be hesitant in sharing political power with their female counterparts. The demand of some sections of the political leadership in this connection is for a further reservation to women from the socially backward communities within the proposed one-third reservation for women.

New Legislative Initiatives

In response to the pressures of commitments made at international forums and of social activists and voluntary agencies at home, Indian government has been striving, if at times half-heartedly, for improving the legislative framework to ameliorate the conditions of women and to hasten the process of their empowerment. As mentioned earlier, a bill to amend the Constitution to provide for reservation of seats in parliament is being contemplated. Another piece of legislation, viz. Domestic Violence (Prevention) Bill, has been introduced and is under debate. As a part of the Women's Empowerment Year, a task force constituted under the chairmanship of Shri K.C. Pant, Deputy Chairman of Planning Commission, reviewed in 2001 the existing laws impacting on women's rights and made recommendations on 22 laws, including labour laws on minimum wages, maternity benefits and equal remuneration and other laws on dowry, sati, family courts and indecent representation of women. Over a year has passed since these recommendations have been made, but implementation has, as usual, been tardy due to lack of political will, apathy and bureaucratic delays.

Institutional Framework

The legislative structure for securing the rights of women and protecting them against social evils has, thus, gradually been improving during last fifty years. An institutional edifice to ensure implementation of these Constitutional and other legal provisions came up only in 1992 with the establishment of The National Commission on Women with the responsibilities of:

- Overseeing the working of Constitutional safeguards for women
- Reviewing laws and regulations where necessary
- Intervening in select individual cases of violation of women's rights and equality by issuing appropriate directions to the concerned authorities.

Some of the specific matters coming under the purview of the Commission relate to The Commission of Sati (Prevention) Act, sale of minor girls, guardianship law, compulsory registration of marriages, amendment of Hindu Marriage Act, amendment of Child Marriage (Restraint) Act, Criminal Procedure Act, 1973, etc. It is mandatory for the Governments, Central and State, to report to Parliament about the follow-up action taken on the recommendations/directives of the Commission and submit specific reasons where they disagree with the views of the Commission. Several State Governments, including Delhi, also have set up similar State level Commissions.

Two important pre-requisites for poor women seeking judicial remedies for their rights are: (a) an awareness of the rights available and the relevant legal instruments, and (b) the availability of appropriate legal assistance to them. Several programmes of awareness generation are in operation like dissemination of information through mass media, incorporation of relevant modules in the training of local level functionaries like Village Level Workers, Village Health Workers, etc and gender sensitization programmes. A scheme of legal aid was started in 1970 and a Commission for implementing legal aid services was set up in 1979 along with legal aid structures at the State and District level all over the country. The Legal Services Authorities Act, 1987, created structures for aid to specific categories entitled to free legal aid, including women.

Gender Focus in Development Policies

The main thrust in India's developmental efforts has been the realization of rapid economic growth with distributive justice. Gender issues, though identified by the National Planning Committee's Sub-Committee on Women in the pre-Independence days, did not receive much attention in the First Five Year Plan (1951-56), which considered that women needed educational, health and welfare services only. A significant development that had taken place during this period was the establishment of the Central Social Welfare Board (CSWB) in 1953 with counterpart organisations in the States. The CSWB identified the problem of absence of any governmental machinery at various levels for welfare-related activities. CSWB undertook a number of activities to promote welfare of women through voluntary organizations and encouraged women's organizations to take up such activities in partnership with government, leading to the growth of grass root organizations of women at various levels, such as the Mahila Mandals. These organizational entities were used as delivery mechanisms for essential services of education and health, especially maternal and child health, etc. The Second Plan (1956-61), while continuing with this welfare approach, recognized issues like organization of women workers, protection of women against injurious work, maternity benefits and care of working women, equal remuneration for equal work and women's training. However, as pointed out by the Government itself, "This combination of institution building and human resource development was also expected to prepare women to participate in the political and developmental processes. Thus, though the language of these strategies reflected contemporary meaning of 'welfare', there was a conceptual thrust (even though inadequately articulated) towards actively involving and stimulating the participation of women's organizations in the processes of change" (GOI, 1997). Increasing bureaucratic control, top-down designing of programmes, declining resource support to organizations and institutional development from below, however, indicated the low priority attached and the non-serious approach adopted in dealing with the basic issues in promotion of gender equality. Consequent upon the recommendations of the National Committee on Women's Education (1958-59), the Third, Fourth and Fifth Plans (1961-79) paid some attention to girls' education and immunization programmes and supplementary nutrition programmes for children and expectant and nursing mothers. All through this period the emphasis was only on women's education, health and welfare activities. Steps were also initiated to provide a modicum of social security through maternity benefits and widow pensions. An important event during this period was the constitution of the first National Commission on Labour under the chairmanship of Justice P.B.Gajendragadkar in 1966, which submitted its report in 1969 The terms of reference of the Commission were to review the conditions of labour in general since Independence and the existing labour laws, to report on aspects of labour such as the earnings, levels of living, health, safety, welfare, social security, industrial relations, etc. and make appropriate recommendations. Even though the terms of reference did not require specifically so, the Commission considered the issues relating to women-labour important and thought it fit to include a separate chapter on employment of women and children in its report. Its recommendations (GOI, 1969) in regard to women were:

- The right of a woman to employment should in no way be considered subordinate or secondary to that of a man. The necessary training facilities should be created/augmented. Vocational guidance programme will serve a useful purpose in giving required information to women. It will be desirable to give preference to women for training in those trades and occupations for which they have special aptitude;
- Implementation of the principle of equal pay for equal work should be more satisfactory than at present;
- Women will have to be absorbed more and more in skilled categories of work to make their employment more economic to the employer. With proper skill generation and rational distribution of women labour force as a part of social and economic planning, it should be possible for an employer to follow non-discriminatory policy in employing women.

More than thirty years after these recommendations were made, the goal of equal remuneration for equal work is yet to be realized and the discriminatory practices, if not policies, in employment continue to this day.

The approaches and efforts towards development of women in the first two decades of planning were, thus, woefully inadequate. The Committee on the Status of Women in India (CSWI) constituted by the Government in 1971, in its report pointed out *inter alia* the following:

- Majority of women not enjoying the Constitutional Rights
- Declining sex ratio, a process accelerated during the period of planned development
- Wide gap between enrolment of boys and girls in education
- High drop-out rates among girls
- Regional and urban-rural disparities in enrolment of girls
- High maternal and infant mortality rates
- Exclusion of women from active participation in productive processes
- Marginalisation of the large majority of women in the economy and their consequent neglect and devaluation by the society and the state
- Unequal treatment at work places and unequal security of employment
- Threat to the promise of gender equality by escalation of social practices like dowry, continued inequality in personal laws and non-enforcement of existing labour and criminal laws, which sought to offer some protection to women

The Sixth Five Year plan (1980-85) drew inspiration from the Report of the CSWI and, influenced by representations from women's organizations at national level, incorporated for the first time a separate Chapter on Women and Development. This Chapter expressed concern about the declining sex ratio, lower life expectancy among women and the continued low status of women in the society as a result of inadequate opportunities of independent employment and income. To improve women's access to education and training and thereby to more productive work opportunities, educational facilities were created through non-formal education centers exclusively for women, early childhood centers as adjuncts to primary schools, higher rates of scholarships to girls belonging to Scheduled Caste and Scheduled Tribe communities and training-cum- production centers for women. The importance of vocational training for women was recognized and exclusive Industrial Training Institutes/ Centres were set up for them.

The need for participation of women in self-employment pursuits was recognized. The Integrated Rural Development Programme (IRDP), which was expanded nation-wide to tackle rural poverty through development of self-employment opportunities, adopted a family-centred approach and gave preference to female-headed households. It incorporated the Government's promise that in cases of transferred assets such as agricultural and homestead land government shall endeavour to provide joint title to husband and wife. Organisation of groups of women to access credit and pursue self-employment activities was put in place through the scheme for Development of Women and Children in Rural Areas (DWCRA) in 1982-83. A quota of one-third for women was fixed in the programme of Training Rural Youth for Self-employment (TRYSEM). Other points made in the Sixth Plan related to strengthening of voluntary organizations of women at grass root level to enable them to participate in decision-making process, supportive services like child care services to working mothers to promote education of girls, setting up working girls' hostels and improvement in the existing health services. The Sixth Plan, thus, represented a watershed in the approach of development planning in India to issues relating women and marked a definite shift from the earlier welfare approach to an approach that would eventually lead to empowerment of women. During the Sixth and the Seventh Plans, a number of States had set up Women's Development Corporations to promote self-employment among women, particularly from the weaker sections of the society, through training, margin money assistance, marketing support, etc.

The National Commission on Rural Labour (1983) made a number of recommendations to accelerate development of women. Some of the more important recommendations stressed on:

- Promoting occupational diversity among women workers
- Amendment of existing inheritance laws to eliminate discrimination against women; extending co-ownership of property to productive assets and access to common property resources, collection of forest produce, and so on.
- Encouraging voluntary agencies to organize groups of women to pursue productive activities
- Skill training to improve productivity among women
- Protection to women workers from adverse effects of casualisation and contractualisation of employment through appropriate legal measures
- Protection to home-based workers through law to promote their interests and welfare

- Creation of a special Central Fund raised through employers' contributions to pay maternity benefits to rural women
- Generating awareness among employers and workers regarding Equal Remuneration Act

The Seventh Five Year Plan (1985-90) emphasized the need for an integrated approach to development of women, encompassing areas like education, health and family welfare, nutrition and employment. It laid stress on skill training for women for promoting their employment and programmes for awareness generation and confidence building. The Seventh Plan period also witnessed significant developments like the fixing of 30 per cent quota for women under the IRDP, steps to begin gender sensitization as a mandatory part of training of rural development officials, initiation of innovative, flexible programmes for training poor women to enable them to pursue income-generating activities, the creation of a full-fledged Department of Women and Child Development in the Ministry of Human Resource Development, and the incorporation of Education for Women's Equality within the National Policy on Education carrying "the message that along with expanding women's access to all kinds of education, the system, with all its institutions, had to shoulder a major responsibility for genuine empowerment of women, by changing the social construction of gender" (GOI, 1997). Two other significant events that occurred during this period were the preparation of a National Perspective Plan for Women and the constitution of The National Commission for Self-Employed Women to highlight the problems of women working in the informal sector.

The National Commission for Self-Employed Women was constituted under the chairpersonship of Smt. Ela Bhat in 1987 to: (a) examine the current employment, health, educational and social status of women in self-employed sectors, (b) assess the impact of various labour legislations on the self-employed women, specially in respect of maternity benefits, (c) identify the constraints on increase of productivity of self-employed women and the gaps in training, credit, up-gradation of skills and marketing, (d) survey employment patterns, including production relations and assess their impact on the wages of the self-employed women, (e) survey the effects of macro-policies relating to investment, production and technology on the status of self-employed women, (f) consider the link between the productive and reproductive roles of the self-employed women, with special reference to their health status, and (g) suggest measures relating to all sectors for removing the constraints which adversely affect the integration of self-employed women in the national development process. The total focus of the issues referred to the Commission was, therefore, on self-employed women, not covering the other categories of unprotected women workers. The Commission, however, took a wider view of the issue and decided to cover the "entire gamut of unprotected women labour to include self-employed and wage labour, paid and unpaid labour, women labour in informal sector and contract labour". Some of the important recommendations made by the Commission are:

- The definition of women workers should be enlarged to include women engaged in all the activities, paid and unpaid, performed within the home or outside, as an employee or on own account
- Strategies should be devised to enhance the ownership and the control of women over productive assets. It would enhance women's empowerment and their well-being. Such assets may be land, house, trees, etc.
- Adequate funds should be allocated in the development plans to education, health, rural and small industries and basic amenities like drinking water and housing
- Women should be involved in planning, implementation and monitoring development programmmes
- Credit mechanisms should be evolved to assist poor and self-employed women exclusively
- Training of women should be given due emphasis. Training should be linked to employment.
- Health is another area that requires attention. Poor health affects women in work places also. Health should be considered as a full package in the context of the total scenario that affects the conditions of women especially in the informal sector.
- Special steps should be taken to provide education to women and girl children
- Right to work should be made a Fundamental Right
- An Equal Opportunities Commission should be set up with statutory powers of investigation, advice, monitoring, etc.
- Awareness programmes should be organized to make women become aware of their rights
- A central fund should be constituted to provide welfare and social security measures to women workers that should be financed through levies on individual employers as well as major industries.
- Lack of organisation being the root cause of exploitation of women workers in the informal sector, efforts should be made to facilitate and promote organization of women workers.
- The coverage of cooperative movement should be expanded to include areas like farm labour, artisans, cereal processing, fodder

and fuel development, fruit preservation and other agro-based industries.

The Commission made several sector-specific recommendations and also for several categories of women like the destitute, sex workers, etc. While there have been some initiatives to implement some of the recommendations of the Commission like allocation of funds for women's education and health, organization of women by encouraging formation of Self-Help Groups, organizing special training programmes for women, etc., several of the major recommendations like recognition of household work as socio-economic productive work, creation of social security fund for women, recognizing Right to Work as Fundamental Right are yet to be implemented, more than three decades after the recommendations are made.

The National Perspective Plan (NPP) for the period 1988 - 2000 released in 1988 considered that "A parallel sub-stream of women's development, even if possible, will only perpetuate discrimination and subordination" and called for "an alternative strategy of national development which will provide not just some additional space for women, but creates a democratic, egalitarian, secular, cooperative social structure" in which women become equal partners with men. The NPP reviewed the nearly four decades of planned development and made recommendations covering nine sectors, viz., rural development, health, legislation, political participation, communication, voluntary action, support services, education and employment. It called for: (a) adoption of a holistic approach for women's development, (b) inter-linkages and converging strategies for programmes relevant to women in various sectors, (c) formulation of national policies for increasing the participation of women in development plans so as to create productive employment and services for women, (d) setting up of an apex body to revamp and oversee women's training programmes, (e) appointment of a commission for women's rights and enforcement of laws, (f) reservation of 30 per cent of seats in all elected bodies *as a transitory measure* to ensure that women have opportunity to enjoy equal political status with men, (g) recognition of the unpaid work of women in the household and outside and taking into account its value, h) strengthening women's access to productive resources like land and credit inputs, (i) bringing female-headed households above poverty line and ensuring 30 per cent of beneficiaries under IRDP should be women, (j) reviewing property laws to ensure women's rights to property, (k) uniform civil code for all citizens, (l) making demand for dowry a ground for divorce, and (m) ensuring coordination among local community, teachers and educational administrations to promote

- To universalize the on-going supplementary feeding programmes – the Special Nutrition Programme (SNP) and the Mid-day Meals scheme (MDM).
- To ensure easy and equal access to education for women and girls through the commitments of the Special Action Plan of 1998.
- To initiate steps to eliminate gender bias in all educational programmes.
- To institutionalize plans for free education for girls up to college level, including professional courses.
- To equip women with necessary skills in the modern upcoming trades which could help them gainfully engaged, making them economically independent and self-reliant.
- To increase access to credit through setting up a Development Bank for Women Entrepreneurs in small and tiny sectors.

One of the important events during the Ninth Plan period was the constitution of the second National Commission on Labour under the chairmanship of Ravindra Varma in 1999. The Commission was set up against the backdrop of the economic liberalization and integration of the national economy with that of the world. The broad mandate of the Commission was: (a) to review existing labour laws applicable to the organized sector and recommend rationalization of the laws, and (b) to suggest an 'umbrella' legislation for ensuring a minimum level of protection to the workers in the unorganized sector. As a part of elaboration of these broad terms of reference, the Commission was asked to recommend action *inter alia* at "improving the effectiveness of measures relating to social security, occupational health and safety, minimum wages and linking wages with productivity and in particular the safeguards and facilities required for women and handicapped persons in employment." Issues relating to employment of women and children, particularly the perceptions of threats to security and quality of employment in the context of globalisation, were accordingly considered in depth by a special Study Group set up by the Commission. The final report submitted by the Commission to the Government recently contains the following major recommendations in respect of women workers apart from the Commission's general recommendations on aspects like workers in the unorganized sector, social security, labour laws, skill development, etc. which apply to both male and female workers.

- The contribution of women as a category of workers is grossly under-estimated, which manifests itself in disparities in wages, in access to control over resources, in lack of infrastructure support and above all in the work burden. The problems arising from inadequate definitions of work and measuring work participation of women are compounded by difficulties in attaching economic value to the work of women, especially when it is not related to the market. These issues need a fundamental remedy.

- The most important intervention towards improving the economic status of poor women working in the informal sector would be to devise strategies, which would enhance their ownership and control over productive assets.
- Organising is the key to women's development. It helps them to unite, become conscious of their rights and obligations, increase self-esteem and forge channels through which they can avail of financial and credit services and bring their influence to bear on the issues affecting them.
- Government should allow widespread registration of MBOs (Member Based Organisations) of women workers under the Trade Unions Act; promote Mutually Aided Cooperatives Acts (such as in Andhra Pradesh and a few other States) in each State, recognize MBOs as implementing agencies for government schemes, set up Voice Representation Systems for MBOs of women, invest in training and research for building up their capacity and sensitize government functionaries at various levels on issues relating to women. Other agencies like the trade unions and NGOs can help MBOs by playing a promotive or supportive role in mobilizing membership, training, conducting awareness programmes, etc.
- No solution to the problems of women at work would be complete without taking into account their reproductive function, which can be supported through maternity benefits and childcare. Responsibility for this should be borne by all employers, irrespective of whether they employed women or not. If the employer is not identifiable, the responsibility should lie with State. A statutory scheme of maternity entitlements, providing financial support for childbirth, childcare, should cover all women under income criterion. A flexible child care fund may be set up to provide childcare facilities to all women, regardless of income, number of children or other considerations, which may be raised from multiple sources like employees, employers, government, community contributions, etc.
- An Equal Opportunities Commission should be set up with wide powers of investigation, direction, advice and monitoring.
- Industrial subcontracting has increased work opportunities for women but unfortunately the earnings are low. A National Policy on Home-Based work should be formulated in conformity with the

ILO Convention on the subject. Anyone employing workers directly or indirectly should be required to pay at least the minimum wage or assure a minimum income. Minimum rates should be fixed in all work situations including those where there is no clear employer-employee relationship or a piece-rate system of payment is followed. The Minimum Wages Act should be extended to piece-rate work also and piece rates should be so fixed as to enable a worker putting in 8 hours of work earn wages equal to time-rated minimum wage.

- A system of continuous up-gradation of skills should be established to deal with the shrinkage of employment due to introduction of new technology and mechanization. Technologies which increase productivity but which have least adverse impact on employment should be identified and promoted. Skill development is essential for enhancing employment opportunities in various sectors like agriculture, forestry, livestock, handicrafts, food processing, textiles and garments and construction. Increasing micro-finance and direct access to markets are also important for expanding employment.

The National Policy on Empowerment of Women has finally been adopted in 2001. Full text of the Policy is given in the Annexure 4. The Policy identifies for its goals: (a) creating an environment that enables realization of the full potential of women, (b) *de jure* and *de facto* enjoyment of all human rights and freedoms by women on equal basis with men in all spheres, (c) equal access to participation and decision-making in social, political and economic life of the nation, (d) equal access to health care, quality education, employment services, employment, remuneration, occupational health and safety and social security, (e) strengthening legal systems to eliminate discrimination against women, (f) changing societal attitudes and community practices through active involvement of men and women, (g) mainstreaming gender perspective in development, (h) elimination of discrimination and all forms of violence against women and girl child, and (i) building and strengthening partnerships with civil society, particularly with women's organizations. The policy prescriptions identified are: (i) making the legal-judicial system more responsive to women's needs, encourage changes in personal laws relating to marriage, divorce, etc. and in property laws, (ii) ensuring equality in power sharing and active participation in decision making at all levels in all spheres, (iii) ensuring mainstreaming a gender perspective in the development process by establishing appropriate policies, programmes and systems, (iv) economic empowerment of women through addressing women's needs in poverty eradication programmes, strengthening micro-credit mechanisms to ensure easy credit to all women below poverty line, recognizing women's contribution to socio-economic development as producers and workers and to identify it in national accounts, enhancing capacity of women to face the negative social and economic impacts of globalisation, training women in agricultural occupations, support to women workers in industry through legislation, social security and support services and women-friendly personnel policies, and (v) social empowerment ensuring equal access to education and vocational training, universalisation of education, adoption of a holistic approach to women's health including nutrition and health services, attention to the needs of women in programmes for safe drinking water, sanitation, housing, environment and appropriate technologies, special assistance to women in difficult circumstances, strengthening institutions and mechanisms to prevent all forms of violence against women, measures to eliminate discrimination against girl child and use of media to portray a positive image consistent with human dignity of women and girls. The National Policy also outlines operational strategies to translate these policy prescriptions into practice. These include: (a) development of action plans identifying measurable goals, committing resources, assigning responsibilities and establishing efficient monitoring systems, (b) strengthening institutional mechanisms to promote the advancement of women, establishment of National and State Councils to oversee the operation of policies and National and State Resource Centres on women to collect and disseminate information, (c) appropriate management of resources and ensuring flow of funds to women's development, (d) review of existing legislative structure and ensuring strict implementation of relevant legal provisions, prevention and punishment of sexual harassment at work place, effective monitoring of crimes against women, establishment of women's cells in police stations, women police stations, family courts, counseling and legal aid centers, (e) gender sensitization through appropriate training of personnel, (f) involvement of Panchayat Raj institutions in implementation of the policies, and (g) partnership with voluntary organisations in the formulation, implementation and monitoring and review of policies and programmes.

As mentioned earlier in this Chapter, while the 73rd and 74th Constitutional Amendments ensured adequate representation of women in elected local bodies, efforts to enact similar legislation to ensure one-third quota for women in Parliament and State legislatures have so far fallen flat in the absence of a consensus of political opinion and some political parties demanding further reservation for women from socially and economically backward communities within the proposed one-third quota for women. Questions are also raised about the seriousness of the political parties dominated by men in enacting such a far-reaching piece of legislation. The strategy of Women Component Plan within the development plans has been implemented from the Ninth Plan to ensure that not less than 30 per cent of the benefits/funds flowed to women in the programmes of various Ministries and Departments. There have also been some efforts to achieve convergence of programmes for economic empowerment of women. For example, the Integrated Women's Empowerment Project based on formation of Self-Help Groups (SHGs) recast the earlier Indira Mahila Yojana and merged it with Mahila Samriddhi Yojana to achieve holistic empowerment of women through awareness generation, economic empowerment and convergence of various schemes. The paradigm of empowerment through SHGs, spearheaded by National Bank for Agriculture and Rural Development (NABARD) and Rashtriya Mahila Kosh has taken off in a really big way and the number of SHGs has multiplied several-fold in recent years.

The Tenth Plan (2002-07) aims to continue with the process of empowering women through translating the National Policy for Empowering Women into action. A sector-specific three-fold strategy based on the prescriptions of the National Policy, comprising social empowerment, economic empowerment and gender justice, is proposed to be followed. Social empowerment aims at creating "an enabling environment through various affirmative developmental policies and programmes for development of women besides providing them easy and equal access to all basic minimum services so as to enable them to realize their full potential" (GOI, The Tenth Five Year Plan). Economic empowerment would "ensure provision of training, employment and income-generation activities… with the ultimate objective of making all potential women economically independent." (GOI, The Tenth Five Year Plan). Gender justice seeks to eliminate all forms of gender discrimination and enables women to enjoy fundamental rights and freedoms on equal footing with men.

Non-Governmental Action

In an area like progress and development of women, which depends so much on generating awareness, changing attitudes that have been deeply ingrained for centuries, and overcoming resistance from and involving other powerful stake holders, legislation and development programmes initiated by the government alone will not succeed unless accompanied by the active involvement and participation of the people themselves led by voluntary action groups. Such voluntary action has been on the ground since the days of Independence struggle but acquired momentum as the issues relating to women came into sharp focus. In fact, individual social activists and non-Governmental organizations have generally been in the forefront of movement to spur government into action and have been primarily responsible for several of the women-oriented legislative enactments and policies referred to elsewhere. The activities of these organizations can broadly be grouped as: (a) implementing welfare programmes for destitute women, (b) training of women and work-oriented skill development, (c) promoting women's cooperatives and other forms of women organizations (SHGs, for instance) to enable mobilization of finances and other requirements in pursuit of productive self-employment, and (d) taking up issues affecting women, generating awareness, supporting action in individual cases and providing legal aid and other services. Individuals, small local level groups of women like Mahila Mandals and other institutions promoted by individuals, and national level organisations (like The All India Women's Conference, Self-Employed Women's Organisation (SEWA) and Working Women's Forum) contribute equally to this private effort. Most of the governmental schemes aimed at development of women like the programme of Training-cum-Production Centres supported by Norwegian Agency for Development (NORAD), Support to Training and Employment Programme for Women, Mahila Samriddhi Yojana, Old Age Homes for Women are operated through NGOs, and so are the efforts to organize women as SHGs for mobilization of credit and other inputs for their economic activities. SEWA is one of the most successful attempts at organizing poor self-employed women on a cooperative basis and improve their access to credit through self-help. There are today various forms of women's organizations such as trade unions, Member Based Organisations (MBOs), Mahila Mandals, NGOs, etc all working for advancement of women's empowerment. These models of organizing women would be the subject of another Chapter of this book.

Summing up the developments over the past fifty years, it may be concluded that judicial activism, pressures from non-governmental agents catalyzing social change and international commitments have forced the pace of governmental intervention, legislative and developmental, to achieve a greater degree of egalitarianism in the Indian society in so far as gender is concerned. There has been a sea change in the approach too. What in the first half of the past half a century was a condescending welfare-oriented approach was transformed into a grudging acceptance of the empowerment paradigm of women's development. First it was empowerment through education and training, then it was social and economic empowerment and soon empowerment involving sharing in the decision-making process. It is true that the progress has been painfully slow, but considering the fact that the attack is on ideas, customs and beliefs that have existed and taken deep roots over more than two millennia and on social forces and vested interests that have well-entrenched themselves, what has been achieved in fifty years is indeed significant. One may also be disappointed that the progress in basic sectors like education, primary health, sanitation and water supply, poverty and employment has been grossly inadequate and that there is an extent of cynicism in the implementation of well-meant programmes. But there have been winds of change sweeping across the country and there is an increasing section of the society that believes in the imperatives of gender equality and women's development. Another Chapter will look at the achievements in terms of hard quantitative and qualitative evidence.

Welfare to Empowerment Development of Women in India—Important Milestones

Year	*Event*
1950	Adoption of the Constitution
1953	Establishment of Central Social Welfare Board
1955	Enactment of Hindu Marriage Act
1956	Enactment of Hindu Succession Act; Hindu Adoption and Maintenance Act
1961	Enactment of Maternity Benefits Act; Dowry Abolition Act
1971	Constitution of the Committee on Status of Women in India
1976	Enactment of Equal Remuneration Act
1983	Amendment of Rape Laws
1986	Enactment of Indecent Representation of Women (Prohibition) Act; Immoral Traffic (Prevention) Act (amending the earlier SITA)
1987	Constitution of National Commission on Self-employed Women
1988	Adoption of National Perspective Plan for Women 1988 -2000
1992	Constitution of National Commission for Women
1993	Enactment of 73rd and 74th Constitution (Amendment) Act; Establishment of Rashtriya Mahila Kosh; Launching Mahila Samriddhi Yojana
1994	Ratification of Convention on Elimination of All Forms of Discrimination Against Women (CEDAW); Enactment of Pre-Natal Diagnostic Techniques (Regulation and Prevention of Misuse) Act
1995	Launching of Indira Mahila Yojana
2001	Adoption of National Policy of Empowerment of Women

Notes

1 Composer of Manusmriti, around the beginning of the Christian era, prescribing a social code of conduct

2 There are over 50 Central laws dealing with various aspects of labour, let alone the laws enacted by individual States.

III

Empowerment Programmes

A Review

The legislative action and the developmental policy on the part of the state aimed at accelerating the process of empowerment of women in India have been outlined in detail in the previous Chapter. The Fundamental Rights enshrined in the Constitution, the Directive Principles and Constitutional amendments, already carried out or in pipeline, attempt to ensure equality of treatment between the two genders in all matters concerning social, economic and political and legal rights, with provisions calling for supplementary action to correct the existing leeway suffered by women in the matter of economic, social and political development. Various other legislative instruments have been enacted to protect women against social evils and other gender-related crimes and against discrimination in employment, and to provide certain benefits like regulation of employment conditions, maternity benefits and crèche facilities, etc. On the developmental front, a variety of programmes and schemes have been launched from time to time with the objective of sensitizing the society regarding development of women, improving women's access to health and nutrition, education and skill development, and bring about economic empowerment through better access to wage and self-employment and to resources. Content-wise, these programmes aim, to use the terminology of Tenth Five Year Plan, at social empowerment, economic empowerment and gender justice. From an organizational point of view, the programmes can be classified as (a) state-managed and operated, (b) state-sponsored and/or supported and operated by the non-governmental institutions, and (c) managed and operated independently by the private sector, with or without assistance from the state. Another classification, from an operational point of view, would be: (a) general developmental schemes which benefit males and females without distinction, (b) general development schemes meant for all, but with specific benefits/preferences/quotas for women, and

(c) schemes which are exclusively for the benefit of women. A modification of the last classification, classifying schemes as women-specific schemes specifically targeted at women and girls and pro-women schemes having a significant (at least 30 per cent) women component, is adopted in the gender-budget studies commissioned by Department of Women and Child Development in recent years under the coordination of National Institute for Public Cooperation and Child Development. This Chapter will look at the government's commitment to women's development in terms of funds allocated to these schemes and then attempt a review of some of the sector-specific programmes and schemes, which are either exclusively for the benefit of women or those with specific components benefiting women. An assessment of the overall impact of these as well as other general development schemes have had on the status of women will be the subject of the next Chapter.

Allocation of Funds and Gender Budgeting

Even though the need to ensure flow of adequate quantum of development funds to schemes for the benefit of women was highlighted in the Eighth Five Year Plan (1992-97), the first real operational step to monitor this commitment of funds was taken, as stated in an earlier Chapter, in the Ninth Five Year Plan (1997-2002) through the mechanism of Women Component Plan. Governments, both at the Centre and those in the States, have been directed to ensure that not less than 30 per cent of the funds/benefits are earmarked in all the women related sectors. The Women Component Plan of the Ninth Plan of the Central Government, accordingly, proposed flow of funds to the tune of 42.9 per cent of the Plan budgets of women-specific and women-related ministries (Table 3.1).

The National Policy for Empowerment of Women (see Chapter 2) also envisaged introduction of a gender perspective in the budgeting process as an operational strategy. The gender analysis of budgets conducted by the Department of Women and Child Development through the National Institute for Public Cooperation and Child Development (Government of India, Department of Women and Child Development, Annual Report, 2002-03) found that the allocations on women specific schemes increased from Rs.3,260 crores in 2001-02 to Rs.3,358 crores in 2002-03 (by 3 per cent) and further to Rs.3,675 crores in 2003-04 (by 9 per cent). Similarly, the budget allocations for 'pro-women' schemes increased from Rs.10,596 crores in 2001-02 to 13,036 crores in 2002-03 (by 23 per cent). The allocations for these schemes in the budget for 2003-04 reflected a further increase of 7 per cent over 2002-03.

Table 3.1: Women's Component Plan in the Ninth Five Year Plan (1997-2002)

Ministry/Department	*Ninth Plan (Gross Budgetary Support) (Rs. crores)*	*Flow to Women Component Plan (Rs. crores)*	*Percentage of flow to Women Component Plan*
A. Women-Specific (Nodal Department)			
Women and Child Development	7,810.42	7,810.42	100.0
B. Women-related Ministries/Departments			
1. Health	5,118.19	2,581.25	50.4
2. Family Welfare	15,120.20	10,541.26	69.7
3. Indian Systems of Medicine & Homeopathy	266.35	133.18	50.0
4. Education	20,381.64	10,212.44	50.1
5. Labour	899.12	300.85	33.5
6. Agriculture & Cooperation	9,153.82	349.96	3.8
7. Rural Development	41,833.87	17,415.00	41.6
8. Urban Employment & Poverty Alleviation	4,931.22	403.60	8.2
9. Social Justice & Empowerment	6,608.13	814.81	13.2
10. Tribal Affairs	*	60.00	*
11. Science & Technology	1,497.35	7.50	0.5
12. Information & Broadcasting	680.05	30.00	4.4
13. Non-Conventional Energy Sources	2,122.14	401.00	18.9
14. Small-Scale & Agro-Related Industries	3,786.85	868.93	23.0
15. Youth Affairs & Sports	826.09	12.33	1.5
Sub-Total (B)	1,13,225.02	44,132.11	39.0
Grand Total (A +B)	*1,21,035.44*	*51,942.53*	*42.9*

*Included in the Ministry of Social Justice and Empowerment. The total Gross Budgetary Support of all Minstries and Departments for the Ninth Plan was Rs. 2,03,982 crores. The percentage of Women Component Plan funds to this total works out 25.5.

Source: Tenth Five Year Plan (2002-07), Planning Commission, Government of India.

Some studies were conducted in respect of some State budgets also (Government of India, Department of Women and Child Development, Annual Report 2002-03). The available results in respect of 10 States (Assam, Bihar, Gujarat, Jammu & Kashmir, Madhya Pradesh, Maharashtra, Manipur, Meghalaya, Orissa and Rajasthan) indicate that:

- The shares of social sector budget in the total budget varied between 22 and 52 per cent in 2000-01. During 2001-02, the share varied between 18 to 48 per cent only.
- In 2001-02, the provision for social sector was less than 25 per cent in Orissa, Bihar, Jammu & Kashmir and Madhya Pradesh, between 25 and 35 per cent in Maharashtra, Gujarat and Manipur, and between 35 and 50 per cent in Assam, Meghalaya and Rajasthan.
- The percentage of provisions for Women Targetted schemes within the social sector budget was very low, ranging from less than 1 per cent to 11 per cent.
- The provisions for all women related schemes (Women Targetted and Pro-Women) as percentage of total social sector budget varied from a low of 6 per cent in Madhya Pradesh to a high of 41 per cent in Orissa. Meghalaya and Manipur also had relatively high percentages at 29 and 24 respectively.

On the whole, it must be admitted that the development effort targeting women is grossly inadequate, though there has been substantial improvement over the last two decades. As the Government itself mentions (GOI, Department of Women and Child Development, 2002-03), there were only two women-specific development schemes during the first twenty-eight years of planning history, namely, the schemes of Condensed Course of Education and Women and Socio-Economic Programme introduced during the Second Five Year Plan (1956-61) and that of Working Girls' Hostels and Short Stay Homes during the Fourth Five Year Plan (1969-74). Since then a host of schemes aimed at social and economic empowerment have been introduced with expanding scope and outlays. The rest of this Chapter will look at some of the more important of these schemes.

Schemes for Social Empowerment

Programmes directed towards social empowerment of women cover aspects like health and nutrition, education and skill development, old age security and other forms of social welfare. Some of the important programmes in the area of health and nutrition are the Scheme of Primary Health Centres, Reproductive and Child Health Programme and the Integrated Child Development Services. Schemes to promote education and skill development include those of Scholarships for Girl Students from Scheduled Castes and Scheduled Tribes, Mahila Samakhya Yojana, scheme of Hostels for Girl Students, scheme of Vocationalisation of Education and vocational training for women through Industrial Training Institutes and Vocational Training Institutes for Women. Welfare schemes are 'Swadhar', the scheme for Women in Difficult

Circumstances, and the old age pension and the maternity benefits component of the National Social Assistance Programme (NSOP).

Health

Rural Health Infrastructure

The elaborate network of Community Health Centres, Primary Health Centres and Sub-Centres, however rickety it may be, constitutes the backbone of the rural health infrastructure in India. By the year 2002, there were 2,935 Community Health Centres, about 22,975 Primary Health Centres and 1,37,271 village-level Sub-Centres providing the basic health and immunization services in the rural areas. Though plagued by problems of absence of medical and paramedical personnel according to the sanctioned strength, inadequate accessibility of services in remote areas to the desired extent, etc, this rural infrastructure created over the years performs a very useful function in creating health awareness in the villages and in providing essential health care. The services of these Centres are available for both men and women, but spread of family welfare measures being an essential function of the Centres, special attention is paid to the women-related health problems through separate staff like Lady Health Visitors and Auxiliary Nurse/Midwife.

Reproductive Health Care

The Reproductive Health Care programme was launched in 1997 subsuming the earlier schemes of Child Survival and Safe Motherhood and Universal Immunisation Programme. The programme provides access, as far as possible at the community level, to essential as well as emergency obstetric care during the whole period of pregnancy, to better and safe abortion services, to treatment of reproductive tract infections and sexually transmitted infections and to immunization against tetanus through tetanus toxoid vaccination of pregnant women. By 2000-01, about 83.4 per cent of the pregnant women were covered by the immunization programme. A scheme of Training of Dais was also launched in 2000-01 in 142 districts in 17 States.

Integrated Child Development Services (ICDS)

Started on a small scale in only 33 community development blocks in 1975, ICDS has grown over the years into perhaps the largest child development programme in the world, covering now about three-fourths of the community development blocks in the rural areas and over 270 urban slum pockets in the country and aiming at total coverage in a short time. The objectives of the scheme are: (a) to improve nutritional and health status of children below the age of six years, (b) to provide proper conditions for psychological, physical and social development of the child, (c) to reduce the incidence of mortality, malnutrition, school drop-out, etc., and (d) to enhance the capability of the mother to look after the child through proper community education. ICDS also provides nutritional and other assistance to pregnant women and nursing mothers in socially and economically backward villages and slum areas of cities. Operating through the institutional mechanism of 5.8 lakh *Anganwadis* at the community level and through over 4,000 ICDS projects, it now benefits over 5 million expectant and nursing mothers and about 25 million children. The scheme envisages one ICDS rural/urban project for 1,00,000 population and one tribal project for 70,000 population. Currently, the scheme benefits about 332 lakh children in the age group 0 – 6 years and 62 lakh pregnant and lactating women.

The principal components of ICDS are health, nutrition, early childhood care and pre-school education. The health component consists of regular check-ups, pre-natal and post-natal care for pregnant women, immunization against six vaccine preventable diseases, management of malnutrition, treatment of common child diseases and distribution of simple medicines at the *Anganwadis* through the staff of the Primary Health Centres. The nutrition component includes supplementary feeding through provision of food supplements to remove calorie and protein deficiency among children and pregnant and nursing mothers, monitoring of growth and spread of health education. In 1991-92, a new component, titled Adolescent Girls' Scheme, has been introduced into the programme in selected blocks to provide an environment of self-supportive development to girl children in the age group 11 to 18 years who have dropped out of the school system, addressing such needs as nutrition, health, education, literacy recreation, skill formation and self-development. A revamped version of this scheme for adolescent girls titled Kishori Shakti Yojana has been launched in 2000-01 as part of ICDS programme and is being implemented in 2000 ICDS projects. Other initiatives taken to improve ICDS further include opening mini-*Anganwadis* to cover remote areas, integration of Indian systems of medicine, decentralization of activities to provide a flexible response to the needs of women and child care etc. Human resource development needs of the staff involved in the implementation of ICDS have been taken care through the introduction of nation-wide training component through *Udisha.* In sum, the ICDS provides services that include (a) supplementary nutrition, (b) Immunisation, (c) Health check ups, (d) Referral Services (e) Pre-school non-formal education and (f) Nutrition and health education. ICDS, thus, contributes to the development of women in more than one way-directly, through health and nutritional services to pregnant and nursing women and health education, and indirectly through various child care services, which otherwise would have been the responsibility of the mothers.

Rural Water Supply (Swajaldhara)

Women are the main stakeholders in any water supply programme as fetching water for domestic consumption from supply points at far off distances is one of the back-breaking burdens of the daily lives of rural women, impacting adversely on their health and constraining their ability to participate in other productive activities, thus having an important bearing on their empowerment. Three decades of intensive efforts (from 1972-73 when Accelerated Rural Water Supply was introduced) and two in mission mode[1] to ensure that safe drinking water is available within a reasonable distance from the villages have not been sufficient to achieve this basic goal. While the Accelerated Rural Drinking Water Supply scheme continues, some innovative reform initiatives have been taken in recent years (from April 1999) to promote community participation and responsibility in the programmes, thereby ensuring long-term sustainability. The key elements of this reformed component of the rural water supply programme *Swajaladhara* include a shift in the role of government from one of provider to that of facilitator, adoption of a demand-driven approach at the community level, focus on village level capacity building, water conservation measures, and partial capital and full operational and maintenance expenditure by the community. Empowerment of women and promotion of health and environmental awareness are important objective of these reforms. Experience of the pilot phase of these initiatives in operation since 1996 in 357 villages in 7 districts of Bundelkhand region in Uttar Pradesh has been encouraging, with surveys showing (a) an average saving of 2 hours per head time against an expected 30 minutes, (b) women's participation in the Village Water Supply Committees constituted under the scheme to the tune of 36 per cent against 30 per cent envisaged, (c) decline in the incidence of water-borne disease of diarrhoea (d) formation of 501 Self Help Groups, each group on an average saving about Rs. 8,000, etc. Based on this experience, the *Swajaladhara* has now been extended throughout the country from December 2002. By March 2003, 67 districts have been covered by these reformed component of rural water supply programme.

Education

Education is a key element in the process of empowerment of women. Literacy and educational levels in India, irrespective of gender, being lower than international achievements, most schemes for educational development are geared to benefit both males and females. An elaborate network of educational institutions comprising over 6 lakh lower primary schools, 2 lakhs upper primary schools, about 80,000 high schools and about 7,500 colleges for general education and a host of institutions for technical and professional education at various levels has been built up over the years. There are also schemes for non-formal education and adult education. There are, however, considerable and persistent gender gaps even in the relatively low levels of educational attainments in India, larger than in many other countries, including some developing countries. About half of the children remain outside the school system, of whom the majority are girls. There are also regional disparities and between the rural and the urban areas in the levels of educational achievements of women due to socio-cultural factors. The first Educational Commission (1964-66) recommended special attention to girl's education. The first National Policy on Education (1968) emphasized the need for equal educational opportunities for women so that they could become the means of social transformation. The National Policy on Education (1986, revised in 1992) also renewed this emphasis on education to be an instrument towards achieving the goal of women's equality. In order to translate these policy pronouncements into a practical reality, schemes have been launched from time to time specifically aiming at improving the participation of women in the educational process.

Mahila Samakyha Scheme

Mahila Samakhya Scheme, conceived as a women's empowerment project and as a practical move towards the goals of the National Education Policy, was launched in 1989 and is currently implemented in over 9,000 villages in 60 districts in 10 States. It enabled growth of grass root level organizations of women that provide a forum and environment for women's education at the community level in addition to managing Non-Formal Education Centres and Early Childhood-Care Education Centres. The Scheme seeks to bring about a change in women's perception about themselves and that of the society in regard to women's traditional roles and enable them to tackle the larger socio-cultural issues that have traditionally inhibited the participation of women and girls in the educational system. It endeavours to create an environment for women to seek knowledge and information in order to make informed choices and create circumstances in which women can learn at their own pace and rhythm. A key element of the scheme is an area intensive approach to integrate the existing efforts to provide formal and non-formal schooling, adult education, up-gradation of educational qualifications through condensed courses and vocational training. Under the scheme, financial assistance, to the tune of 100 per cent of the cost, is provided by the government to voluntary agencies to implement well-designed field projects for women's empowerment and education and related activities.

The nodal point for all activities under the scheme is the Sangha, a women's group at the village level. There is a leader, designated Sahayogini, for each group of ten villages acting as the motivator, supporter and guide, mobilizing and organising women into Sanghas and coordinating the programme in the ten villages under her charge and providing linkages with the educational support structure and the district level institutions. The scheme is said to have generated demand for literacy and education among girls and women.

District Primary Education Programme

The District Primary Education Programme (DPEP), was taken up in 1994 with assistance from a number of international agencies in 14 States that have a low level of female literacy. Though not confined to girls only, the programme has a gender perspective built into it. It provides for flexible school timings to suit the girls' needs, residential schools, gender-sensitive text books and recruitment of female teachers to encourage participation of girls in the primary education process. There are now 21,000 new formal schools and over 67,000 alternative schools covering 25 lakh children.

Sarva Shiksha Abhiyan

Universalisation of elementary education is still an unrealized goal and a number of schemes intended to accelerate the approach towards this goal have been in place for several years. These include, apart from the Mahila Samakhya and DPEP mentioned above, schemes like Mid-day Meal Scheme, Non-formal Education with focus on out-of-school children and innovative projects like the Shiksha Karmi and Lok Jumbish in Rajasthan, Janshala and other projects elsewhere in the country. Most of these schemes and projects have a gender focus. Sarva Shiksha Abhiyan has been launched in the Ninth plan as an umbrella programme to bring about universal elementary education in a time-bound integrated manner synergizing all the on-going prorammes in such a way that (a) all children are in schools by 2003, (b) all children to complete five years of schooling by 2007 and eight years of schooling by 2012, (c) universal retention of children in schools by

2010 and (d) eliminating all gender and social disparities at primary stage by 2007 and at upper primary level by 2010. The programme has a special focus on the education of girls among other groups with special needs.

Skill Development

Vocational skills are imparted under two institutional streams—the vocational education component at the post-secondary school educational system operated by the Ministry of Human Resources Development and the vocational training scheme operated by the Ministry of Labour. Under the vocational education scheme of the Ministry of Human Resources, currently implemented at the +2 stage in about 6,700 schools through the State governments, over 150 vocational courses are offered. In addition, NGOs are given assistance to take up innovative programmes to promote vocational education. The scheme has not been a great success primarily in view of the preference of the students for general education but also due to inadequate infrastructure and inadequate attention from the educational authorities. Though the vocational education stream is open to both sexes, there is perhaps even less enthusiasm among girls to go in for it, only a quarter of the total enrolment in the vocational stream being girls.

The Ministry of Labour operates programmes for training in vocational skills through its Craftsmen Training Programme, Apprenticeship Programme and Vocational Training Programme for women. The Craftsmen Training Programme provides institutional training in 43 engineering and 24 non-engineering trades through a network of about 4,500 Industrial Training Institutes (March, 2002) run both by the State governments and private organizations, with a total seating capacity of 6.58 lakhs (March, 2002). Some of these (211 in March, 2002) are exclusively for women while some others (534 in March, 2002) have a separate women's wing attached to them. The total training capacity of all these facilities for women in the Industrial Training Institutes is less than 50,000 (46,750 in March, 2002). The participation of women in the training under the Apprenticeship Training programme is still more inadequate, with only 4,100 training places out of a total of 1.61 lakhs located (in June 1998) having been taken by women. The Ministry of Labour also runs a National Vocational Training Institute and 10 Regional Vocational Training Institutes for Women for training in specialized trades and advanced skills, but their combined capacity is only 2,050 seats making insignificant impact.

Others

National Old-age /Widow Pension Scheme

Old age pensions and widow pensions were being paid by a number of States since the seventies. Under the National Old Age Pension Scheme launched in 1995 as a component of National Social Assistance Scheme, Central government provides assistance to the States to meet their expenditure on monthly pension up to Rs. 75 to men and women aged 65 or above and have no regular means of livelihood. It is open to the States, and in fact many States do, to pay pension at higher rates. Around 7.7 million women, constituting 24 per cent of the aged, were benefited under the scheme during the period 1997-2002. The scheme is budget-driven and not need-driven and consequently all the eligible old people cannot avail of the benefits.

Women in Difficult Circumstances (Swadhar)

This scheme was launched in 2001-02 to help women in difficult circumstances, like destitute widows, deserted by families, women prisoners released from jails and without support, survivors of natural disasters rendered homeless, rescued trafficked girls/women, victims of sexual crimes, mentally disordered women, etc. . The assistance under this programme includes shelter, food, clothing, health care, and counseling. Social and economic rehabilitation services are also provided to these women. The scheme, implemented through Government departments, local bodies, trusts, other organizations with adequate experience in the field of rehabilitation and with adequate infrastructure, has seven project modules having provision of shelters of different capacities for inmates, family counseling, medical centres, and training centres, family and help line for women in distress. During the year 2002-03, about Rs 347 lakh were released benefiting more than 200 women.

National Maternity Benefits Scheme

The National Maternity Benefits Scheme, launched as a component of the National Social Assistance Scheme in 1995, is meant for financially assisting expectant mothers with a grant of Rs. 500 for each of the first two live births. Since the inception of the scheme, about 6.5 lakh women have been benefited under it.

Short-stay Homes for Women and Girls

This scheme was launched in 1969 to provide temporary shelters to provide security for women and girls who are at risk due to family problems, mental mal-adjustment, and are subjected to various types of exploitation. Under this programme, implemented by the Department of Women and Child Development till 1999 and through Central Social

Welfare Board since then, services like counseling, medical care, psychiatric treatment, occupational therapy, education cum vocational training, etc. is provided. The scheme aims at helping the women to rehabilitate themselves during their short stay at these homes. It is operated through voluntary agencies and grants are given to such voluntary organizations that run these homes. 289 Short-stay homes were given grants till the end of 2002 covering about 8 thousand beneficiaries.

Balika Samriddhi Yojana

The objective of Balika Samriddhi Yojana, which was launched in 1997-98, was to raise the status of the girl child in the family and to bring about a positive attitudinal change towards her in the community as a whole. Under this scheme, up to two girl children born after 15 August 1997 in families below poverty line are covered and a grant of Rs. 500 is given to the mother in each case. The scheme was recast in 1999 providing for (a) the deposit of the post delivery grant of Rs. 500 in interest-bearing bank/post office account in the name of the child, (b) additional scholarship money ranging from Rs. 300 for Class I to Rs. 1000 for Class X for each class successfully completed, which will also be deposited in the same account, and (c) payment of the accumulated amount in the account to the girl when she attains the age of 18 years and remains unmarried till then.

Mahila Mandals

This programme was started in 1961-62 by the Central Social Welfare Board in the areas where there were no voluntary organisations to implement welfare schemes for women and children. Mahila Mandals work like NGOs and the welfare services taken up at grass root level through these organizations include balwadis for children, craft activities, social education, maternity services for women, etc. During 2002-03, funds to the tune of 29.40 lakhs were released to 92 Mandals covering about 20,000 beneficiaries.

Schemes for Economic Empowerment

Economic empowerment of women depends on their participation in productive activities leading to independent incomes. This is sought to be achieved through improving their access to wage and self-employment, meeting their credit, marketing and organizational needs, and introducing to the benefits of technological advances.

Sampoorna Grameen Rojgar Yojana (SGRY)

Wage employment schemes to provide supplementary employment opportunities in the rural areas have been in operation for over a quarter of a century. Beginning as rural works programmes on a relatively small scale, they have evolved first as National Rural Employment Programme and Rural Landless Employment Guarantee Programme, then as Jawahar Rojgar Yojana and Employment Assurance Scheme, then as Jawahar Gram Samriddhi Yojana and Employment Assurance Scheme, and finally from 25th September 2001 as an integrated rural wage-employment programme in the form of Samporna Grameen Rojgar Yojana (SGRY). SGRY is a comprehensive programme to take care of requirements of additional wage employment, food security and village infrastructure in the rural areas. The programme, run by Ministry of Rural Development through the States, has an annual outlay of Rs. 10,000 crores to meet the cost of about 100 crore mandays of employment expected to be created annually, half the amount in wages and the other half as foodgrains. Labour-intensive activities for creating durable assets like drought proofing, watershed development, promoting traditional water resources, aforestation, construction of link roads, school buildings, marketing infrastructure etc. are to be taken up under the Programme. Zilla Parishad is the implementing agency at district level and Panchayat Raj institutions are fully involved in execution. Contractors are not allowed to take up any work in this scheme.

SGRY is a self-targeting programme for the benefit of Below Poverty Line families, with special focus on providing wage employment to women, scheduled castes, scheduled tribes and parents of children withdrawn from hazardous occupations. The programme stipulates that 30 per cent of the wage employment opportunities created should be reserved for women. Similarly, during 2002-03, up to November, 2003, out of a total of 3,130 lakh mandays of employment created, about 759 lakh mandays were for women.

Swarnjayanti Gram Swarojgar Yojana (SGSY)

The Swarnjayanti Gram Swarojgar Yojana (SGSY) is an anti poverty programme which was launched during 1999 amalgamating and restructuring a number of schemes like the former Integrated Rural Development Programme (IRDP), the Scheme for Training Rural Youth for Self-employment (TRYSEM), the scheme for Development of Women and Children in Rural Areas (DWCRA), the scheme for Supply of Improved Toolkits in Rural Areas (SITRA), Ganga Kalyan Yojana (GKY) and the Million Wells Scheme (MWS). These schemes have, in fact, been going on for over two decades. Unlike the earlier schemes, the combined and restructured programme SGSY is conceived as a holistic programme to provide sustainable income to the poor families in the rural areas through establishing micro-enterprises, covering aspects such as organization into groups, capacity building, training, selection of key self-employment activities in each area, technology and marketing support and infrastructure building. It is envisaged that families under this programme can be brought above poverty line within a period of three years. It is a credit-cum-subsidy programme. Four or five viable activities are to be identified in each block and self-help groups (SHGs) of 10 to 20 persons from Below Poverty Line families have to be formed. Facilities for training, credit, technology, infrastructure, marketing, etc. have to be provided in the identified activities. The scheme is based on participatory approach and emphasizes social mobilization at grass root level. Group activities have to be given preference and gradually all funding under the programme would be to SHGs.

The scheme is implemented through District Rural Development Agencies (DRDAs) with involvement of Panchayat Raj Institutions, Banks, Line Departments and NGOs. SGSY stipulates that 50 per cent of all the self-help groups formed should be exclusively for women. Further it is expected that efforts would be made to involve women members in each SHG. During the last three years (1999-2000 to 2002-03), the percentage of women among all persons assisted under the programme averaged 43.5, the highest being 47.3 in 2002-03, against a target of at least 40 per cent.

Swarna Jayanti Shahari Rozgar Yojana (SJSRY)

Swarna Jayanti Shahari Rozgar Yojana (SJSRY) provides wage and self-employment opportunities to the urban poor, especially those below poverty line. While one of its components, namely, Urban Self Employment Porgramme (USEP), provides assistance to the urban poor, especially women living below poverty line, another, namely the scheme for Development of Women and Children in the Urban Areas (DWCUA) launched in 1997, provides assistance in the form of revolving fund to groups of poor women in urban areas to take up self-employment. The revolving fund is for the purposes of purchase of raw materials, marketing, infrastructure support, child-care activities, etc. Between 1997 and 2003, about 20,000 groups have been formed under DWCUA and nearly 34,000 women have been assisted into group self-employment.

Support to Training and Employment Programme for Women (STEP)

This programme was launched in 1987 to upgrade the skills of poor and asset-less women in the sectors of agriculture, animal husbandry, dairying, fisheries, handlooms, handicrafts, khadi and village industries, sericulture, forestry and waste land development. The basic objective was to enhance their productivity and incomes by increasing their employability through wage-paid employment and also self-employment. Besides training, the scheme includes other support services like linkages with marketing and credit facilities. Under this programme, women are encouraged to organise themselves in homogenous groups to start some income generating activity. The programme is in operation in 20 States of the country. About 6.5 lakh women have been covered under 138 projects up to 2002-2003 in various States. Due to higher demand in dairying, handlooms, handicrafts, sericulture and poultry, more support is being provided for these sectors under this programme.

Swavlamban

This programme, earlier known as Women's Economic Programme, was launched in 1982-83 with the help of Norwegian Agency for Development (NORAD) and is rechristened Swawlamban during 2002-03. It aims at equipping women with skills and subsequently to take up wage- or self-employment. Financial assistance is provided to public sector undertakings, autonomous bodies, corporations, and voluntary organisations to train women in non-traditional areas such as electronics, watch-making, garment-making, computer programming, embroidery, etc. The assistance is to cover costs on hiring training cum production units, training costs, stipend to trainees, equipment etc. The maximum limit of this assistance is Rs.8,000/- per trainee.

Swayamsidha

The two earlier programmes of Indira Mahila Yojana and Mahila Samriddhi Yojana have been combined and recast as Swayamsidha in 2001 as an integrated programme for empowerment of women by ensuring their direct access to and control over resources through a sustained process of mobilization and convergence of all the on-going sectoral programmes. Its objectives include formation of self-help groups of women, creation of confidence and generation of awareness among the members of SHGs, strengthening saving habit, improving access to micro-credit, involvement of women in local level planning and convergence of services of various departments.

Swa-Shakti

Swa-Shakti was launched during 1998-99 with the support of World Bank and International Fund for Agricultural Development to enhance women's access to resources and quality of life through time-saving and drudgery-reducing devices, health, literacy and confidence building. It envisages establishment of women's self-help groups of 15 to 20 members each, developing linkages between SHGs and financial institutions to ensure access to credit, involvement of women in income generating activities, and provision of technology inputs to save time and reduce drudgery in work. It also aims at sensitizing the support agencies to women's needs. Till 2002-03, a total of over 17,500 SHGs were formed in 7,288 villages under the scheme through 231 NGOs and with a membership of about 2,50,000.

Rashtriya Mahila Kosh

Rashtriya Mahila Kosh (RMK) has been established in 1993 to facilitate credit support or micro-finance to poor women. The support is provided through NGOs, Women Development Corporations, Cooperative Societies and other Block Mahila Samitis and other State government agencies. Its ultimate aim is to initiate socio-economic change and development in the lives of women. Apart from lending to eligible NGOs that help women's groups in meeting their credit needs, RMK has a number of promotional and innovative schemes like loan promotion scheme to assist potentially capable but as yet ineligible NGOs, micro-credit for education and skill up-gradation in newly emerging opportunities in the information technology sector, support for crop credit and off-farm activities to women, support for small consumption loans,etc. RMK also supports its NGOs to form women thrift & credit societies/self-help groups. Since its inception on 13th March, 1993 upto 31st December, 2002, a sum of Rs.118 crores was sanctioned by RMK for about 4.35 lakh women beneficiaries through 1066 NGOs/organisations. Rate of recovery of RMK loan is quite high at more than 90 per cent.

Socio-economic Programme of Central Social Welfare Board

Under this programme launched in 1956 by the Central Social Welfare Board, women are encouraged to take up a wide variety of income generating activities. Women's voluntary organizations, women's cooperatives, etc. are given grants to set up production units and agro-based units like dairy, poultry, piggery, etc. to provide employment to women from the marginalized sections of the society. Self-employment is promoted through supply of sewing machines, etc.

Science and Technology for Women

This scheme, launched by the Department of Science & Technology, aims at promoting research and development and adaptation of technology to improve the life and working conditions and opportunities for gainful employment for women, especially in rural areas and increasing the contribution of women in science and technology and development. Some of the priority areas identified under the scheme, *inter alia*, include specific science and technology application programmes to solve the problems of women in different regions, involvement of women in low cost preservation and processing of horticulture produce, association of women in wasteland development schemes, involvement of women in regional health practices and minimizing occupational hazards to women, etc.

Trade Related Entrepreneurship Assistance and Development Scheme for Women (TREAD)

The Department of Small Scale Industries and Agro & Rural Industries, Ministry of Industries, launched this scheme during 1996-97 to economically empower poor women in rural and urban areas by providing financial assistance to them through NGOs who could help such women to set up gainful enterprises. The project covers women in the unorganized sector. Assistance is provided in establishing enterprises in the products involving processed food, leather goods, readymade garments, coir works, hand-made paper and processing minor forest produce.

Working Women's Hostels

The Department of Women and Child Department initiated a scheme for working women's hostels in 1973 to facilitate their stay in the places where they are working outside their family security. Under this scheme, financial assistance is made available to voluntary organisations and local bodies for construction of hostels for the women who move outside their home for employment and technical training. The basic aim of the scheme is to provide cheap and safe accommodation to these women, especially to single working women, widows, divorcees, etc. Girl students studying in professional courses may also avail this facility. These hostels also have day-care facility for children. 889 such hostels have been constructed up to January 2003 all over the country to benefit about fifty two thousand women. 316 hostels have day-care centre facilities with a capacity of keeping more than 8000 children.

Creches for Children of Working and Ailing Women and National Creche Fund

General creches were started in 1975 for giving proper care to children in the age-group of 0-5 years in the absence of their mothers to help those working in casual, migrant, agricultural and construction employment. The scheme provided for recurrent grants and non-recurring grants for purchase of equipment to voluntary organizations that set up a crèche unit for 25 children. The National Creche Fund was set up in 1994 with a corpus fund of 19.90 crores out of the Social Safety Net Adjustment Credit from World Bank. 25 per cent of the Centres had to be Anganwadi cum creche centres to be assisted by these funds, while 75 per cent of the centres would be general crèches. Children of parents, whose monthly income does not exceed Rs. 1,800/- are eligible for enrolment. The scheme is implemented through voluntary organisations and Mahila Mandals. Services provided under this programme are day care facilities, supplementary nutrition, immunisation, medical and health care and recreation.

Ownership of Assets

Indira Aawas Yojana

Indira Aawas Yojana (IAY) was launched in 1985-86 to provide housing assistance to rural families below poverty line belonging primarily to disadvantaged sections like Scheduled Castes and Scheduled Tribes and freed bonded labour. From 1993-94, the scheme has been thrown open to other rural families below poverty line with the restriction that the number of such beneficiaries should not be more than 40 per cent of the total. An amount of Rs. 20,000 (Rs. 22,000 in hill areas) is granted for construction of each dwelling unit to be constructed by the beneficiary him/herself. Assistance is also available for up-grading the dwelling unit to a limit of Rs. 10,000 per unit. Beneficiaries are selected by the Gram Sabha. Priority is to be given to widows and unmarried women. The important provision in IAY in so far as empowerment of women is concerned is the stipulation that the houses constructed under the scheme are to be allotted in the name of the female member of the beneficiary household or in the joint names of the husband and the wife.

Organisation

A key element of the current strategy in empowering women is to organize them into groups. It is considered, and rightly so, that organising women is extremely important in the process of realisation of their rights and in reaping their just share of the fruits of development, as it would provide a platform to raise their collective voice which may not be possible when they are not united. Such organisation takes a wide variety of forms – informal groups, NGOs, cooperatives, trade unions, etc. Even though the process of organisation of women began during the course of freedom movement itself, it was mainly as a part of the general mobilization of opinion against the colonial government. As a movement to strengthen the voice of women against gender injustice, to implement development programmes meant for them and to avail of the facilities made available by the state to enhance their incomes and quality of life, it has a shorter history. Beginning with loose associations like Mahila Mandals in the early sixties, organisations of women soon made their presence felt in the form of DWACRA groups and unions like Self-Employed Women's Association (SEWA). In the recent past, the country has witnessed proliferation of NGOs which, though at times set up not entirely out of altruistic considerations, have no doubt helped mobilisation of marginalised groups. They have succeeded as people and international funding agencies have more confidence in non- governmental agencies than in the government machinery for various reasons. It is felt, for example, that since NGOs function at grass root level, usually with local participation, and have day to day interaction with local people, they are at a distinct advantage in delving deep into the issues concerning local people and in mobilising them. Sometimes NGOs work as a bridge between the government and the community and help in implementation of developmental schemes apart from organising the marginalised groups. They have been able to reach the remote areas of the country and have addressed several social problems such as child labour. Plenty of funds flow these days to the NGOs from various national and international agencies for a variety of activities. The anti-arrack movement in Andhra Pradesh sought to tackle the issue of domestic violence against women from drunken husbands. The campaign against child labour is another successful movement organised through NGOs. However, as hinted earlier, formation of NGOs and their way of functioning have not remained beyond the pale of criticism. In 1996, about 150 NGOs were blacklisted by Council for Peoples' Action and Rural Technology (CAPART), an autonomous agency under the Ministry of Rural Development, which works through NGOs. NGOs are sometimes criticized as autocratic, not accountable to anyone, helping a few or the elite only, etc. It has also been observed that many politicians and retired bureaucrats or their relatives open NGOs and make their own lives comfortable through government grants. Moreover, it is sometimes felt that their impact is not significant in the national context. Streeten (1998), for example, studied the situation in Bangladesh and found that the Gramin Bank in Bangladesh, which used to be considered a model NGO in the area of rural micro-credit, accounts for only 0.1 per cent of the national credit of Bangladesh and all NGOs in that country together provide only 0.6 per cent of the total credit.

Organising women through cooperatives is another form where women can gain control over their assets and manage their own organisations. Through cooperatives they can raise credit and access the markets, which otherwise are not accessible to them as individuals. In some European countries, the experience of workers' cooperatives was an enriching and enlightening one. A large number of such cooperatives in our country are also promoting and generating incomes for poor. The examples of Sonali Tea Estate in West Bengal, cooperatives in tea plantations in Tripura, cooperatives in Madhya Pradesh, etc. are some such examples. Workers' cooperatives are autonomous organisations and are not subsidiary to other firms. Workers are able to become members of the enterprise generally by nominal holding of share capital and can participate in decision-making process. Worker members share in the incomes after payments of all costs of production. There were 8,714 women's cooperatives in the country in 1998 accounting for only 1.8 per cent of all cooperatives in the country. Women workers being illiterates find it difficult to register themselves as cooperatives under the Cooperative Societies Act due to long and cumbersome legal formalities and involved procedures. Sometimes initiative is also lacking among women to form cooperatives due to their lack of self-confidence and lack of awareness.

Women have participated in labour movement even before Independence. The movements of jute workers in Bengal, textile workers in Bombay, plantation workers in North East, etc. all involved women workers as active participants. Gradually, the trend shifted to formation of trade unions to bargain on the part of the workers. There are about 60,000 registered trade unions which are affiliated to the Federations/Central Trade Unions at national level but the membership of women in these unions is negligible. There are also trade unions which are not affiliated to any Central Trade Union such as Self-Employed Women Association (SEWA), National Alliance of Construction Workers, National Alliance of Street Vendors, etc. These unions generally are area- specific and, therefore, isolated. SEWA was registered in 1972 as a trade union for organisation of poor and self-employed women workers. A number of activities have been started by SEWA aimed at organisation for collective strength and capital formation to have access to functional services, capacity building through access in market infrastructure, education, knowledge skills, etc. and social security in terms of health care, child care, etc. The efforts of SEWA have been a great success, and its activities have been expanding and diversifying. Originally confined to Gujarat, the activities of SEWA have now spread to other States too. As a consequence, its membership has increased from about 46,000 in 1972 to 2,15,000 in 1999 in the country as a whole. In Gujarat itself, the membership rose from about 26,000 in 1990 to 1,48,000 in 1999. Street vendors, home-based workers, manual labourers and service providers comprise the membership of SEWA. Working Women Forum (WWF) in Chennai, Annapurna Mahila Mandal, Mumbai, etc. are other examples of successful efforts to organise urban poor women who were self employed as vendors. Bankura project was started on the similar lines for organising rural poor women.

In Kerala's Alleppy model, women have organised themselves as a society, titled Community Development Society, for implementing anti-poverty programmes. This is a society of poor women. Community identifies poor families and nutritional and health services are provided to the poor women. Women plan and implement the programme through a self-help approach. The organisation has a three-tier system. At Panchayat level, there is an apex body called Community Development Society, at ward level it is Area Development Society and at local area level it is known as Neighbourhood Group. Funds are mobilised through NABARD and other Banks, through thrift and credit societies or pooling resources. The model, working in various parts of the State with a focus on rural population, is based on participatory approach with a community base for sustainable development of women.

Political Empowerment

An important pre-requisite for accelerating the process of economic and social empowerment is the adequate participation of women in the political process at all levels.

While women constitute half of the population, their political representation at national level is below 10 per cent, which is a matter of concern. At regional level, in some States the situation is much worse. The bill to give one-third reservation to women in parliament is in doldrums and yet to be tabled. Political parties raise huc and cry about women's share in membership but when the question of distribution of tickets comes in, virtually no party adheres to their commitment for giving adequate representation to women and, thus, women's participation in actual decision making remains no where near equality.

The position at local level also needs some analysis. Panchayati Raj system in the country was introduced in 1959 to expedite the community development programme. The 73rd amendment of the Constitution has given 30 per cent reservation to women in all the three tiers of Panchayat System. The representation of women at Panchayat level was extremely poor especially in the States of Assam, Bihar,

Jammu & Kashmir, Kerala and Orissa before this Constitutional amendment. There are examples which show that women have potential for delivering the desired results in the Panchayat system. The examples of Kerala and Maharashtra may be cited in this connection. But the experience of Orissa, Madhya Pradesh and Uttar Pradesh tell a different story. Another indicator of political empowerment of women is their participation in the poll process. Equality in exercising the right to vote has been granted but the question is whether women will come out of their houses to vote or be able to exercise this right independently. Many a times, they vote according to the desires and under the influence of the male members of the family/society. All these issues and the impact of the measures to enhance the participation of women in the political process will be discussed further in the next Chapter.

A Critical Review

There are, thus, a number of programmes and schemes in the areas of women's empowerment through promotion of health, education and skill development, through income generating activities, generation of awareness and gender sensitisation, etc. which have been launched by Central and State Governments. It is not the intention to provide a compendium of all such schemes and programmes. What is attempted in the rest of this Chapter is a general review of the schemes.

There is, first of all, a tendency among different government departments to launch schemes of their own without taking into account similar schemes already going on elsewhere and, if that is pointed out to them, to defend themselves indicating some minor differences between the two schemes. As a result, quite often, duplication of effort creeps in as, for example, in the case of self-employment promotion assistance programmes. In this process, the limited resources available get spread too thinly over a number of schemes to have any significant impact. Inter-departmental rivalries at the policy and implementation levels and one-up-man-ship prevent emergence of any real convergence of effort in practice, even though the need for it is mentioned often. Lack of holistic approach in designing and implementing programmes is again a symptom of what ails development effort in the country. Different schemes look at different aspects of the problem and are geared to tackle only that ignoring the interactions and inter-connections between different aspects. It is indeed heartening to see a move towards integration of all rural development programmes in the form of *Sampoorna Grameen Swarozgar Yojana* and coordination of all effort to universalize elementary education under the *Sarva Shiksha Abhiyan*.

Another point of concern is the lack of proper monitoring of performance in the real sense. There is no doubt that a system of monitoring is built into most schemes as that is required by funding agencies but how truthful is the monitoring is open to question. A point in case is the performance of enrolment in primary classes, though the same can be said of several other schemes. On paper all targets get achieved and 99 per cent enrolment is shown out of modesty instead of 100 per cent. In reality, it is a known fact that primary school teachers, whose salaries are linked to achievement of enrolment targets, often visit households and write out the names of all children in the registers. Independent and objective observation and assessment is indeed lacking.

Sometimes, the scheme is well thought out and perhaps well implemented too, but the effort is too slight to impact on the real need. An example is the vocational training scheme for women. A total seating capacity of 50,000 in the Industrial Training Institutes and of 2,000 in the National/Regional Vocational Training Institutes is hardly adequate, even taking into account the fact that skill formation no doubt takes place under a variety of programmes.

Administrative costs are too high in the developmental programmes implemented by the government. There is no real cost-benefit analysis and the tendency is to expand the bureaucratic set up. Costs on salaries and other office expenses may not be as much as 85 per cent as pointed out by the late Prime Minister Rajiv Gandhi in relation to rural development programmes, but they do lower the impact of the programmes substantially.

Political interference with the implementation of the schemes is another problem. The involvement of politicians with NGOs running various developmental institutions and their close association with the top echelons of the government, be it in the area of education, skill development, welfare or awareness generation, makes it difficult for the bureaucracy to objectively evaluate the competence and integrity of the organization while entrusting the work or in assessing performance and in releasing or withholding grants subsequently. Many a time this leads to corrupt practices as well benefiting the bureaucracy and the implementing organizations but not necessarily the targeted population for whom the scheme is intended.

Organisation of women into small self-help groups through the medium of NGOs has been a fairly successful experiment in meeting their micro-credit needs. SHG is also currently the basic unit in the implementation of several developmental programmes. Formation of such groups had been there in the past also as, for example, in the case of DWACRA, but is now the most preferred strategy for delivery of micro-credit. The advantages in this arrangement, as put forward by Karmarkar (1999), are that "Individually, a poor person tends to be rather tentative, uncertain in his behaviour, but group membership smoothens the rough edges of his behaviour pattern, making him more reliable as a borrower. Membership in a group gives him a feeling of protection, a source of guidance and help in case of need from people he knows.... Group imposes discipline, enhances self-confidence..." The advantages are, therefore, to both the lender and the borrower. There have been several success stories of working through SHGs and the Annual Reports of various Ministries and Departments of Government are replete with them. It is said that the incomes of women have risen significantly in several States in this new paradigm of economic empowerment of women. Andhra Pradesh is one of the major beneficiaries of the experiment and it is even said that one of the reasons for the overall development and decline in population growth in this State in spite of low female education levels is this process of economic empowerment through group approach. It must, however, be remembered that NGOs constitute the king-pin in the whole exercise and the extent of success achieved rests mainly on the commitment to cause, competence and integrity of these organizations. There has been an unhealthy proliferation of NGOs in recent times, particularly since the State has started using this channel for the delivery of services to the community and quite a few have emerged as instruments to siphon off public resources into private pockets. It is, therefore, necessary for the government to exercise strict vigilance in the selection and verification of the credentials of NGOs before committing funds to them and regular monitoring of their performance over time.

It is not that nothing is all right with the conception, designing and implementation and monitoring of the development schemes. The effort has produced its effect, although not to the extent one would have wanted it, but nevertheless it is there. The extent and the desired goals that have been achieved, is the subject matter of the next Chapter.

Notes

1 National Drinking Water Mission from 1986, rechristened Rajiv Gandhi National Drinking Water Mission in 1991

IV

Women in India

How Far Have They Come?

Before we pat ourselves on our backs for the legislations enacted to protect the interests of women, the institutional structures put in place to oversee their implementation and the developmental policies and programmes adopted to sustain the effort to bring women at par with men in all walks of life, it is essential to have a look at the hard facts that give an indication of the real impact of these measures on the status of women in the country. It takes two things for visible changes to take place in the approach to gender parity—enabling environment created by measures such as those listed above and, perhaps more importantly, real changes in the social attitudes. No doubt, there have been social and sociological changes of significant magnitudes in the past fifty years. The liberation, partial if not total, of Scheduled Castes and Scheduled Tribes and other socially backward communities, rapid urbanization, growth of services sector in the economic structure and the declining importance of agriculture, increasing entry of women into higher education and non-household employment and that increasingly in areas uncharted by them earlier, breakdown of the traditional joint family system and the emergence of simple biological families, have all had their impact on the social life of the country. Old values, some good and some bad, have yielded place to newer ones, some bad and some good. While the break-down of joint family system and the emergence of nuclear families, for example, resulted perhaps in women having a greater say in the household affairs, the trend has posed newer forms of threats to the traditional social security arrangements for the elderly and care of the children. Again, increasing participation of women in non-household employment might have opened up opportunities for their development, but without significant reduction in their share of burden of domestic chores, which often heightened their workload and added to their stress. The immediate relative costs and benefits of these forces arrayed on the opposite sides are hard to evaluate and their overall impact can be seen only in a historical perspective, a few decades hence.

Societal attitudes hardened over ages do not change easily. Even if change *per se* is accepted in principle, the deep-rooted prejudices do die hard. A majority of people, men and women alike, still have a preference for a son over a daughter and indulge in the banned activity of pre-natal sex-determination, pay relatively little attention to the girl child in the matter of education and health and look upon her as someone else's property. If they encourage her to pursue higher education and allow her eventual entry into a job, it is only partly out of a liberal attitude and partly out of an expectation that education and employment would make it that much easier for them to find a suitable husband and at a lower dowry. While the feeling of male superiority has received a jolt with the consistently better performance of women in various fields and at various levels, it still pervades over wide areas of employment and is exhibited in a number of ways—choosing female staff as subordinates, allotment of work with a lower level of responsibility to women, paying lower wages, etc. Even if women are made heads of local bodies through Constitutional Amendments, their men folk still breathe down their necks and control affairs indirectly, taking advantage of the lack of experience, education and training among women and the social attitudes in the country side. At family level too, women, even when they are the major contributors to family incomes, have relatively less say in the application of family resources and other areas of decision making. Household duties are not generally shared by the husband but are considered the exclusive responsibility of the wife even when she has a job outside the home, leaving her struggling with dual responsibilities. Her work at home goes mostly unaccounted for in the statistics and is often not considered work at all. Domestic violence against women continues without any complaint and goes mostly unreported. Crimes like molestation and rape, sexual harassment at work places continue despite prohibitory legislation. While it is not possible to assemble and present statistical facts on all these aspects, we could look at some of the indicators of the state of affairs as regards the status of women in the country and the trends in these indicators.

Sex Ratio

Even though at birth boys outnumber girls by a fraction of about 105[1] to 100 the world over, under conditions of low fertility, low maternal mortality, equal treatment of boys and girls as they grow up, proper access to safe drinking water and sanitation and gender-neutral health care, all of which are characteristics of a developed gender-egalitarian society, the mortality rates among females would decline relatively fast beyond a particular age because of their biologically stronger constitution and eventually they tend to outnumber men in the population as a whole. The ratio of the number of women per thousand men in the population, the sex-ratio, is, therefore, a summary indicator of the gender equality in a society. As seen in an earlier chapter, the sex-ratio in the developed countries is over 1,000 women per 1,000 men. It is currently (in the year 2002) 1,139 in Russian Federation, 1,028 in the United States of America, 1,045 in Japan, 1,053 in France and 1,029 in United Kingdom. Thailand, a newly emerging economy, has a sex-ratio of 1,022 and Vietnam and Ethiopia, two relatively poor countries, have ratios of 1,007 and 1,010 respectively. In India, by contrast, Census 2001 results give a ratio of 933, which is well below even the 1,000 mark.

What is more worrisome is the well-known fact that the sex-ratio in India has been declining steadily, while the other major countries in South Asia region have shown improvement (Table 4.1). The decline in the sex-ratio in India is not a post-Independence phenomenon. It has been occurring throughout the twentieth century. From a level of 972 in 1901, the ratio fell steadily to 930 in 1971, showed some improvement to 934 in 1981, only to fall again to 927 in 1991 but regain the loss and climb up to 933 in 2001. There are also considerable spatial and temporal variations in the sex-ratio (Table 4.2). For instance, in 2001, Kerala had the highest sex-ratio at 1,058, the only major State with more females than males, and it has also shown a healthy improvement over the previous decade from 1,036 in 1991. The other major Southern States of Tamilnadu, Karnataka and Andhra Pradesh had ratios over 960 in 2001 and registered a distinct improvement over 1991. This is in sharp contrast to the relatively more prosperous States of Maharashtra, Gujarat, Punjab and Haryana (including the smaller Chandigarh and Delhi), all having a sex-ratio of less than the national average of 933 in 2001 and in all of which the ratio declined sharply during the inter-census decade 1991-2001. This again corroborates the view that economic prosperity *per se* may not change the people's outlook about gender issues. It may also be pointed out that the record of the Southern States of Tamilnadu, Andhra Pradesh and Karnataka had not been a happy one prior to 1991. In all these States, the sex-ratio declined from much higher levels in 1901 (Andhra Pradesh from 985 in 1901 to 972 in 2001, Tamilnadu from a healthy 1,044 to 986 and Karnataka from 983 to 960). Kerala alone has the unblemished record of rising sex ratio over the entire twentieth century – 1,004 in 1901, 1,028 in 1951 and 1058 in 2001. The reasons for this healthy state of affairs in Kerala in so far as sex ratio is concerned will have to be looked for in the relatively high level of empowerment of women in the State due to its long tradition of women's education and health services fostered by

As pointed out by Mishra (1996), "Designed for the detection of genetic abnormality in the unborn child, the technology of amniocentesis has put in to the hands of some crazy parents and unscrupulous medical practitioners, a means to detect and summarily eliminate female foetuses. It was estimated that 78,000 such abortions took place during the period 1979-83." Sex determination before birth has since been banned with the enactment of the Pre-Natal Diagnostic Techniques (Regulation and Prevention of Misuse) Act in 1994, but there is evidence to show that the practice continues. As pointed in the Human Development Report 2002 and quoted earlier in this book, "a study of a clinic in Bombay found that 7,999 of the 8,000 aborted foetuses were female". According to the report of National Crime Records Bureau, the number of such registered foeticide cases in 1999 was higher than that in 1995 (the year after the enactment of the preventive legislation) by 60.5 per cent. It is, of course, possible that with the enactment of the Act, registration of cases increased sharply irrespective of what might have actually happened to the practice. A disturbing feature is that the evil is prevalent to a greater extent in the more prosperous regions/ sections of the country and population who are more aware of the technical possibilities and have greater access to the facilities. Increasing acceptance of the two-child or sometimes one-child norm without acceptance of and commitment to the notion of equality of genders could play havoc on the female foetuses. The second factor, viz., changes in the sex ratio at birth, may not necessarily be an independent one but may in fact be related to the practice of female foeticide discussed above. Sex-ratio at birth in India has been around 900 females per 1,000 males against an accepted norm of 943 to 952. There is some evidence of a decline in this ratio in recent years. Based on the data from the Sample Registration Scheme, Registrar General of India (2001) pointed out that sex-ratio at birth which was 900 during the decade 1981-90 had declined to less than 900 during the next decade (1991-2000).

Foeticide Slur on Posh Delhi

After Punjab and Haryana, Delhi too provides statistical proof that the wealthier the area, the greater the discrimination against the girl child. The latest data to emerge from the 2001 census reveal that the areas in Delhi with the largest number of 'missing' girls—girls who are never born because of female foeticide—are also some of the most posh ones.

Times of India, New Delhi, 19 Sept. 2002

Killing of girl children during the early ages is another pernicious practice prevalent in parts of the country. While reliable estimates of such instances of infanticide are not available for obvious reasons, Mishra (1996) referred to a study by Biswajeet Banerjee in Muri and Bharwadi Block of Uttarkasi, which brought out the "gory details of a barbaric practice, according to which a girl child is put to eternal sleep soon after birth by the Dai (mid wife) even without the knowledge of the mother" and to another conducted in Salem district of Tamilnadu, in which out of the 501 women respondents 316 had killed infant daughters through poisoning, strangulation, etc.". The Human Development Report 2002 referred to a recent survey in India which found 10,000 cases of female infanticide a year. All this is reflected in a slightly lower Infant Mortality Rate (number of deaths of infants less than one year in age to 1000 live births, IMR) for males than for females (Table 4.3). Further, even though IMR has been falling steadily over the years, both for males and females, the ratio of the rate for females to that of males still remained above unity in 1999.

Table 4.3 Infant Mortality Rates by Sex

Year	*Infant Mortality*			*Ratio of Female to Male Rate*
	Female	*Male*	*All*	
1985	98	96	97	1.02
1990	81	78	80	1.04
1995*	76	73	74	1.04
1999	71	70	70	1.01

Source: Registrar General of India, Sample Registration System;

* Excludes Jammu & Kashmir.

While actual killing of female children may be somewhat uncommon, neglect of the girl child, who is often looked upon by the parents rather as a liability than asset, is more ubiquitous. It takes so many forms—denial of adequate nutrition and access to health facilities, utilization in domestic chores even at a very tender age, etc. All this could lead to deaths of the female children before they reach the school-going age. Mishra (1996) also referred to a study by UNICEF, according to which "females experience greater probability of dying as the age of the child advances in 172 districts. In 224 districts the female child is exposed to a much greater risk of death than a male child between the third and fifth year." Death rates have always been higher for girls in the age group 0 – 4 than for boys of the same age group. An unfortunate trend is that though the rates have been steadily declining both for males and for females, the relative gap between them has been increasing, instead of closing, over the years. In fact the mortality rate for female children was higher than that for male children by a factor 1.07 in 1991 and crept upward to 1.15 by 1998.

Chart 4.2: Mortality Rates by Sex for Age Group 0 – 4

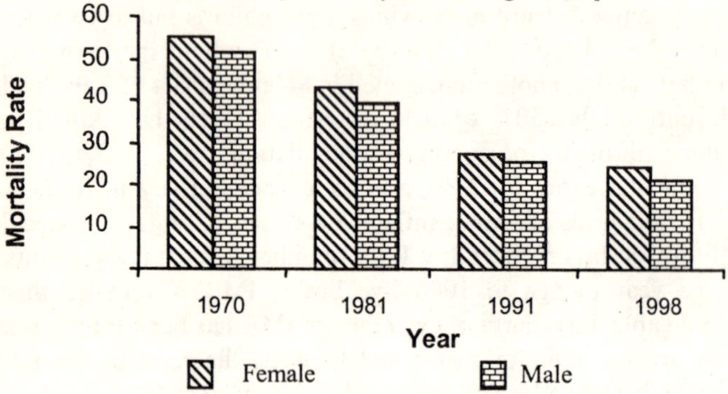

Source: Sample Registration System (SRS)—Fertility and Mortality Indicators for respective years, Registrar General of India.

As mentioned above, neglect of the girl child in providing the required nutrition is the main cause for the relatively higher mortality among girls. That gender biases are widely prevalent in the allocation of food and health care is a well-documented fact. Mishra (1996) refers to a study in Tamilnadu, which found that male children were breast-fed for 5 months longer than female children in landed families and for about 10 months more than male children in agricultural labour households, and to another study of children under five by the Institute of Health Management, Pachod, which showed that disparity in nutritional status is the highest in the age group of 1 – 3 years. The same study also showed that the percentage of severely mal-nourished female children was consistently 2-3 times higher than that of boys. Mishra points out that "The sex based discrimination is extended from nutrition to health care. Several studies indicate that (a) fewer resources are invested in the health of the girl child, (b) girl children are taken to health centers less often, (c) higher mortality figures for girls in hospitals indicate that they are brought in for treatment late, and (d) girl children and married women in Bihar, Uttar Pradesh and Rajasthan are not sent to hospitals on the ground that they tend to get corrupted by the vile forces existing outside home." The impact of this is seen in the summary measure of sex-ratio for the age group 0 – 6 (Table 4.2). For the country as a whole, the Under-6 sex-ratio was 927 in 2001 against the ratio of 933 for the population as a whole. More importantly, Under-6 sex-ratio declined from 945 in 1991 to 927 in 2001, while the overall sex-ratio improved marginally. This has happened in all the major States (except Kerala), including those that recorded an improved sex ratio in 2001, a fact that has ominous implications for the overall sex ratio in years to come.

Higher mortality among females continues beyond the childhood into the childbearing ages. It is only after the age of 30, that mortality forces work stronger on males (Table 4.4). While neglect of the girl child in matters of nutrition and health and domestic duties are responsible for the higher female mortality below the age of 15, it is the early marriages, high levels of fertility coupled with inadequate access to quality health services and the resultant unacceptable levels of maternal mortality that result in higher female mortality rates till the age of 30 years.

Table 4.4: Age-Specific Mortality Rate by Sex, 1998

Age Group	*Mortality Rate*	
	Female	*Male*
0 – 4	24.1	21.0
5 – 9	2.4	2.1
10 – 14	1.2	1.0
15 – 19	2.0	1.7
20 – 24	2.7	2.3
25 – 29	2.6	2.6
30 – 34	2.8	3.2
35 – 39	3.0	4.2
40 – 44	3.8	5.6
45 – 49	5.2	7.4
50 – 54	8.8	12.9
55 – 59	13.7	18.9
60 – 64	23.8	32.8
65 69	35.8	47.6
70 +	77.6*	89.7*
All Ages	8.6	9.2

Source: Registrar General of India, Sample Registration System.

* Relate to 1997.

The average age at marriage of a female has steadily increased from about 15 to about 20 years during the last half a century and the law prohibits marriage of a girl before the age of 18. Nevertheless, enforcement of the Child Marriages (Restraint) Act is loose and early marriages do take place. Data from Sample Registration System indicated, for example, that in 1992, about 1.3 per cent of the females in the age group 10 – 14 and 30 percent of the females in the age group 15- 19 were married. Data for 1998 showed some improvement with none in the age group 10 – 14 and 25 per cent of the females in the age group 15 –19 having been married. A UNICEF study conducted in 12 North Indian villages showed that of the 400 girls in the age group 10 –16 surveyed, 45 per cent were either married or engaged or their marriages were under consideration. Fertility among Indian women has been on the decline over the years. Total Fertility Rate (TFR), for example, has come down from over 5 in 1970 to about 3 currently. Though this is less than the TFR (5 to 6) in some other South Asian countries like Pakistan, Nepal and Bhutan and some North African countries like Ethiopia, Democratic Republic of Congo and Nigeria by a significant margin, it is still a little higher than the rate (1 to 2) obtaining in the developed countries and some of the newly industrialized countries like Republic of Korea and Thailand.

In general, morbidity affects females more than the males in India. According to the National Sample Survey Organisation, morbidity rates (number of ailing persons per 1000 population) in the rural areas were 54 for males and 57 for females, while in the urban areas they were 51 and 58 respectively during 1995-96 (GOI, NSSO, 2000). In spite of the numerous programmes for reproductive health care and improved nutrition initiated on a substantial scale, about half (47.8 per cent) of the adolescent married girls suffer from mild to severe anaemia (GOI, National Family Health Survey- II, 1998-99). This is also substantiated by the findings of the National Nutrition Monitoring Bureau (GOI, The Tenth Five Year Plan) which found that 47 per cent of the pregnant women suffered from moderate to severe form of anaemia in 1996. But what adds to the problem is the prevailing sorry state of primary health services and the extent to which they are availed of by the pregnant women, particularly in the rural areas. Unlike in the urban areas where over 90 per cent of the live births are attended to by trained health personnel (doctor or trained mid wife or trained nurse, etc.), less than half (46.2 per cent) of the live births in the rural areas were attended to by trained health personnel in 1998 (GOI, Registrar General of India). Though this no doubt represents a significant improvement over the situation two decades earlier when the rural proportion was less than a quarter (24.3 per cent), it is important to realize that even today more than half of the live births are those attended to by untrained persons. Illegal abortions conducted by quacks constitute another contributory cause for maternal deaths. The combined effect of all this is reflected by the level of Maternal Mortality Rate (MMR) of over 400 maternal deaths per 100,000 live births. MMR has no doubt fallen steadily from 468 in 1980 to 437 in 1993 and to 407 in 1998 (GOI, The Tenth Five Year Plan) but it is unacceptably high when compared to 10 to 20 in the developed countries and less than 100 in countries like even the relatively less-developed Thailand.

As mentioned earlier, the mortality forces work more against males than females beyond the age of 30 (Table 4.4) and the difference in the age-specific mortality rates for the two sexes widens considerably in favour of females as the age advances further. This offsets the higher risks to female lives in the earlier age groups to a large extent and the expectation of life at birth for women is now higher than that for men. Life expectancy for women, which was about 24.0 years at the beginning of the twentieth century (against 23.6 years for males), has risen to around 59.7 years (against 59.0 years for males) during 1989-93, and further to 65.3 years (against 62.3) for males) during 1996-2001. This is consistent with the international pattern, though in absolute value the expectation of life at birth in India, both for males and females, is way behind the level attained in many countries, advanced and some not so advanced (Table 4.5).

Chart 4.3: Trends in Expectation of Life at Birth

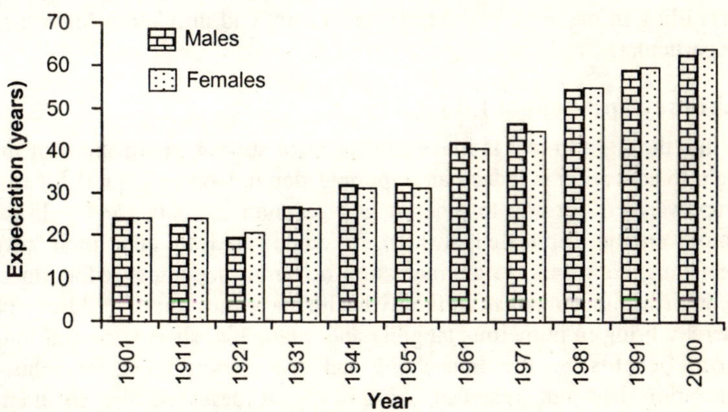

Source: (a) Registrar General of India: (i) Decennial Census Reports, (ii) Sample Registration System; (b) UNDP: Human Development Report, 2002.

To sum up this section, there have been significant advances made by the country in containing the forces of mortality at all levels. both for men and women, due largely to some improvement in avail-

Table 4.5: Expectation of Life at Birth in India and Selected Countries (2000)

Country	*Expectation of Life at Birth (years)*	
	Female	*Males*
Norway	81.5	75.6
United States of America	79.9	74.1
Japan	84.4	77.4
United Kingdom	80.2	75.2
Republic of Korea	78.6	71.2
Mexico	76.0	70.0
Russian Federation	72.5	60.1
Thailand	73.2	67.3
Vietnam	70.6	65.9
China	72.8	68.5
Pakistan	59.8	60.2
Bangladesh	59.5	59.4
India	63.8	62.8

Source: Human Development Report, 2002, UNDP.

ability of health services, though still weak, and life saving drugs. However, social forces like neglect of the girl child in various forms still work against the health of females. The country has, therefore, to traverse considerable distance to catch up with the levels of longevity prevailing in many other countries in general and in relation to women in particular.

Literacy and School Education

While the right to live is important for mere survival, realization of the right to education is indeed an important step in women's quest for true empowerment leading to other stages—economic, social, and political empowerment. Educated women, if empowered to take their own decisions, contribute to augmentation of family incomes, reduction of childbirths, improvement in family health and education of children and thereby bring in numerous tangible and intangible, short term and long term, benefits to the household and the society. Yet, somehow, education had not received the priority it deserved for so many centuries or, if it did, it was confined only to relatively minor segments of the society. The cumulative impact of the neglect of education for the vast majority is seen in the low levels of literacy and education inherited at the time of Independence, not only among the women but among the entire population in general. Indian Constitution makers put education on a high pedestal and set universal primary education as a goal to be achieved within a time span of fifteen years. It is another matter that fifty years after the Constitution was adopted we are nowhere near that goal.

India has the dubious distinction of having the largest number of illiterates in the world. The 2001 Census enumerated a total of 296 million illiterates (107 million males and 196 million females), a number larger than the populations of most countries. The number of female illiterates declined only by 10 million from 200 million to 190 million over the decade 1991 to 2001. About 58 million female illiterates (about a third of the total) in 2001 were found in the two States of Uttar Pradesh (36.5 million) and Bihar (21.1 million). A depressing fact is that during the inter-Census decade the number of illiterate women in Bihar actually increased by 2 million while in the neighbouring Uttar Pradesh they declined only by 0.3 million. Apart from these two States, four other States had sizable number of illiterates—Andhra Pradesh (16 million), West Bengal and Maharashtra (13 million each) and Madhya Pradesh (12 million).

Literacy rates (percentage of population who can read and write a simple letter) have no doubt improved over the years. In 1951, only 18.33 percent of the Indian population aged 5+ was literate – 27.16 per cent of the males and a mere 8.86 percent of the females. By 2001(Registrar General of India, 2001)[2], these rates have improved to 65.38 percent for the entire population, 75.85 per cent for the males and 54.16 per cent for the females, mainly due to the national drive during the last two decades to achieve total literacy in a mission mode. With the growth in the literacy rate among the females being 6 times against a growth of less than three times among males, the gender gap has also narrowed down substantially, the ratio of female to male literacy rates having improved from 0.33 to 0.71 during the fifty years 1951 – 2001. Despite this improvement, literacy rates among Indians, male or female, are far below those in the developed countries as well as countries like Vietnam, Philippines or Thailand with over 90 percent literacy for both sexes (Table. 4.6).

The national averages, of course, hide substantial regional variations between Kerala's literacy rate of over 90 percent (91 for the population as a whole, 94 for men and 88 for women) to Bihar's less than 50 per cent (48 for the population, 60 for men and 34 for women) (Table 4.7). Female literacy rates are over 80 percent only in Kerala, the adjacent Lakshadweep and the far off Mizoram. They are below 50 per cent in 7 States (Rajasthan, Uttar Pradesh, Bihar, Jammu & Kahsmir, Arunachal Pradesh, Jharkhand and Dadra & Nagar Haveli).

Chart 4.4: Literacy Rates in India 1951 – 2001

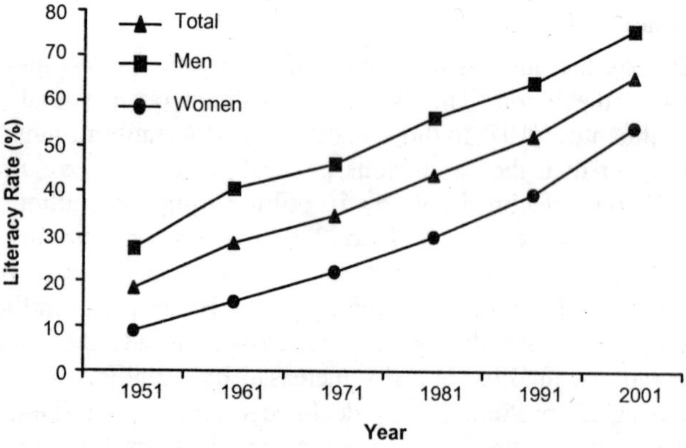

Table 4.6: Adult Literacy Rates in Selected Countries (2000)

Country	*Adult (aged 15+) literacy Rate*		*Ratio of Female to Male Rate*
	Male	Female	
Republic of Korea	99.1	96.4	97.3
Mexico	93.4	89.5	95.8
Russian Federation	99.7	99.4	99.7
Thailand	97.1	93.9	96.7
Philippines	95.5	95.1	99.6
Vietnam	95.5	91.4	95.7
China	91.7	76.3	83.2
Pakistan	57.5	27.9	48.5
Bangladesh	52.3	29.9	57.2
India	*68.4*	*45.4*	*66.4*

Source: UNDP: Human Development Report 2002.

In 12 of the States/Union Territories (Kerala, Goa, Meghalaya, Mizoram, Nagaland, Punjab, Delhi, Tripura, Andaman and Nicobar Islands, Chatisgarh and Lakshadweep) the female literacy rate is over 80 per cent of the rate for males, indicating a reasonable achievement of gender parity. However, only Kerala, Punjab and Delhi among these 12 are of substantial size. Interestingly, there is reasonable gender parity even though the rates for males and females are not very high in Punjab, Nagaland, Meghalaya and Tripura. Among the major States, gender parity in literacy is low in Bihar, Rajasthan, Orissa and Uttar Pradesh with the female literacy rate constituting only 50 to 60 per cent of the rate for males.

Table 4.7: Literacy Rates in Different States and Uniton Territories, 2001

State / Union Territory	*Literacy rate (% of literates among population aged 7+)*			*Female to male rate (%)*
	Total	*Men*	*Women*	
Andhra Pradesh	61.11	70.85	51.17	72.22
Assam	64.28	71.93	56.03	77.90
Bihar	47.53	60.32	33.57	55.65
Chatisgarh	65.18	77.86	52.40	67.30
Goa	82.32	88.88	75.51	84.96
Gujarat	69.97	80.50	58.50	72.67
Haryana	68.59	79.25	56.31	71.05
Himachal Pradesh	77.13	86.02	68.08	79.14
Jammu & Kashmir	54.46	65.75	41.82	63.60
Jharkand	54.13	67.94	39.38	57.96
Karnataka	67.04	76.29	57.45	75.30
Kerala	90.92	94.20	87.86	93.27
Madhya Pradesh	64.11	76.80	50.28	65.47
Maharashtra	77.27	86.27	67.51	78.25
Manipur	68.87	77.87	59.70	76.67
Meghalaya	63.31	66.14	60.41	91.34
Mizoram	88.49	90.69	86.13	94.97
Nagaland	67.11	71.77	61.92	86.28
Orissa	63.61	75.95	50.97	67.11
Punjab	69.95	75.63	63.55	84.03
Rajasthan	61.03	76.46	44.34	57.99
Sikkim	69.68	76.73	61.46	80.10
Tamilnadu	73.47	82.33	64.55	78.40
Tripura	73.66	81.47	65.41	80.29
Uttaranchal	72.28	84.01	60.26	71.73
Uttar Pradesh	57.36	70.23	42.98	61.20
West Bengal	69.22	77.58	60.22	77.62
Andaman & Nicobar	81.18	86.07	75.29	87.48
Arunachal Pradesh	54.74	64.07	44.24	69.05
Chandigarh	81.76	85.65	76.65	89.49
Dadra Nagar haveli	60.03	73.32	42.99	58.63
Daman & Diu	81.09	88.40	70.37	79.60
Delhi	81.82	87.37	75.00	85.84
Lakshadweep	87.52	93.15	81.56	87.56
Pondicherry	81.49	88.87	74.13	83.41
All India	*65.38*	*75.85*	*54.16*	*71.40*

Source: Registrar General of India: Census 2001, Paper 1.

Literacy rates by themselves do not reveal accurately the educational attainment of the population. These rates are computed with reference to people's ability to read and write a simple letter. In actual census operations, in all probability, even this liberal criterion gets further watered down to ability to sign. Nevertheless, literacy level is an important attribute of the population and provides a basic measure of people's access to education. It would, however, be useful to supplement by looking at other measures like enrolment at various stages of education, the composition of the population by educational attainment, etc. in order to gauge the extent to which women have real access to instruments of personal development that accelerate their progress on the path of empowerment.

Table 4.8 gives the trends in gross enrolment ratios[3] at different stages of education (primary or Class I to V, middle or Classes VI to VIII and high/higher secondary or Classes IX to XI/XII) as percentage of the number of children in the age groups appropriate to the stage of education (6 – 11, 11 – 14 and 14 – 17 years respectively). Clearly, at all stages of school education, the gross enrolment rates have improved substantially over the years, but faster among the girls compensating to some extent for their late start. Primary school enrolment of boys in the age group 6 –11 has always been nearly complete over the past three decades, but the coverage of girls is still one-fifths short. Less than half of the girls in the age group of 11 –14 are enrolled in Classes VI to VIII against two-thirds of the boys in the same age group. Enrolment in the high and higher secondary level as percentage of those in the age group 14 – 17 is low both for boys and girls, but the ratio for girls is only half that of the boys.

Table 4.8: Gross Enrolment Ratios at Different Stages of School Education

Year	*Primary Classes (I – V) Age group 6 - 11 years*		*Middle Classes (VI – VIII) Age group 11-14 years*		*High/Higher Secondary Classes (IX – XI/XII) Age group 14 - 17*	
	Boys	*Girls*	*Boys*	*Girls*	*Boys*	*Girls*
1971	92.6	59.1	46.5	20.8	27.1	10.2
1981	95.8	64.1	54.3	28.8	23.1	11.1
1991	115.3	86.0	73.4	46.1	31.2@	16.3@
2000	104.1	85.2	67.2	49.7	N.A	N.A

* Provisional.

@ Relate to 1990. Data for subsequent years not available.

Source: Institute of Applied Manpower Research: Manpower Profile India, Year Book 2001.

Chart 4.5: Gross Enrolment Ratio of Girls as Percentage of Gross Enrolment Ratio of Boys

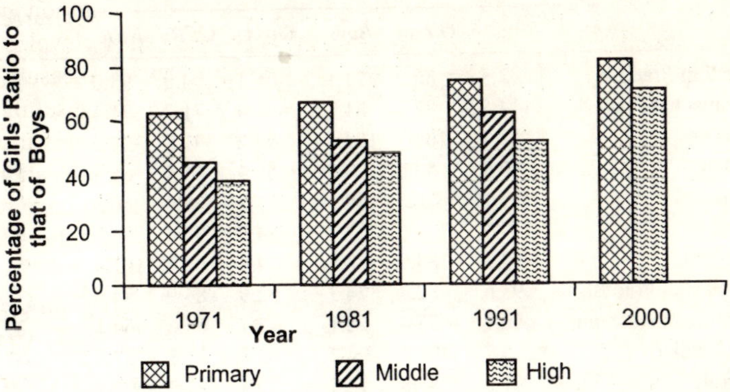

Between 1981 and 2000, enrolment of girls as a percentage of total enrolment advanced from 38.6 to 43.6 at the primary level, from 32.8 to 40.4 at the middle level and from 29.4 to 39.2 at the secondary/ higher secondary level. Even though gender gaps are closing in enrolment at various stages of school education they are still wide, particularly at the post-primary stage. A more revealing picture emerges when the net enrolment ratio instead of the gross ratio is considered. Data available for 1997 give the following picture (Table 4.9). It would be observed that in the rural areas the enrolment ratios are very low and the gender gaps are also high. On the other hand, gender gaps seem to have more or less disappeared in the urban areas (last two rows of Table 4.9).

As in the case of literacy levels, the achievements or non-achievements in raising enrolment ratios are not evenly spread all over the country. Table 4.9 shows the gross and net enrolment ratios at primary level in different States and Union Territories for 1997-98. While at one end there are Kerala and a few smaller States/Union Territories with primary school enrolment ratios over 90 per cent, there are others like Bihar, Rajasthan, Madhya Pradesh, Uttar Pradesh and Orissa where in rural areas the enrolment ratios at that stage of school education were less than 60 per cent.

Apart from low enrolment ratios, one of the disturbing features of school education in India is the prevalence of high levels of dropouts. About 40 percent of the boys and girls entering schools in the first year of primary stage leave the school system before they complete that stage. About 50 to 60 percent of those who enter the middle stage do

Table 4.9: Gross and Net Enrolment Ratios at Primary Level, 1997

State/Union Territory	*Gross Enrolment Ratio (GER)*		*Net Enrolment Ratio (NER)*		*Gender Parity Index*		*Percentage of female teachers*
	Boys	*Girls*	*Boys*	*Girls*	*GER*	*NER*	
Andhra Pradesh	92.3	86.8	71.1	66.1	94.0	93.0	33.2
Arunachal Pradesh	114.5	82.1	81.7	58.4	71.7	71.4	28.6
Assam	113.8	104.3	102.5	94.2	91.6	91.9	25.0
Bihar	90.9	59.5	90.9	59.4	65.4	65.4	19.5
Goa	97.1	76.8	68.3	55.2	79.0	80.8	67.3
Gujarat	119.9	114.5	87.7	84.7	95.4	96.7	47.0
Haryana	83.1	84.9	72.5	74.4	102.2	102.6	51.7
Himachal Pradesh	98.6	82.7	74.3	62.9	84.0	84.6	38.6
Jammu & Kashmir	82.7	53.4	68.1	43.7	64.6	64.1	37.2
Karnataka	120.7	105.5	94.2	82.8	87.3	87.8	47.2
Kerala	91.3	88.8	72.5	70.4	97.2	97.1	69.5
Madhya Pradesh	114.5	89.4	97.4	78.2	78.1	80.3	27.4
Maharashtra	115.7	110.0	86.2	82.5	95.1	95.8	50.3
Manipur	99.7	74.1	77.7	59.5	74.4	76.5	34.8
Meghalaya	101.9	96.1	54.5	46.8	84.6	85.8	45.4
Mizoram	123.0	104.6	77.7	67.6	85.0	87.1	47.4
Nagaland	103.6	86.3	64.0	53.6	83.3	83.7	39.3
Orissa	104.5	76.1	81.0	58.0	72.9	71.6	25.9
Punjab	80.4	83.1	68.8	72.7	103.4	105.7	61.0
Rajasthan	111.3	81.0	82.6	59.3	72.7	71.9	28.8
Sikkim	116.7	110.0	63.4	59.3	94.2	93.5	45.5
Tamilnadu	109.8	107.3	85.7	83.6	97.8	97.6	44.1
Tripura	103.4	75.3	92.0	68.6	72.8	74.5	21.0
Uttar Pradesh	74.1	49.0	56.0	36.4	66.1	65.0	25.0
West Bengal	98.6	85.6	59.2	51.8	86.9	87.4	24.8
Andaman & Nicobar Islands	99.6	76.2	72.1	56.7	76.5	78.6	47.7
Chandigarh	85.9	73.2	65.1	55.2	85.2	84.8	96.4
Dadra & Nagar Haveli	111.0	81.3	79.0	61.4	73.3	77.7	31.1
Daman & Diu	110.9	88.8	81.6	67.8	80.1	83.1	57.1
Delhi	97.2	81.6	74.0	61.7	84.0	83.4	62.4
Lakshadweep	112.8	96.3	77.2	68.4	85.4	88.7	42.3
Pondicherry	105.8	83.0	83.4	65.2	78.5	78.3	58.6
India	*98.5*	*81.5*	*77.7*	*64.0*	*82.7*	*82.3*	*35.8*
India—Urban	*91.0*	*86.8*	*71.7*	*68.2*	*95.5*	*95.0*	*35.8*
India—Rural	*101.1*	*79.6*	*79.7*	*62.5*	*78.7*	*78.4*	*35.8*

Source: National Institute of Educational Planning and Administration, Ministry of Human Resource Development, Government of India: Education For All, Year 2000 Assessment, 2000.

not complete that stage. Similarly two-thirds of the children entering secondary stage do not go on to complete that level. In effect, therefore, out of 100 girls enrolled in Class I, less than 10 only complete the high school/higher secondary stage. It is only slightly better in the case of boys. Gender differences in the dropout rates are not very large, but always against the girl students, though, over the years, the dropout rates have been coming down, more rapidly in the case of girls.

Chart 4.6: Drop-out Rates in School Education by Stage and Sex

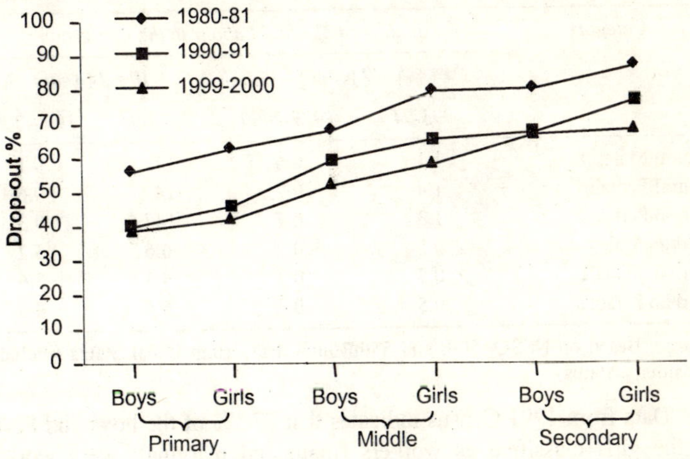

Source: IAMR, Manpower Profile India Year Book, 2001.

The low ratios of enrolment of girls in primary schools and the high rates of dropouts at various stages of school education are the consequence of interplay of forces both on the demand and supply side. Important supply side factors are: (a) not having a school, particularly a school exclusively for the girls, close to home, (b) lack of female teachers and (c) inadequacy of the education in terms of quality and relevance. The demand side factors are: (a) well-entrenched prejudices against education of women on the ground that women are required only to tend the family, (b) the widely prevalent notion that a girl is eventually to be married off and that there is no use investing in her education, (c) costs involved in education, (d) dowry to be paid, (e) the advantage in having girl children available for household work and also for wage-paid work, (f) anticipated difficulties in finding suitable grooms for educated girls, and (g) lack of perception about the ultimate benefits of girl's education. Thus, lack of proper educational infrastructure including female teaching staff, parental apathy, socio-cultural norms, direct and indirect costs and benefits, inadequate appreciation of the true costs and benefits of girls' education, all contribute to deprive girls of their right to schooling. In contrast, in the case of boys, the possible loss of immediate wage labour would be the only limiting factor (Sen and Dreeze). More girls than boys are made to attend to not only domestic chores but also to work as child labour in the rural areas (Table 4.10).

Table 4.10: Incidence of Child Labour 1993-94 and 1999-2000 (Percentage)

Category	*Incidence of Child Labour in the Age-group*			
	5 – 9 years		*10 – 14 years*	
	1993-94	*1999-2000*	*1993-94*	*1999-2000*
Rural Male	1.1	0.6	13.8	9.1
Rural Female	1.4	0.7	14.1	9.6
Rural Persons	1.3	0.7	14.0	9.3
Urban Male	0.5	0.3	6.6	5.2
Urban Female	0.5	0.2	4.5	3.6
Urban Persons	0.5	0.3	5.6	4.3

Source: Based on NSSO, 50th and 55thRound data, using Usual Status (including Subsidiary Status)

Data from 1991 Census indicates that 77.5% of the boys and 82.7% of the girls classified as workers (main and marginal) were working in agricultural activities and 20.4% of the boys and 12.7% of the girl workers were working in household manufacturing activities, while 2.1% of the boys and 4.6% of the girl workers were engaged in other activities.

Higher and Vocational Education and Technical Training

What about the participation of women in tertiary education and in vocational streams, which is important from the point of view of enhancing the employability, quality of employment and participation in other forms of social development? Enrolment of girls at the 'post-matric but below graduate' stage of general education increased from 228 thousand in 1971 to about 3.7 million in 2000 or by over 15 times in three decades. At the degree level of general education too there has been a substantial growth from 396 thousands to an impressive 3.1 million during the same period. In the field of professional and technical education too girls' education has been making rapid strides though not as spectacular as in the case of general education (Table 4.11). Enrolment of girls at the 'post-matric but below graduate stage in the professional/technical streams has gone up by about two and a half times while that at the degree and above levels increased faster having gone up by about 7 times during the three decades: 1971 to 2000.

Table 4.11: Enrolment of Girls in Post-Matric Education

Level of Education	*1971*			*2000 (P)*		
	Total enrolment (000)	*Enrolment of girls (000)*	*% of girls in total*	*Total enrolment (000)*	*Enrolment of girls (000)*	*% of girls in total*
General Education						
(a) Post-matric but below degree level*	1,041	228	21.9	9,633	3,679	38.2
(b) Degree and above	1,647	396	24.0	7,731	3,082	39.9
Professional/Technical Education						
(a) Post-matric but below degree level	448	0.81	18.1	1,001	195	19.5
(b) Degree and above	378	51	13.5	1,427	350	24.5

P – Provisional;

* includes 10+2, Intermediate, Junior colleges, Pre-university

Source: Ministry of Human Resources Development and University Grants Commission reproduced in IAMR, Manpower Profile India Year Book, 2001.

Chart 4.7: Percentage of Enrolment of Girls in Higher Education in Enrolment of All Children

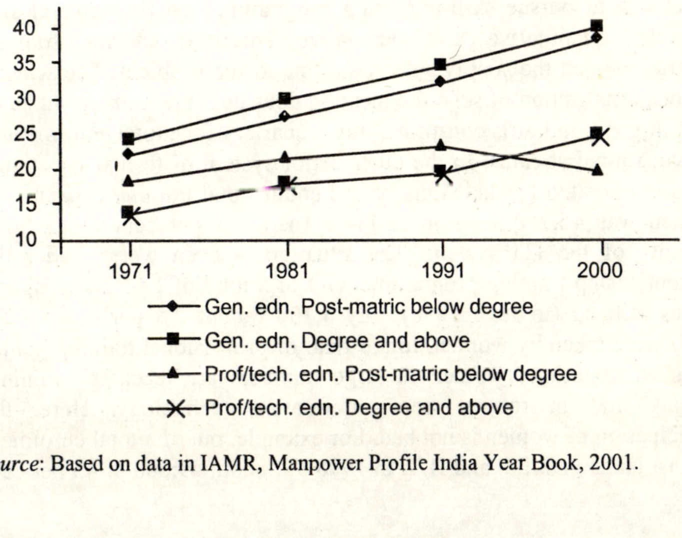

Source: Based on data in IAMR, Manpower Profile India Year Book, 2001.

Table 4.12 shows the progress of university education among girls in different fields of study. While the improvement has been across the board in all fields of study, it has been highly impressive in the faculties of commerce and engineering/technology in which girls increased their share from almost nil to a substantial level bridging the gap between these and the other fields. This augurs well for increased participation of women in quality employment in the fields of financial services and information technology related activities.

Table 4.12: Enrolment of Girls as Percentage of Total Enrolment in Higher Education

Faculty	*1970-71*	*1980-81*	*1990-91*	*1999-2000*
Arts	33.5	37.5	39.8	44.9
Science	18.8	27.9	36.8	37.4
Commerce	2.8	15.2	24.0	37.4
Education	37.3	46.7	44.2*	42.6*
Engineering/Technology	1.0	4.6	10.9*	22.1*
Medicine@	21.3	23.8	34.3*	37.8*

*Only for degree level, not post-graduate.
@ Excludes dentistry, public health, nursing, midwifery and pharmacy.
Source: IAMR, Manpower Profile India Year Book, 2001.

While commendable progress has, thus, been made in the area of higher education of girls, the achievements thus far seem to be inadequate in the area of vocational education and skill development. The problem again lies on both demand and supply sides. The general preference for degree-oriented education and the corresponding reluctance to pursue skill-imparting programmes on the demand side and the quantitative and qualitative shortfalls in the training programmes on the supply side contribute to the problem. The scheme of vocationalisation of school education does not attract many students, boys or girls, and girls constitute only a quarter of the total enrolment in the vocational streams. In the other major system of formal vocational training operated by the Ministry of Labour, total training capacity for women was 46,750 seats in 2002—a mere 7.1 per cent of the total capacity of the ITI system. The situation is even worse under the apprenticeship training programme. Out of a total of 1.61 lakh training places utilized (in June 1998) only 4,100 (about 2.5 per cent of the total) were taken by women. In the field of professional training, major areas which attract women in large numbers are teachers' training, nursing and in recent years information technology. Here, the participation of women is not bad. For example, out of a total enrolment of 1.14 lakhs in B.Ed. and B.T. in 1998-99, about 49,000 or 43 per cent were women (GOI, Ministry of Human Resources Development, 1998-99). The situation is even better in the case of enrolment in the teacher training schools (certificate level), with women accounting for 47 per cent of the total enrolment of 1.28 lakhs in the same year. Among the annual turn-out of 22,000 nurses and other paramedical personnel[4], women form the bulk. According to the 1991 Census, the overall level of certified skill attainment among Indian working women is, however, negligible with only 0.55 per cent of the women main workers having either a technical or non-technical diploma or certificate not equal to a degree (Table 4.13). That the percentage is only slightly less than that for men (0.68 per cent) in the country as a whole is not a matter of consolation. However, the fact that a greater percentage of women workers were formally trained than men in the urban areas in both technical and non-technical fields is reassuring.

Table 4.13: Percentage of Main Workers with Technical/Non-Technical Diplomas/Certificates, 1991

Educational level	*Rural areas*			*Urban areas*			*All areas*		
	Females	*Males*	*Persons*	*Females*	*Males*	*Persons*	*Females*	*Males*	*Persons*
Non-technical Diploma/ Certificate not equal to degree	0.10	0.13	0.12	0.76	0.18	0.25	0.18	0.14	0.15
Technical Diploma/Certificate not equal to degree	0.18	0.28	0.26	1.62	1.33	1.37	0.37	0.54	0.51
Total	*0.28*	*0.41*	*0.38*	*2.38*	*1.51*	*1.62*	*0.55*	*0.68*	*0.66*

Source: Registrar General of India, 1991 Census, reproduced in IAMR, Manpower Profile, 2000.

There are also a number of informal programmes of skill development among women. Apart from the transfer of traditional skills that takes place from one generation to the other within the households, a number of development schemes operated by the government as well as NGOs have an in-built training component. In terms of coverage, however, all the existing formal and informal channels of skill development put together are grossly inadequate. Table 4.14 would show that in 1993-94 only 6.3 per cent of the female population in the rural areas and 11.2 per cent in the urban areas has some marketable skill or the other (acquired formally or informally).

Table 4.14: Percentage Distribution of Persons by Possession of Marketable Skills: 1993-94

Possessing	*Rural*		*Urban*	
	Male	*Female*	*Male*	*Female*
No Skill	89.9	93.7	80.4	88.8
Some Skill	10.1	6.3	19.6	11.2
Total	100.0	100.0	100.0	100.0

Source: NSSO Report No. 409 on Results of 50th round (1993-94) survey on Employment and Unemployment.

Employment

The crucial factor in the economic empowerment of women is the extent to which they have access to employment and generation of incomes and control over means of production. The issues that emerge in relation to women and their participation in production of goods and services include:

- Proper assessment of the economic contribution of women.
- Lower participation rates of women in production of goods and services measured in a traditional conceptual framework.
- Quality of women's employment.
- Stereotyping of women's activities.
- Unequal remuneration and other forms of discrimination.
- Harassment and other problems at work place.
- Organisation and protection of rights.

Evaluation of Women's Economic Contribution

The value of the contribution of women to production of goods and services and consequently to the national product had gone unrecognized for ages, not only in India but all over the globe. The problems are partly conceptual as the traditional national income accounting takes into account only those economic activities that lead to products and services that can be exchanged in market. To a large extent, women's participation in economic activities is 'non-market' and is confined to their own households, and the households themselves are the beneficiaries of the fruits of their unpaid activities. The national income would (as pointed out by Pigou) fall if a woman employed as a paid housekeeper by a person marries him and becomes unpaid member of the family and would rise if two women from separate households teach each other's children (or cook each other's food) for payment instead of teaching their own children (or cooking food for themselves). According to the data from Human Development Report, 2002 presented in Table 1.6, females constitute the majority of the unpaid workers contributing to household economic activities in the developed as well as the developing countries (82 per cent in Japan, 75 per cent in Germany, 66 per cent in Thailand and 74 per cent in Bangladesh). Also, time-use studies conducted in seven countries (mostly advanced) during 1995-99 showed that women continued to spend substantially more time on unpaid work than men. Difficulties in evaluating the contribution by putting an appropriate price tag on these unpaid activities, social attitudes against treating women's activities as work and biases against reporting work done by women confound the issue further. Moreover, women often combine both economic and domestic work playing dual roles and their personal contribution gets merged with that of the family. The resultant invisibility of women's work and the need for a proper appreciation and evaluation of its contribution to national production is one of the aspects that attracted international attention during the past three decades. The Beijing Platform of Action called on the national and international statistical organizations to "devise suitable means to recognize and make visible the full extent of the work of women and all their contributions to the national economy, including their contribution in the unremunerated and domestic sectors, and examine the relationship of women's unremunerated work to the incidence of and their vulnerability to poverty"(United Nations). The 1993 Revision of SNA (System of National Accounts) includes within its production boundary "all production actually destined for market, whether for sale or barter. It also includes all goods or services provided free to individual households or collectively to the community by the government units" and all household "production of goods for own use" but not "production of services for own final consumption within the households (except for the services produced by employing paid domestic staff and the own-account production of housing services by owner-occupiers" (United Nations Statistical Division). Though this definition is an improvement over the earlier version, it still excludes a number of activities from its scope which contribute to production and consequently have a justifiable claim for being included in the SNA production boundary. Such activities are, in fact, those in which women are engaged to a substantially larger extent than men.

The Indian system of national accounts conforms to the international practice and takes account of activities covered within the United Nations SNA Boundary. The population censuses and the labour force surveys conducted by the National Sample Survey Organisation (NSSO) generally adopt a corresponding approach in classifying persons as in and out of labour force depending on whether their activities fall within or outside SNA boundary. However, in recent years conscious attempts are being made to identify some of the unpaid activities that have economic consequence and to elicit as much information as possible on women's participation in economic activities through probing questions. The introduction of the concepts of 'marginal work' in the censuses and of 'subsidiary status work' by the NSSO and the measurement of labour force participation through Current Day Status approach by the latter constitute some of the attempts to capture women's work to a greater degree than before. Further, as a part of its effort to identify the unpaid activities of economic consequence engaged in by those (mainly women) classified as 'out of labour force', sub-categories like 'attended domestic duties only', 'engaged in free collection of goods (vegetables, fruits, firewood, cattle feed), etc. have been introduced in the 'out-of-labour force' category. Thus, according to the 55th Round of the NSSO, about 11 per cent of all the rural women were engaged in domestic duties but at the same time contributing to the family income by free collection of goods (Table 4.15).

Table 4.15: Distribution of Persons by Usual Status* 1999-2000 (Percentage)

Activity status (UPSS)	*Rural areas*			*Urban areas*		
	Male	*Female*	*Persons*	*Male*	*Female*	*Persons*
Workers	53.1	29.9	41.7	51.8	13.9	33.7
Seeking /available for work	0.9	0.3	0.6	2.4	0.8	1.7
Out of labour force (Total)						
(a) Domestic duties only	0.3	17.9	8.9	0.3	37.1	17.9
(b) Domestic duties + free collection of goods	0.2	11.3	5.6	0.0	6.2	3.0
(c) others out of labour force	45.5	40.6	43.2	45.5	42.0	43.7
Total out of labour force	46.0	69.8	57.7	45.8	85.3	64.6
Grand total	*100.0*	*100.0*	*100.0*	*100.0*	*100.0*	*100.0*

Source: National Sample Survey Organisation, Report on Employment and Unemployment, 55th Round (July 1999 – June 2000).

It is obvious that for a fuller appreciation of the economic participation of women, it is not enough to go by the time spent on productive activities that fall inside the SNA production boundary only. Instead an 'extended SNA boundary' which takes into account the unpaid services performed at home, mostly by women, like: (a) household upkeep, management, shopping, etc., (b) care of the children, old, or the disabled in the family, and (c) community services needs to be used. Ghosh (1990) points out that even though female participation in economically productive activities is low, her total hours of work, including work within the household, are not less than the total time of work by the male. He estimates that, on an average, a man spends about 9.47 hours and a woman about 9.53 hours per day on various activities that qualify to be enumerated as work in an extended sense. A detailed Time-Use Survey conducted by the Central Statistical Organisation (2000) in six States (Haryana, Madhya Pradesh, Gujarat, Orissa, Tamilnadu and Meghalaya) has led to similar conclusions. Based on the results of this Survey, Hirway (2002) showed that (a) of the total daily person's hours of work (on SNA and extended SNA activities combined), about 47.5 per cent was shared by men and a higher burden of 52.5 per cent by females, and (b) that while men work mostly (90 to 95 per cent of the total work time) on SNA activities, 60 to 70 per cent of the work time of women is on extended SNA activities (Table 4.16 and Charts 4.8) and concludes: "This implies that about 60-70 per cent of their *(women's)* time, which is spent on working for the family's well being, is not counted in the national accounts. However, if any of these services are satisfied by markets through hired labour, they would be counted in the national accounts. It is quite likely that some of these services move in or outside the market, depending on the specific economic conditions of the family or the overall economic environment."

Table 4.16: Percentage of Hours Spent on SNA and Extended SNA Activities by Sex (Percentages)

State	*Percentage of hours spent on*					
	Men			*Women*		
	SNA activities	*Extended SNA activities*	*Total*	*SNA activities*	*Extended SNA activities*	*Total*
Haryana	94.99	5.01	100.00	40.63	59.37	100.00
Madhya Pradesh	90.47	9.53	100.00	35.68	64.32	100.00
Gujarat	93.19	6.81	100.00	31.05	68.95	100.00
Orissa	89.98	10.02	100.00	32.35	67.65	100.00
Tamilnadu	93.02	6.98	100.00	38.38	61.62	100.00
Meghalaya	86.52	13.48	100.00	43.28	56.72	100.00
Six States Combined	92.00	8.00	100.00	35.09	64.91	100.00

Source: Central Statistical Organisation: Report of the Time Use Survey, 2000.

Lower Work Participation Rates

Even if the conceptual issue of whether only SNA activities or both SNA and extended SNA activities should be included for measuring national accounts and labour force is ignored and only the traditional approach of including only SNA activities is followed, there is still

Chart 4.8: Percentage Share of SNA and Extended SNA Activities

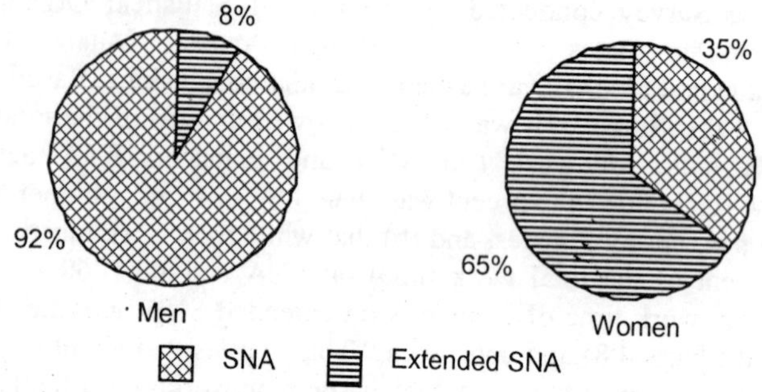

considerable under-estimation of the productive work performed by women. Hirway (2002) identifies three reasons why women's work goes under-enumerated in India: (a) the seasonal, intermittent and uncertain nature of work and the mix up of domestic work and economic work, separation of which poses conceptual and operational problems, (b) the high pedestal on which domestic work is placed and the low esteem attached to women engaged in manual employment outside the home under the prevailing socio-cultural milieu, leading to women under-reporting their economic activities, and (c) a belief among women themselves that their work is not important enough to be reported. While these reasons are peculiar to some of the other developing countries as well, even in the developed world the female work force participation rates are lower than the rates for the males. For instance, in the OECD countries the work force participation rate in 1999 was 76.6 for men and only 55.4 for women (Table 4.17). Data for the 23 highly populated countries on economic activity participation rates (in 2000) given in Table 1.6 of Chapter 1 indicate that the ratios in respect of the rates for women to those of men were high (over 80 per cent) only in Vietnam (91 per cent), China (86 per cent), Thailand (85 per cent), Russian Federation (82 per cent) and USA (81 per cent). In the first three of these countries, the rates for females were high not only relative to the rates for men but in absolute terms as well being around 73 per cent. At the other extreme, in Pakistan, Iran and Egypt the economic activity rates for women were in the range of about 30 to 35 in absolute terms and around 40 per cent of the rates for men. The choice between and relative importance attached by women to leisure, domestic work and gainful work outside the homestead are influenced by a complex set of economic, demographic, social and cultural considerations, while in the case of men it is primarily the economic

Table 4.17: Work Force Participation Rates in OECD Countries by Sex

Sex	*Work Force Participation Rate (%)*		
	1990	*1998*	*1999*
Men	78.2	76.0	76.6
Women	52.5	54.4	55.4

Source: OECD : Employment Outlook 2000, cited in International Labour Office: World Employment Report, 2001.

factors that govern the choice. The extent to which traditions of patriarchal family systems and values which assign the bread-winner's role to men and care of the household to women have been weakened, the educational attainments and skill endowments of women, rate of marriage, household size and composition, household assets and income, levels of unemployment, wage rate for women-absolute as well as relative to that of men, extent of urbanization are some of the important factors that seem to have an effect on the work participation rates of women.

Estimates of work force participation rates in India are available from two sources, viz., the decennial population censuses and the five-yearly (approximately) labour force surveys conducted by the National Sample Survey Organisation. Though the two sources measure the work participation in somewhat differing conceptual frameworks, the results from the two broadly explain the same phenomenon. Two measures of work participation are available from the censuses – one as the ratio of 'Main' workers to the population and the second using the ratio of 'Main' and 'Marginal' workers taken together to the population. The NSS surveys estimate participation using three different approaches, namely, 'Usual Status', 'Current Weekly Status' and 'Current Day Status'. Within the Usual Status, a further distinction is made between Principal Status and Subsidiary Status activity, which broadly correspond to the census categories of 'Main' and 'Marginal' workers.

Table 4.18 indicates the work participation rates from the 1981, 1991 and 2001 censuses for each sex and place of residence, taking into account: (i) all workers (Main and Marginal workers), and (ii) Main workers only. The data on all workers would indicate: (a) low participation by women in comparison to men, (b) a steady increase in the participation rates for females, both in the rural as well as the urban areas, and (c) a more or less stagnant or even slightly falling rates for males. Consequently, female work participation rate as a percentage of the rate for males improved substantially from 37.5 in 1981 to 49.5 in 2001. Such improvement is visible both in the rural as well as the urban areas. Even so, the participation rates for women are low in absolute

Table 4.18: Work Participation Rates in India by Sex (1981 – 2001) (Percentages)

Yerar	*Rural Areas*			*Urban Areas*			*All Areas*		
	Female	*Male*	*Persons*	*Female*	*Male*	*Persons*	*Female*	*Male*	*Persons*
Total (Main + Marginal) Workers									
1981	23.1 (42.9)	53.8	38.8	8.3 (16.9)	49.1	30.0	19.7 (37.5)	52.6	36.7
1991	26.8 (51.0)	52.6	40.1	9.2 (18.8)	48.9	30.2	22.3 (43.2)	51.6	37.5
2001	31.0 (59.2)	52.4	42.0	11.6 (22.8)	50.9	32.2	25.7 (49.5)	51.9	39.3
Main Workers									
1981	16.0 (30.7)	52.6	34.8	7.3 (14.9)	48.5	29.2	14.0 (27.1)	51.6	33.5
1991	18.6 (35.9)	51.8	35.7	8.1 (16.7)	48.6	29.5	15.9 (31.3)	50.9	34.1
2001	16.8 (37.7)	44.5	31.0	9.1 (19.2)	47.5	29.3	14.7 (32.4)	45.4	30.6

Source: Census of India, 1981Census of India, 1991 and Census of India, 2001: Provisional Population Totals, Registrar General of India, Government of India.

Figures in brackets are percentages of rates for females out of the rates for males.

* Ratio of workers to the total population.

terms and particularly so in the urban areas where hardly a tenth of the women are counted as workers. The observed rural-urban differences are understandable as the rural women take part in almost all the agricultural operations and household industries along with their domestic work. By contrast, urban women, though more educated than their rural counterparts, are more circumscribed by middle class traditions. Development of education in the urban areas has mainly been in the middle class families, where the attitude to women's work outside the home has generally been more restrictive. Paucity of employment opportunities commensurate with their educational endowments could well be another reason. As Myrdal (1968) pointed out, "That participation rates are not higher has at least as much to do with considerations of status and prestige as with the absence of jobs for those who seek but cannot find them. It is of course conceivable that a more progressive and expanding society could elevate the position of women and change attitudes towards female work. But an economy whose capacity to absorb men of working age is strained does not encourage the elimination of traditional forms of discriminations against economic activity by women." A more revealing picture emerges if only Main Workers are considered. Women's participation as Main worker is only 14.7 (less than one-third of the rate for men) – 16.8 in the rural areas and a mere 9.1 (less than one-fifth of the rate for men) in the urban areas. Work participation rates based on only Main workers had fallen during the nineties both for men and women, a feature important in the context of the process of globalization and liberalization in operation during this period, and to which there will be an occasion to return to later. About 43 per cent of all women workers in 2001 were working only as Marginal workers compared to about 29 per cent in 1991, indicating further deterioration in the quality and visibility of female employment.

A look at the work participation rates based on 2001 census for different States (Table 4.19) would show that while the rates for men varied in a narrow range across the States and between urban and rural areas, there are considerable differences in the rates for women between States and between rural and urban areas. Ten States/Union Territories (Lakshadweep, Delhi, Daman and Diu, Chandigarh, Andaman and Nicobar Islands, West Bengal. Uttar Pradesh, Kerala, Punjab and Bihar) had an overall female participation rate less than 20 and Delhi and Lakshadweep among them had less than 10 per cent of the female population working. It is indeed strange to find progressive States like Delhi, Kerala and Punjab keeping company of relatively backward Uttar Pradesh and Bihar. Another important feature is that female participation rates are fairly high in Himachal Pradesh, Chatisgarh, Manipur, Mizoram, Sikkim, Arunachal Pradesh and Nagaland which have sizeable rural populations. The rates in the urban areas are invariably lower than those in the rural areas and are abysmally low at less than 10 in Jammu & Kashmir, Jharkhand, Orissa, Punjab, Rajasthan, Uttaranchal, Uttar Pradesh, Delhi and Lakshadweep. While it is possible that a substantial part of the work done by females in these States might not have got reported in the census data, a broad picture that emerges is that economic prosperity (Punjab, Delhi), high levels of urbanization (Delhi, Chandigarh) and even advances in social development (Kerala) do not seem to guarantee high levels of work participation of women. High household incomes and higher levels of urbanization appear to depress female work participation.

The results from the 55th Round of the labour force surveys of the National Sample Survey Organisation (July 1999 to June 2000) (Table 4.20 and 4.21) tell much the same story of women in the urban areas being engaged in economic activities (as measured through the traditional approach) to a lesser degree than their rural counterparts.

Table 4.19: Work Participation Rates by Sex in Different States and Union Territories, 2001

State/Union Territory	*Work Participation Rates (Main +Marginal)*					
	Females			*Males*		
	Total	*Rural*	*Urban*	*Total*	*Rural*	*Urban*
1. Andhra Pradesh	34.93	43.24	12.62	56.44	58.48	51.10
2. Assam	20.80	22.28	10.29	49.93	49.77	51.03
3. Bihar	18.84	20.19	6.86	47.73	48.43	41.93
4. Chatisgarh	40.04	46.59	12.96	52.97	54.28	47.95
5. Goa	22.24	26.37	17.96	54.86	54.85	54.86
6. Gujarat	28.03	39.04	9.11	55.02	55.59	54.12
7. Haryana	27.31	34.18	10.27	50.49	50.88	49.52
8. Himachal Pradesh	43.69	46.47	14.96	54.70	54.74	54.38
9. Jammu & Kashmir	21.96	25.84	9.50	49.83	49.14	51.80
10. Jharkhand	26.40	31.86	6.29	48.21	49.91	42.57
11. Karnataka	31.88	39.86	16.06	56.87	58.32	54.11
12. Kerala	15.28	15.88	13.55	50.36	50.22	50.78
13. Madhya Pradesh	33.10	40.68	11.70	51.62	53.08	47.64
14. Maharashtra	32.59	46.52	12.72	53.49	54.18	52.60
15. Manipur	40.51	43.20	32.28	48.91	50.07	45.17
16. Meghalaya	35.02	38.92	19.15	47.76	50.09	38.19
17. Mizoram	47.63	54.73	40.50	57.45	59.52	55.32
18. Nagaland	38.25	42.92	14.87	46.82	47.08	45.70
19. Orissa	24.62	27.10	9.76	52.75	53.38	49.37
20. Punjab	18.68	23.15	9.74	54.10	54.45	53.42
21. Rajasthan	33.48	40.70	9.24	50.07	50.82	47.64
22. Sikkim	38.59	40.67	21.42	57.58	57.75	56.27
23. Tamil Nadu	31.32	41.33	18.42	58.06	59.38	56.37
24. Tripura	21.02	22.86	12.09	50.81	50.61	51.78
25. Uttaranchal	27.09	33.32	7.28	46.42	45.99	47.58
26. Uttar Pradesh	16.28	18.89	6.19	47.26	47.84	45.08
27. West Bengal	18.08	20.70	11.13	54.23	54.30	54.07
28. Andaman & Nicobar	16.45	18.50	12.09	56.73	57.05	56.09
29. Arunachal Pradesh	36.45	41.33	16.69	50.69	51.13	48.99
30. Chandigarh	13.72	10.32	14.06	56.10	63.96	55.12
31. Dadra & Nagar Haveli	38.68	45.10	14.35	62.38	61.29	65.74
32. Daman & Diu	18.34	19.76	16.48	65.56	70.89	53.83
33. Delhi	9.15	10.12	9.08	52.21	49.71	52.40
34. Lakshadweep	7.19	6.07	8.61	42.51	40.70	44.75
35. Pondicherry	17.00	23.78	13.61	53.28	54.47	52.68
All India	*25.68*	*30.98*	*11.55*	*51.93*	*52.36*	*50.85*

Source: Census 2001 (Electronic Data), reproduced in The Indian Journal of Labour Economics, Vol. 45, No.1, 2002.

The figures for All India and Gujarat exclude the entire Kachh district and certain Talukas of Rajkot and Jamnagar Districts.

Table 4.20: Usual Status (Principal and Subsidiary) Work Participation Rates (1977-78 to 1999-2000) (Percentages)

Year	*Usual Status Participation Rates*			
	Females		*Males*	
	Rural	*Urban*	*Rural*	*Urban*
1977-78	33.1	15.6	55.2	50.8
1983	34.0	15.1	54.7	51.2
1987-88	32.3	15.2	53.9	50.6
1993-94	32.8	15.4	55.3	52.0
1999-2000	29.9	13.9	53.1	51.8

Source: National Sample Survey, 55th Round (July 1999 – June 2000), Employment and Unemployment in India, Key Results, 2000.

Chart 4.9: Usual Status (Principal and Subsidiary Work Participation Rates by Sex

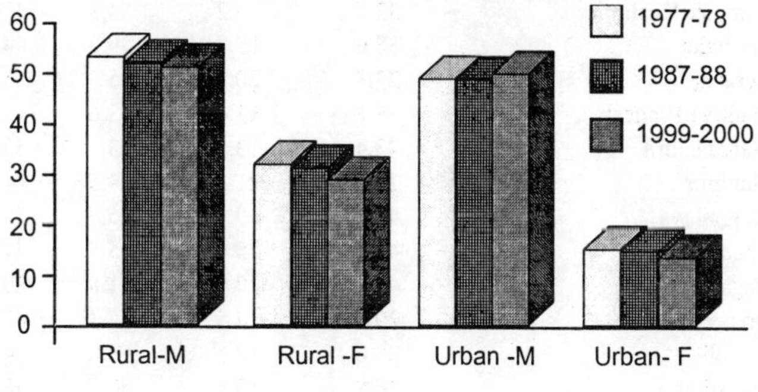

Unlike the census-based data, which exhibited a firm increasing trend in the female work participation rates over the last two decades (which in part could be due to constant endeavours on the part of the census authorities to net as much of women's work as possible through adequate questioning), the labour force survey data showed marginal fluctuations in both directions till 1993-94 but recorded a steep fall in the subsequent period (1993-94 to 1999-2000). While the small fluctuations prior to 1993-94 could be brushed off as insignificant as data is subject to sampling errors also, the same cannot be said of the changes in the subsequent period. Several explanations have been put forth for this decline in the participation rates which, though visible among both males and females, had been particularly sharp among the latter. Increasing pursuit of school and higher education, decline in participation in subsidiary activities, inability of the surveys to capture female work participation through the traditional approach, the rates for

1993-94 being outliers and not fitting well into the series, etc are some of these explanations other than the effects of job losses in the wake of economic liberalization (Sunderam, 2001 and Hirway, 2002).

Table 4.21: Usual Status (Principal and Subsidiary) Work Participation Rates by Sex in Different States and Union Territories, 1999-2000

State/Union territory	*Females*		*Males*	
	Rural	*Urban*	*Rural*	*Urban*
1. Andhra Pradesh	47.8	17.8	60.5	51.1
2. Assam	15.1	11.2	52.9	52.2
3. Bihar	17.3	7.5	49.2	43.2
4. Goa	18.1	10.6	53.9	49.8
5. Gujarat	41.3	13.5	58.4	53.6
6. Haryana	20.2	9.8	47.5	50.6
7. Himachal Pradesh	47.1	13.0	53.6	49.9
8. Jammu & Kashmir	32.7	6.2	54.8	47.8
9. Karnataka	38.0	17.8	59.5	54.5
10. Kerala	23.8	20.3	55.3	55.8
11. Madhya Pradesh	38.2	13.4	53.6	48.8
12. Maharashtra	43.4	13.7	53.1	53.2
13. Manipur	25.3	21.1	49.5	44.5
14. Meghalaya	41.8	19.7	55.7	39.3
15. Mizoram	44.0	25.9	55.5	47.1
16. Nagaland	44.1	19.9	51.8	39.3
17. Orissa	29.9	14.5	55.1	47.5
18. Punjab	28.0	12.5	53.0	54.9
19. Rajasthan	38.8	13.8	50.0	48.6
20. Sikkim	24.1	20.0	50.2	51.9
21. Tamil Nadu	43.0	21.5	59.4	56.3
22. Tripura	7.3	7.5	50.4	49.4
23. Uttar Pradesh	20.1	9.4	48.1	49.0
24. West Bengal	16.0	11.7	53.4	56.7
25. Andaman & Nicobar	18.0	20.6	54.7	63.2
26. Arunachal Pradesh	31.0	10.0	42.2	39.9
27. Chandigarh	12.8	13.6	78.4	54.7
28. Dadra & Nagar Haveli	35.4	11.2	58.2	65.6
29. Daman & Diu	30.0	18.6	65.5	54.9
30. Delhi	2.9	10.5	52.0	52.8
31. Lakshadweep	11.5	17.9	49.7	43.2
32. Pondicherry	28.7	16.9	56.0	55.5
All India	*29.9*	*13.9*	*53.1*	*51.8*

Source: National Sample Survey, 55th Round (July 1999 – June 2000), Employment and Unemployment in India, Key Results, 2000.

A look at the work participation rates by educational level indicates that the decline in participation rates between 1993-94 and 1999-2000 had been primarily in the "Below Matric' category (Table 4.22). Either more children in the primary stage of education are going in for further education instead of joining labour force, or there are fewer opportunities for this category of workers.

Table 4.22: Usual Status Work Participation Rates, 1993-94 and 1999-2000

Educational Category	*Year*	*Usual Status Work Participation Rate*			
		Females		*Males*	
		Rural	*Urban*	*Rural*	*Urban*
Below Matric	1993-1994	35.6	18.0	87.6	80.8
	1999-2000	26.8	12.2	57.3	50.0
Matric	1993-1994	15.5	11.4	66.6	63.4
(incl. Hr. Secondary)	1999-2000	15.9	10.6	70.1	63.3
Graduate and above	1993-1994	29.3	28.2	79.2	80.7
	1999-2000	27.8	25.2	80.3	79.7

Source: National Sample Survey Organisation, Sarvekshana, Vol. XX and Report No. 458

Quality of Women's Employment

Despite vastly enhanced access to education and skill development over years and increased visibility in diverse high profile occupations in areas considered the male preserve in the past, women's employment is still by and large characterized by greater instability and insecurity, lower skill levels and creativity, lower incomes and less satisfying career development. According to 2001 census, about 43 per cent of all female workers (46 per cent in the rural areas and 22 per cent in the urban areas) were only Marginal workers with intermittent work, the corresponding percentage for men being only 13. Nearly three-quarters (72 per cent) of all female workers (Main and Marginal) are engaged in agricultural activities (either as cultivators or as agricultural labourers, the latter being more preponderant), about 6 per cent in activities connected with household industries and the remaining 22 per cent in non-household industry and services (Chart 4.10). By contrast, only 52 per cent of the male workers are engaged in agricultural activities, a mere 3 per cent in household industry and the remaining 45 per cent in the industries and services outside the household. The share of women engaged in non-agricultural activities outside the household is, thus, about half the corresponding share for men.

Chart 4.10: Percentage Distribution of Women Workers by Industrial Categories, 2001

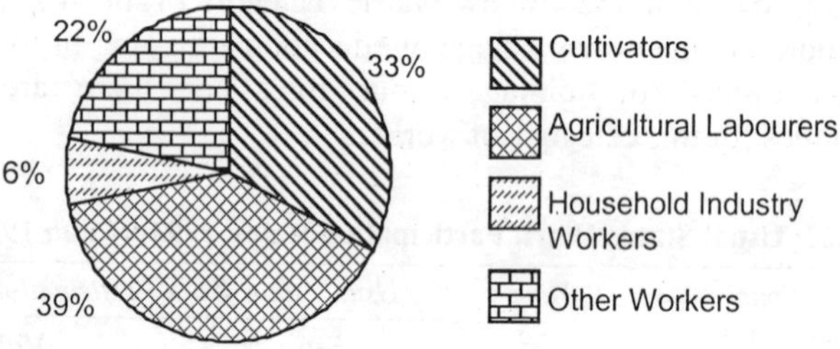

Source: Census 2001

The National Sample Survey data provide a distribution of the work force by the status of the worker, *i.e.*, whether he/she is a self-employed or a regular wage/salaried employee or a casual labourer. These data (Table 4.23) clearly show that a greater percentage of women workers than men are working as casual workers in both rural and urban areas. Only a third of the female workers in the urban areas and a mere 3 per cent in the rural areas were regular employees. Over half (57 per cent) of the rural female workers and 45 per cent of their urban counterparts have been categorised as self–employed. In the rural areas, almost all of them (about 84 per cent) were engaged in agricultural activities, being either cultivators or helping in agricultural operations on household land. In the urban areas, 20 per cent of the female workers classified as self-employed worked in that capacity in agricultural activities, 35 per cent in mining, manufacturing and construction and 45 per cent in various types of services, most of them perhaps low paid ones like domestic services, street hawking or home-based production for others. A positive feature thrown up by these data from successive surveys is that the share of regular employees among the female work force in the urban areas has been showing a steady upward trend, having increased from 25.8 per cent in 1983 to 27.5 per cent in 1987-88, to 28.6 per cent in 1993-94 and to 33.3 per cent in 1999-2000.

Table 4. 23: Distribution of Women Workers* by Employment Status (1999-2000) (Percentages)

	Self-employed	*Regular employees*	*Casual labour*	*Total*
Rural Males	55.0	8.8	36.2	100.0
Rural Females	57.3	3.1	39.6	100.0
Urban Males	41.5	41.7	16.8	100.0
Urban Females	45.3	33.3	21.4	100.0

Source: National Sample Survey, 55th Round (July 1999-June 2000).

*Usual (Principal & Subsidiary) Status.

Another measure of women's access to secure and stable employment is their share in the employment in the organized employment[5] (Table 4.24). Hardly 4 per cent of the total female work force is employed in the organized sector while the overwhelming majority is engaged in the unorganized and unprotected activities. What is more, even though the presence of women in the organized sector has been increasing over the last two decades in absolute numbers (col. 6 of Table 4.24), the increase is at such a slow pace relative to the total female work force that the last two decades witnessed a decline in the percentage of women working in the organized sector from 4.29 in 1981 to 4.16 in 1991 and further to 3.89 in 2001. This decline, however, is not confined to women only, the male work force also having witnessed similar shift in the relative shares of the organized and unorganized sectors. In fact, this shift has been sharper in the case of men than women with the result that women have been improving their share of the organized pie relative to men.

Table 4.24: Employment in Organised and Unorganised Sectors

Year (March of)	*Total Workers (million)*[1]			*Workers in organized sector (million)*[2]			*Share of organized sector in total work force (%)*		
	Men	*Women*	*Persons*	*Men*	*Women*	*Persons*	*Men*	*Women*	*Persons*
1981	185.89	65.01	250.81	20.09	2.79	22.88	10.81	4.29	9.12
1991	226.63	90.78	317.36	22.65	3.78	26.73	9.99	4.16	8.42
2001	275.74	127.39	403.61	22.84	4.95	27.79	8.28	3.89	6.89

Source: 1. Based on population (including estimates for Assam in 1981 and Jammu & Kashmir in 1991) and work participation rates by sex for the respective years given in The Tenth Five Year Plan (2002-07), Planning Commission. The figures in cols. 2 and 3 may not add up exactly to those in col. 4 which have been independently derived. 2. Annual Employment Reviews 1980-81 and 1990-91 and Quarterly Employment Review 2000-01, Ministry of Labour.

Considering that the organized sector excluded agriculture and household economic activity, it might be interesting to look at the share of the employment in the organized sector in the total non-agricultural, non-household employment. Table 4.25 gives the latest available data. Even after the exclusion of these two sectors, the share of the workers in the organized sector is just 18 per cent of all workers within the non-agricultural, non-household workers. Interestingly, this percentage is more or less gender-neutral.

Table 4.25: Percentage Distribution of Workers by Industrial Category and Sector (2001)

Category	*Percentage of workers in the category to total workers*		
	Men	*Women*	*Persons*
1. Agriculture	52.16	71.94	58.40
(a) Cultivators	31.34	32.51	31.71
(b) Agricultural Labourers	20.82	39.43	26.69
2. Household Industry	3.02	6.36	4.07
3. Others	44.82	21.70	37.52
(a) Organised sector	8.28 (18.47)	3.89 (17.92)	6.89 (18.37)
(b) Un-organised sector	36.54 (81.53)	17.81 (82.08)	30.63 (81.63)
Total workers	100.00	100.00	100.00

Source: Based on Census 2001 population data given in The Tenth Five Year Plan (2002-07), work force participation rates and distribution of workers by categories reproduced in The Journal of Labour Economics, Vol.45, No. 1, Jan-Mar 2002 and The Quarterly Employment Review Jan-Mar 2000, Directorate General of Employment and Training, Ministry of Labour

Figures in brackets are the percentages of workers in the organized and unorganized sectors within the category of 'Others'.

Though very low for decades, the percentage of women in the total employment in the organized sector has been going up continuously. Data for the past three decades would show that the share of women in the employment in the organized sector improved from 11 per cent in 1971 to about 18 in 2001. The improvement in the share of women in the employment in the organized sector is both in the public and private sectors (Table 4.26). An important point to be observed is that in the post liberalization period (from 1991) the absorption of women in the organized private sector has gone up substantially and the percentage of women in that sector increased by over 4 percentage points from 18.9 to 24.2 during 1991-2001 against a rise of only 1.5 percentage points from 17.5 to 18.9 in the previous decade.

Chart 4.11: Percentage of Women Employees in the Organized Sector

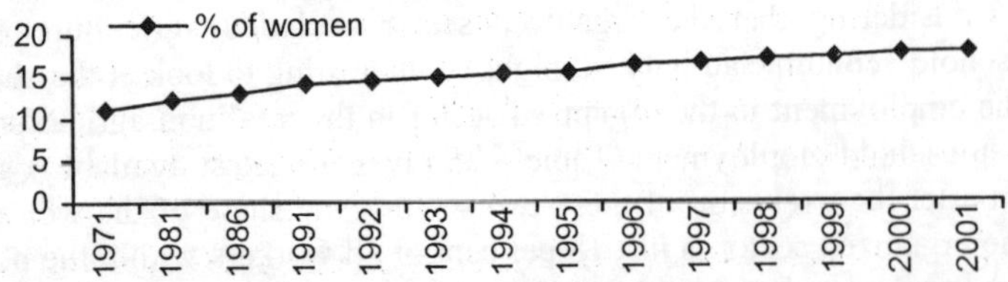

Source: Employment Reviews 1971, 1981 and 1998; Quarterly Employment Reviews January-March 1999 and 2001.

Table 4.26: Employment of Women in Public and Private Sectors (1981-2001)

Year (March of)	Employment (lakhs) in					
	Public Sector			Private Sector		
	Total	Women	Percentage of women in total	Total	Women	Percentage of women in total
1981	154.84	14.99	9.7	73.95	12.94	17.5
1991	190.57	23.47	12.3	76.76	14.34	18.9
2001	191.38	28.59	14.9	86.52	20.90	24.2

Source: Employment Reviews 1981 and 1991 and Quarterly Employment Review Jan-Mar 2001, Directorate General of Employment and Training, Ministry of Labour

The overall picture that emerges is that even though women are constantly improving their share in employment in the organized sector *vis-à-vis* men, practically all of the female workers are engaged in activities connected with agriculture, household industry and in the unorganized segment of other industries and services, without employment or income security. What is more, there is evidence to show that as percent of the total female work force, the number of employees in the organized sector has been steadily declining over the years.

How do women workers in the unorganised sector fare in relation to men? Some results from a nation-wide survey on Non-agricultural Enterprises in the Informal Sector[6] conducted by the National Sample Survey Organisation as part of their 55th Round in 1999-2000 are given below in Table 4.27. These data indicate that a) over 84 per cent (against 67 per cent for male workers) of the female workers in the informal sector are engaged mainly in own account enterprises (which do not hire any labour for most part of the operating period) and only 16 per cent (against 33 per cent of male workers) are engaged in establishments that hire labour. Further, while over 90 per cent of the male workers are full-time workers, over one-fourth of the female workers are part-time workers. This shows that the female workers in the informal sector attach themselves rather loosely to the labour market.

A survey of informal sector in Ahmedabad City conducted jointly by the Gujarat Institute of Development Research and Self-Employed Women's Association, Ahmedabad, in 1998-99 showed that home-based workers accounted for about a third (32 per cent) of the female non-agricultural workers against only 5.8 per cent among the males. Three quarters of these home-based workers were dependent on work orders from outside contractors. Home-based workers including unpaid helpers constituted half (50.7 per cent) of the female workers against only 7.9 per cent among the males.

Table 4.27: Structure of in Informal Sector, 1999-2000 (Percentages)

Nature of employ-ment	*Own Account Enterprises*		*Establishments*		*All Enterprises*	
	Male Workers	*Female Workers*	*Male Workers*	*Female Workers*	*Male Workers*	*Female Workers*
Full time	90.8	70.5	94.3	85.3	92.0	72.8
Part time	9.2	29.5	5.7	14.7	8.0	27.2
All	100.0 (67.0)	100.0 (84.4)	100.0 (33.0)	100.0 (15.6)	100.0 (100.0)	100.0 (100.0)

Source: Based on National Sample Survey, Survey on Non-agricultural Enterprises in the Informal Sector, 55th Round (July 1999 – June 2000)

Figures are percentages of the respective column totals. Figures in brackets in col. 2 and 4 are percentages to those in col. 6 and those in col. 3 and 5 are percentages to those in col. 7.

Occupational Segregation of Women

The concentration of female work force in unorganized economic activities is further complicated by its concentration in certain low-end occupations. Such occupational segmentation of female workers is a phenomenon that cuts across spatial and temporal boundaries. It is both horizontal as well as vertical. Horizontal segregation connotes concentration of men and women in different types of occupations while vertical segregation refers to such concentration at different hierarchical levels within the same occupation. A typical instance is the concentration of women in occupations like school teachers, nurses, domestic servants, etc. and in jobs generally requiring repetitive skills within the same occupation. Rothboeck and Acharya (1999) point out that gender-specific occupational segregation is regarded as a stable and rigid phenomenon that exists in traditional as well as modern societies and that various studies underline the persistence of gender segregated labour markets globally, as being independent of the level of industrial development or occupational diversification. A recent study (reported in Times of India, New Delhi, 6 May 2003) based on census data by the American Association of University Women found that women in the United States of America today are more educated and employed at higher levels than ever before but remain largely confined to traditional "pink-collar" jobs, with the highest proportions of college-educated working women being in teaching and nursing occupations, neither of which appearing in the list of most common occupations for their male counterparts. Several models have been postulated to explain this phenomenon of occupational segregation (Agarwal, 1993). Some of these models (overcrowding model) centre round labour market demand factors explaining why some employers prefer to engage women workers in certain occupations and at certain levels and supply factors why women workers prefer to work in certain occupations and at certain levels. Others (human capital model) postulate that women, who have to strike a balance between their roles within and outside the family, tend to avoid occupations requiring large investments in human capital accumulation, particularly when such capital depreciates fast in value during the time spent out of labour force. Yet another approach to explain gender-based occupational segregation involves the hypothesis that labour market has evolved over time into distinct gender-based segments composing of non-competing groups and with restricted mobility across the segments, and concentrates on factors that determine career mobility and job security. Finally, other theories seek to explain the phenomenon in sociological terms and the disadvantages to which women are subjected to in a patriarchal society in general and in the labour market in particular. A separate chapter in this book attempts to delve deep into this phenomenon.

In a traditional society like India, where female work participation is often frowned upon and is at best accepted as only a source of secondary employment in the household, the tendency towards occupational segregation could be expected to be stronger. As already seen (Table 4.25) above, according to the 2001 census, about 72 per cent of the female work force was engaged in agricultural activities, either as cultivators or as agricultural labour, a greater part as the latter. If those engaged in activities like animal husbandry, fisheries, etc. are added, the proportion of women workers in agricultural and allied occupations would be around 80 per cent. This is what the occupational distribution of the female workforce obtained from the censuses and the labour force sample surveys indicate (Table 4.28).

Table 4.28: Occupational Distribution of Female Workers (Percentages)

Occupational Division	*1981 (Census)*		*1991 (Census)*		*1999-2000 (NSSO)*	
	Persons	*Females*	*Persons*	*Females*	*Persons*	*Females*
(1)	*(2)*	*(3)*	*(4)*	*(5)*	*(6)*	*(7)*
0-1 Professional, Technical and Related Workers	3.2	3.2	3.6	3.9	3.5	3.1
2. Administrative, Executive and Managerial Workers	1.1	0.1	1.0	0.2	2.9	1.5

Contd.

(1)	*(2)*	*(3)*	*(4)*	*(5)*	*(6)*	*(7)*
3. Clerical and Related Workers	3.3	1.0	3.4	1.4	2.9	1.1
4. Sales Workers	4.6	1.5	5.8	1.7	6.6	2.7
5. Service Workers	3.0	2.7	2.9	2.5	3.9	4.2
6. Farmers, Fishermen and Related Workers	68.7	81.2	66.6	80.8	61.1	75.6
7-8-9: Production and Related Workers, Transport Equipment Operators and Labourers	15.1	9.6	15.5	9.0	19.0	11.8
10. Workers not Classified by Occupation	1.0	0.7	1.2	0.5	—	—
All Occupations	100	100	100	100	100	100

Source: Registrar General of India, 1981 and 1991 censuses, and National Sample Survey, 55th Round, July 1999-June 2000.

The census data relate to Main workers and the NSS data to Usual Principal Status workers.

Considering that female workers constituted less than a fourth of all workers, the above data indicate a clear concentration of female workers in the Farmers, Fishermen and Related workers, Professional and Technical and Related workers and Service workers categories. The concentration is somewhat less pronounced among Clerical and Related workers and Production and Related workers, Transport Equipment Operators and Labourers. There are clear differences in the occupational patterns in the rural and urban areas, the former being overwhelmingly dominated by agricultural workers. Table 4.29 would show that in the urban areas, the areas of concentration are clearly demarcated. A greater percentage of women than men work in professional and technical, service and farming occupations. About 30 per cent of the women workers are production workers or labourers. Some of the specific occupations where there is a large concentration of women are school teachers and nursing personnel in the professional and technical category, clerical and secretarial workers in railways, posts, communications and other government departments, banks, insurance and other financial institutions, sales workers, sweepers, cooks and other service workers, labour in tea and coffee plantations, coal mining workers, food processing workers, *bidi* workers, weavers and garment makers, construction workers, telephone operators, and loaders and other types of unskilled labour in the industry. Though increasing number of women have been entering professional and technical fields like scientific research, teaching in higher educational institutions, airline pilots and even locomotive drivers and computer professionals, judicial and legal services, high profile jobs in financial institutions and advertising and other services, police services and holding higher administrative and managerial positions, their number is still small in comparison to men.

Table 4.29: Occupational Pattern of Workers (Usual Principal and Subsidiary Status) in Rural and Urban Areas, 1999-2000 (Percentages)

Occupational Division	*Rural areas*		*Urban areas*	
	Male	*Female*	*Male*	*Female*
0-1: Professional, Technical and Related Workers, of whom	2.3	1.4	7.6	14.4
a) Nurses and other health technicians	0.1	0.2	0.4	2.2
b) Teachers	1.3	1.0	2.3	10.3
c) Others	0.8	0.1	4.9	1.8
2: Administrative, Executive and Managerial Workers	1.7	0.8	9.0	5.8
3: Clerical and Related Workers, of whom	1.9	0.3	9.4	6.5
a) Clerical workers	1.5	0.3	8.3	6.1
b) Transport & communications workers (conductors, postal workers and telephone operators, etc.)	0.4	—	1.1	0.5
4: Sales Workers	5.0	1.8	18.4	8.8
5: Service Workers, of whom	2.4	2.3	7.9	16.5
a) Housekeepers, cooks, maids, sweepers	0.3	1.0	2.4	13.0
b) Washermen, barbers, etc.	1.0	0.9	1.2	1.8
c) Protective and other service workers	1.1	0.3	4.2	1.7
6: Farmers, Fishermen and Related Workers	70.5	84.5	7.0	18.4
7-8-9: Production and Related Workers, Transport Equipment Operators and Labourers, of whom	16.2	8.9	40.7	29.6
a) Construction workers	2.8	0.7	2.9	4.3
b) Labourers	3.1	1.0	4.3	4.9
c) Other production workers	10.3	7.2	33.5	20.4
All Occupations	100.0	100.0	100.0	100.0

Source: National Sample Survey, 55th Round, Report No. 458, Employment and Unemployment in India 1999-2000, Part I.

Unequal Remuneration and Other Forms of Discrimination

Despite international Conventions and national legislations to the contrary, the phenomenon of sex differentials in remuneration for similar or even the same work is more or less a universal one. That discrimination against women in compensation for work exists even in developed countries is amply demonstrated by the data on earnings of women as percentage of men's earnings in European Union countries presented in Table 4.30, which show that women's earnings were 20 to

40 per cent short of the men's earnings. Data in Table 1.6 (col.8) in Chapter 1 in respect of 23 of the most populous countries in the world, developed as well as developing, also lead to the same conclusion. Silvera (2000) points out that "One cannot but wonder about the persistence of gaps of this magnitude despite considerable legislative action at the national, European and international levels. A review of studies on the question in France and a number of other countries led us to the conclusion that traditional explanations are quite inadequate. For instance, in most econometric models, the portion of the gap unaccounted by the conventionally applied variables remains stable and even tends to increase when the gaps close! At present, irrespective of the country or the models used, approximately one half of differentials are not justified by these variables. In other words, everything else being equal (that is, educational level, experience, job category, age, presumably equivalent sectors, etc.), women still earn between 10 to 15% less than men in France." She points out that social and cultural aspects like the traditional division of roles within the family, including unequal access to education and training, unequal sharing of domestic work, existence of a 'male breadwinner wage' and consideration of women's earnings as only secondary income etc are very important factors contributing to the gender gap in earnings. These attitudes outlive development in purely economic terms.

Table 4.30: Earnings of Women Industrial Workers as Percentage of Earnings of Men in E.U. Countries (1996, unless otherwise stated)

Country	*Women's Wages as Percentage of Men's Wages*	
	Women workers (hourly rate)	*Women employees (monthly wages)*
Belgium (1995)	75.6	65.2
Denmark (1993)	84.5	—
Germany (former West)	74.8	69.4
Germany (former East)	79.1	74.5
Greece (1995)	77.0	69.5
Spain	71.6	63.4
France	82.1	71.1
Ireland	72.6	—
Italy	—	—
Luxembourg	70.2	64.0
Netherlands (1994)	77.9	68.4
Austria	65.5	64.8
Portugal	70.4	70.5
Finland (1995)	—	78.8
Sweden	—	76.1
United Kingdom	69.2	60.3

Source: Harmonised statistics on earnings in Eurostat (1996) cited in The Gendering of Inequalities: Women, Men and Work.

There is considerable documentation of the wage differentials on the basis of gender in India too. For instance, according to the surveys of National Sample Survey Organisation, the average wage received by female causal labourer in rural India was about 65 per cent of that received by the males in 1999-2000 and in the urban non-agricultural casual wage employment, the wage rate for females was about 60 per cent of the rate for males (Tables 4.31 and 4.32). Moreover, the gender gap seems to have remained more or less unaltered between 1993-94 and 1999-2000 in the rural areas, except in the case of casual labour in public works where the gap has substantially narrowed, possibly because of the government's interventions. In the urban areas, considerable gender gaps exist across the board in all industries in the wage rates for casual labour. While most of the secondary sector industries and tertiary sector industries like trade and transport have shown improvement in this respect over the period 1993-94 to 1999-2000, the situation in financial and business services and in community services seems to have been worsened.

Table 4.31: Average Wage Received per Day by Causal Labourers in Rural India by Type of Operation, 1993-1994 and 1999-2000

Category and Type of operation	*1993-94*			*1999-2000*		
	Average Daily Wage (Rs.)			*Average Daily Wage (Rs.)*		
	Male	*Female*	*% of female wage to male wage*	*Male*	*Female*	*% of female wage to male wage*
A: Casual labourers in public works	24.70	14.75	59.72	48.14	38.06	79.06
B: Casual labourers in other types of works						
(a) Manual work in cultivation	20.66	14.75	71.39	39.09	27.91	71.40
(b) Manual work in other agricultural activities*	23.65	16.05	67.86	44.84	30.65	68.35
(c) Manual work in non-agricultural activities	29.66	17.08	57.59	58.71	36.19	61.64
(d) Non-manual work	21.50	14.82	68.93	42.80	29.30	68.46
All Categories	22.82	15.15	66.39	44.84	29.81	66.48

*Forestry, plantations, animal husbandry, fisheries and other activities allied to agriculture.

Source: NSSO, Report No. 409 and Report No. 455.

Table 4.32: Average Wage per Day Received by Casual Wage Labourers in Urban India

Industry Division	*1993-94*			*1999-2000*		
	Average Daily Wage (Rs.)			*Average Daily Wage (Rs.)*		
	Male	*Female*	*% of female wage to male wage*	*Male*	*Female*	*% of female wage to male wage*
0. Agriculture, hunting, forestry and fishing	25.19	16.28	64.63	49.14	32.15	65.43
1. Mining and quarrying	28.45	21.59	75.89	75.65	54.67	72.27
2. Manufacturing	33.10	15.66	47.31	62.88	35.64	56.68
3. Manufacturing	31.64	15.15	47.88	69.13	50.69	73.33
4. Electricity, Gas and Water	40.17	23.17	57.68	74.24	-	-
5. Construction	37.63	24.97	66.36	69.00	50.20	72.75
6. Wholesale and retail trade& hotels and restaurants	27.74	20.14	72.60	53.65	45.63	85.05
7. Transport, storage and communication	34.42	19.77	57.44	63.64	49.63	77.99
8. Financial, insurance, real estate and business services	28.47	25.80	90.62	64.85	32.83	50.62
9. Community, social and personal services	26.90	18.67	69.41	55.19	28.95	52.46
All Industry Divisions	31.81	18.07	56.81	62.26	37.71	60.57

Source: Same as for Table 4.31.

Such gender gaps in remuneration are prevalent in regular wage/salaried employment as well. The data from NSSO show that in both rural as well as urban areas wages/salaries received by regular women employees in the age group 15 – 59 years and who are illiterates averaged only slightly above half of what male illiterate employees earned. In the case of literates up to middle school level education, urban wages for females averaged 60 per cent of the wages for males. The rural picture for this educational level seems to be an aberration, being consistent with neither general experience at other educational levels, nor with the data from the earlier Round (50th Round, 1993-94) of National Sample Survey[7]. At higher educational levels (secondary and graduate) the male-female gaps are narrower—the female earnings being around three-fourths or more of the corresponding male earnings

(Table 4.33). Using the results of the Diploma Holders and Technical Persons survey conducted along with the 1981 Census, Duraiswamy and Duraiswamy (1999) found that in various science and technology fields, the monthly earnings of females averaged around 78 per cent of the male earnings, while in social sciences and other professional fields the ratio was 84 per cent. These differences between the sexes in the remuneration received for similar jobs are sought to be explained to a large extent through varying access to different occupations and different levels of jobs and responsibilities within the same occupation as discussed earlier. Women's role as participants in economic activity tends to be secondary to or at best no more important than their role in the domestic sphere, and when they take up economic activity, it is usually such as would not come into conflict with the domestic role. In the process, women forego stable, better- paid employment and career advancement in exchange for overall family happiness. For instance, most women employees in banks are known to lower their aspirations in career and prefer to stay where they are rather than accept promotions which involve transfers, additional responsibilities and late working hours. From the demand side, employers tend, for various reasons, to engage women more often in repetitive jobs and at lower levels of responsibility. Taking the case of bank employees again, Rao (2001) refers to a number of studies indicating complaints of career-minded women in senior positions that they were not assigned challenging and strategic postings such as in foreign exchange or personnel departments, field or inspection jobs, allowing them no opportunity to show their mettle and thereby denying them professional advancement. A wide-spread feeling that because women employees are hard workers and submissive by nature, all work involving drudgery and of urgent nature gets assigned to them, is also widely prevalent among the female employees.

This situation is not exclusive to financial services sector alone. It happens in *bidi* rolling and other areas of tobacco processing industry, in plantations, in construction, in data processing services and a host of other activities. Even though The Equal Remuneration Act, 1976 has been in force for over a quarter of a century, its impact in curbing male-female differences in remuneration for similar work and other forms of discrimination does not appear to be significant. As amended in 1987, the Act prohibits gender-based discrimination in matters of recruitment, remuneration, promotions, training and equal opportunities for growth in profession. In theory, it applies to all industries and sectors (organised and unorganized) and class of permanent, temporary or even casual) employment. Problems that have been cited (Acharya, 1996) as

of tenure (contract, home-based work, etc.) make it difficult for the unions in seeking a common ground for taking up issues that revolve round gender inequality. One of the unions *(Lal Nishan)* whose views were projected by Acharya states that women's organizations generally are more committed to problems relating to women's human rights, wife abuse, divorce, separation, property disputes and the like and pay relatively little attention to work-related problems.

Trends on the membership of women in recognized unions are blurred by varying rates of response on which the statistics for different years are based but seem to indicate some improvement over the years (Table 4.34). One of the significant development in the matter of organisation of women in recent years has been the new paradigm of Self Help Groups (SHGs), in which small groups of women join together to seek credit and other inputs to enhance the scale and productivity of their self-employment ventures, often aided and guided by an NGO. More on this has already been said in the previous chapter.

Table 4.34: Registered Trade Unions and their Membership by Sex (1977-97)

Year	*No. of registered trade unions*	*Percentage of the unions submitting returns*	*Percentage of male members*	*Percentage of female members*
1977	30,810	39.9	91.9	8.1
1978	32,361	38.5	93.0	7.0
1979	34,430	39.7	92.5	7.5
1980	36,507	18.9	94.1	5.9
1981	37,539	45.6	92.9	7.1
1982	38,313	35.1	94.1	5.9
1983	38,935	44.6	92.4	7.5
1984	42,609	28.8	91.4	8.6
1985	45,067	31.5	90.6	9.4
1986	45,904	16.7	92.5	7.5
1987	49,329	36.9	90.6	9.4
1988	50,048	33.5	89.6	10.4
1989	52,210	34.1	88.3	11.7
1990	52,016	46.4	88.1	11.9
1991	53,535	36.8	90.3	9.7
1992	55,680	26.3	89.6	10.4
1993	55,784	26.3	84.1	15.9
1994	56,872	25.3	79.1	20.9
1995	57,952	24.6	86.8	13.2
1996	58,805	20.2	75.9	24.1
1997	59,968	28.6	87.7	12.3

Source: Indian Labour Year Books, 1989, 1991 and 1999, Labour Bureau, Ministry of Labour.

Participation in Political Process

Increasing participation in the political process and in legislative activity is at the same time an indicator of one aspect of empowerment as well as enabling agent for empowerment in a broader sense. Though a number of prominent women participated in the Independence movement and even thousands of ordinary women had been drawn into it under the influence of the national leadership at that time, it was a very special event. But it contributed to the increasing political awareness and participation of women in the political sphere on a regular basis in the post-independence democratic process in the country. A measure of this participation at the national level is provided by (a) the voter turnout of women in elections, both in absolute terms and also in relation to that of men, and (b) representation of women in legislature.

As regards voter turn out, the last national elections (to the 13th Lok Sabha held in 1999) witnessed an overall voter turn out of 60 per cent, while the turn out ratio for women was a shade lower at 56 per cent. The corresponding rates were 62 per cent for all voters and 58 per cent for female voters in the elections to the 12th Lok Sabha held in 1998. These percentages of females turning out to vote in recent elections is a substantial improvement over the female voter turn out of 37 per cent in the elections to the 1st Lok Sabha held in 1952 and 40 per cent to the 2nd Lok Sabha in 1957, but have not shown any improvement after the seventies.

Table 4.35: Women in Parliament (Lok Sabha)

Lok Sabha Sl. No. and year	*Total number of seats*	*Number of women members*	*Percentage of women members to total*
1st (1952)	499	22	4.4
2nd (1957)	500	27	5.4
3rd (1962)	503	34	6.8
4th (1967)	523	31	5.9
5th (1971)	521	22	4.2
6th (1977)	544	19	3.5
7th (1980)	544	28	5.1
8th (1984)	544	44	8.1
9th (1989)	517	27	5.2
10th (1991)	544	39	7.2
11th (1996)	544	40	7.4
12th (1998)	543	43	7.9
13th (1999)	543	49	9.0

Source: KBK Pollgraphics, New Delhi 1999, and Election Commission of India.

Table 4.36: Women in Parliament (Rajya Sabha)

Year	*Total seats*	*Women members*	*Percentage of women*
1990	245	24	9.8
1992	245	17	6.9
1994	245	20	8.2
1996	245	18	7.3
1997	245	18	7.3
1998	245	19	7.8
1999	245	19	7.8
2000	245	22	9.0

Source: Election Commission of India, 1999.

The last three decades have not seen any significant improvement in the representation of women in the highest decision-making body of the nation, namely, the parliament. While their representation in the lower house has shown some improvement, the percentage of women members having increased from about 4 to 9 in the last fifty years, their share in the upper house has fluctuated between 7 to 10 per cent. In 2002, the combined representation of women in both the houses of Indian parliament was 8.9 per cent, up from 7.2 in 1998 and 8.5 in 1999 and 2000 (GOI, The Tenth Five Year Plan) compared to 44 in Sweden, 31.0 in Germany, 21.8 in China, 17.2 in Philippines, 17.1 in U.K., 15.9 in Mexico, 13.8 in U.S.A., 10.9 in France and 10.4 in Vietnam (UNDP, 2002). As of now there are only ten countries in the world (Sweden, Denmark, Finland, Norway, Iceland, Netherlands, Argentina, Germany, Mozambique and South Africa) where more than 30 per cent of the parliamentarians are women. In the State legislatures too the representation of women as Members of Legislative Assemblies is poor. For example, in Karnataka, which once had reserved 25 per cent of the seats in its Legislative Assembly for women during the eighties, there are now only six female members, below 5 per cent of the total. In Gujarat, there are only 12 women legislators in a house of 182, while West Bengal has 28 women in a total of 294. It is in this context that the proposed legislation to amend the Constitution to reserve one-third of the seats in parliament and State legislatures for women is to be considered.

While the above legislative proposal for reservations for women at the national and state levels faces stiff opposition from some quarters delaying its enactment, similar reservation in the local bodies has become a reality at national level for about a decade now with the enactment of 73rd and 74th Constitution (Amendment) Acts 1993 for the Panchayats and municipalities respectively. Earlier Karnataka introduced reservation of seats for women in Panchayats in 1985 while Andhra Pradesh reserved the post of chairman of Panchayat for women by rotation from term to term. There are now (as of October 2001) about 7.25 lakh women in Panchayat Raj Institutions (PRIs) in the country accounting for about 27 per cent of the total (GOI, The Tenth Five Year Plan). On the effectiveness of the presence of women in the PRIs, the experience of the initial years seems to have been unsatisfactory. Rao and Prasad (2002) refer to a study by Niraja Gopal which found "plenty of evidence of surrogate and proxy representation of husbands and other male relatives who not only canvas for their women but also receive notices and attend meetings in their places" and to another study in Meerut that "Pradhanis never attended any meetings or made any decisions about allocation of funds to various individuals or to schemes. They merely sign the papers sent to them after decisions are taken." The authors' experience in some villages of Uttar Pradesh and Madhya Pradesh during the course of a social impact survey conducted in connection with a highways project (1997) corroborated this, with the women Sarpanches mostly depending on their men-folk in discharging their responsibilities. This was perhaps to be expected, given the base from which the rural women started. Over the years the situation has changed somewhat for the better due to achievements in areas of generation of awareness and self-belief and other aspects of social empowerment of women. Individual differences also exist. For instance, Rao and Prasad (2002) cite the case of Fatima Bee, a woman Sarpanch, who was selected by the UNDP for her outstanding contribution for the development of the village by initiating schemes on her own. Their study of 50 women Sarpanches in Guntur district of Andhra Pradesh indicated that after over four years of being in the position, a substantial majority of the female Sarpanches did not find their jobs inconvenient, followed what was going on in the meetings, could represent the problems of the village to higher officials and became familiar with the Panchayat Raj administrative work. The study further found that while only 6 women Sarpanches were involved in and only 3 initiated the meetings at the time of their installation, 34 were involved and 4 initiated the meetings at the time of study. Reviewing the performance of women representatives in Panchayats in States like Andhra Pradesh, Maharashtra and West Bengal, Joseph (2001) concluded that "Examples cited above show beyond doubt that women are capable of performing excellently in Panchayat Raj

Institutions. The apprehension that women might not be able to cope up with the pressures is proved to be unfounded."

Sarpanches on a Unique Mission

Of course, these women from far-flung rural areas have not had it easy when they ventured into the volatile world of politics. Yet, they have battled on gamely and many have emerged triumphant to narrate their success stories.

Take the case of Krishna Devi from Kaurian village of UP's Faizabad district. Being a woman and a scheduled caste was a double handicap for her. "Although I am a sarpanch, they insist that I sit on the floor during the meetings", she said.

Taradevi from Samarada village of Rajasthan's Bikaner district has been sarpanch for over two years but her male predecessor has not handed over the official documents to her. "It becomes very difficult to function in such circumstances", she says but she, too, refuses to give up.

Times of India, New Delhi, 8 March 2003

Women in Decision-making Positions

Political Parties

Despite the positive postures taken up by various political parties overtly in support of the increased participation of women at various levels of the political process, there is not much evidence of translating it into a practical reality when it comes to female representation in their policy-making bodies. Participation of women in such platforms of decision-making is virtually absent among the major left-wing parties, with the Communist Party of India (Marxist) having no woman in their Politbureau and the Communist Party of India having no female member on its Secretariat. The radical nature of the policies of these parties (at least before Independence and a few years thereafter), difficulties in combining such participation with household affairs, and historically lower level of political awareness (whatever the reasons might have been) than men could be the contributory factors. The Indian National Congress seems to be the only political party, perhaps for reasons of history) with a semblance of sincerity in giving a role to women in political decision-making (Table 4.37).

Table 4.37: Women in Decision-making Bodies of Some Political Parties (2002)

Party	*Organisation*	*Total members*	*Women*	*Percentage of women*
1. Communist Party (Marxist)	1. Politbureau	17	0	0
	2. Central Committee	79	5	
2. Communist Party of India	1. Secretariat	9	0	0
	2. National Executive	37	4	10.8
	3. National Council	131	6	4.6
3. Indian National Congress	1. Congress Working Committee	39	6	15.4
	2. All India Congress Committee – Office bearers	8	3	37.5
	3. AICC Central Executive Committee	13	4	30.1
4. Bharatiya Janata Party	1. Parliamentary Board	9	1	11.1
	2. Election Committee	17	2	11.8
5. Telugu Desam Party	1. Politbureau	12	1	8.3
	2. State Committee	17	4	23.5

Source: www.indiannationalcongress.org; www.cpim.org; www.bjp.org; www.telugudesam.prg

Government

There had never been any bar on women being the heads of governments in India, either in the days of monarchies of the pre-colonial period or in the days of democracies later. If Razia Sultana and Chand Bibi provide instances of the past, erstwhile Prime Minister Indira Gandhi is an example of the modern era. There have been women Chief Ministers in the States (*e.g.* Tamilnadu, Uttar Pradesh, Delhi, Bihar and Orissa), some having been elected on more than one occasion. Women have also occupied gubernatorial positions though none has become a President yet. Ministerial posts have been given to women, both in the Union Government as well as in the States, but not in adequate numbers. For example, in 2001, the Union Cabinet had 8 women ministers out of the total ministerial strength of 74, *i.e.*, 10.8 per cent, marking a slight improvement over 1985 when only 4 out of the 40 ministers (10 per cent) were women. One cannot, however, view this as indicating a trend towards higher representation to women in the cabinets. The situation is no better in the States, including those with women as Chief Ministers. In Bihar, for example, there are (in 2003) only two female members in the cabinet of 63 and in Tamilnadu and Gujarat there is only one and in West Bengal five. The low percentage of women in the cabinets is perhaps understandable given the small number of women legislators available to choose from, which again points to the urgency in expanding the share of women in Parliament and State legislatures.

Administrative Services

The representation of women in the Indian Administrative Service (IAS) and other all-India services is a good indicator of the extent to which women participate in the administrative process in the government. In the elite IAS, considered the backbone of bureaucracy in India, women constituted only about 10.4 per cent of all the officers in the cadre in 2000, up from 7.5 per cent in 1987. Their percentage in the Indian Police Service (IPS) is substantially lower at about 3.3 per cent in 2000, but showed a significant trebling over the level of less than 1 per cent in 1987, indicating higher levels of induction of women as police officers.

Table 4.38: Representation of Women in Some All-India Services

Year	*Indian Administrative Service (IAS)*			*Indian Police Service (IPS)*		
	Total members	*Women*	*Percentage of women*	*Total members*	*Women*	*Percentage of women*
1987	4,204	339	7.5	2,418	21	0.9
1997	4,991	512	10.2	3,045	67	2.2
2000	5,159	535	10.4	3,301	110	3.3

Source: Ninth Five Year Plan (1997-2002) and Tenth Five Year Plan (2002-07), Planning Commission, Government of India.

Judiciary

Only 16 of the 526 Judges in the Supreme Court and various High Courts in the country were women in 1996. In the Supreme Court and in almost every High Court, excepting the High Court of Mumbai, the number of female judges was no more than 1 (Table 4.39).

Management in Industry

In most countries, including the developed ones, participation of women in the top management of industrial undertakings is minimal. It is reported that only 12.4 per cent of all Board Directors of the top 500 companies in United States of America are women, though 87 per cent of these companies have at least one female director. Even in Scandinavian countries, which have a very high representation of women in their parliaments, no more than about10 per cent of the Board

Directors are women, and Sweden sees the need to enact a law reserving a percentage of positions of Board Directors for women. In India too, there is a move to expand the participation of women in the management of companies. The proposed Companies (Amendment) Bill, 2003, envisages that public companies with a paid up capital of Rs. 5 crore or more should have a certain number of women directors on their boards.

Table 4.39: Women Judges in Supreme Court and High Courts in India (As on 1 October 1996)

Name of the Court	*Number of Judges*			*Percentage of women judges to all*
	Total	*Men*	*Women*	
A. Supreme Court of India	25	24	1	4.0
B. High Courts				
1. Allahabad	63	62	1	1.6
2. Andhra Pradesh	37	36	1	2.7
3. Mumbai	51	48	3	5.9
4. Calcutta	40	39	1	2.5
5. Delhi	28	27	1	3.6
6. Gauhati	17	16	1	5.9
7. Gujarat	29	28	1	3.4
8. Himachal Pradesh	8	7	1	12.5
9. Jammu & Kashmir	10	10	—	—
10. Karnataka	30	30	—	—
11. Kerala	23	22	1	4.3
12. Madhya Pradesh	28	27	1	3.6
13. Madras	23	23	—	—
14. Orissa	14	14	—	—
15. Patna	33	32	1	3.0
16. Punjab & Haryana	33	32	1	3.0
17. Rajasthan	32	31	1	3.1
18. Sikkim	2	2	—	—
Total	526	510	16	3.0

Source: Department of Justice, Ministry of Law & Justice, Government of India

Broadly speaking, workers classified into Division 2 of the National Classifications of Occupations comprising Administrative, Executive and Managerial Workers (excluding Occupational Group 20, representing elected officials) may be taken as those who have some say in decision-making in various organisations. While data on the detailed occupational pattern of workers from the 2001 Census are still awaited, the 1991 Census data indicate that less than 5 per cent of the Administrative, Executive and Managerial Workers were females. The only data available in some detail for a subsequent period are those based on the Occupational Pattern of Employment in the Public Sector brought by the Ministry of Labour for the year 1996. These two sets of data are shown in Table 4.40, and they broadly support each other.

Table 4. 40: Percentage of Females in Administrative, Executive and Managerial Workers

Occupational Group	*Percentage of women workers in the total*	
	1991 (Public and Private together)[1]	*1996 (Public Sector)*[2]
1. Administrative, Executive Officials, (Government and Local Bodies)	4.7	6.0
2. Working Proprietors, Directors, Managers (Wholesale and Retail Trade)	4.2	4.6
3. Directors and Managers (Financial Institutions)	4.5	4.9
4. Working Proprietors, Directors, Managers (Mining, Manufacturing and Construction)	2.9	2.1
5. Working Proprietors, Directors, Managers (Transport, Storage and Communication)	2.7	5.0
6. Working Proprietors, Directors, Managers (Other Services)	6.5	6.9
7. Other Administrative and Managerial Workers	8.4	6.8
All Administrative and Managerial Workers[3]	4.1	5.2

Source: 1. Population Census, 1991

2. Occupational Pattern of Employment in Public Sector, 1996, Directorate General of Employment and Training (DGE&T), Ministry of Labour.

Notes: 1. Census does not indicate information separately for public and private sectors.

2. DGE&T collects the information for public and private sectors in alternate years. However, the latest year for which private sector data are available is 1991.

3. Excluding Elected Officials,etc. covered under the National Classification of Occupations Group 20.

Crimes against Women

Numerous legislations aimed at preventing crimes against women outlined earlier not withstanding, such crimes continue unabated. For example, according to report of the National Crime Records Bureau, the number of recorded foeticide cases in 1999 registered an increase of 60.5 per cent over the number in 1995. On an average, 64 housewives committed suicide each day in 1999. Crimes against women are registered under various Sections of the Indian Penal Code (IPC) as well as under various special legislations dealing with specific aspects of welfare of women discussed in an earlier Chapter. Table 4.41 shows the trends in these registered crimes during the nineties. Crimes against women have been accounting for an increasing proportion of all crimes registered under IPC in recent years, the percentage having increased from 4.4 in 1991 to 7.0 in 1999. There could be reasons for this increase apart from actual increase in crime against women, like greater vigilance against such crimes brought about by NGOs and other social activists taking up the cause, stricter enforcement of the legislation, etc. The magnitude of increase in the number of registered cases, however, suggests that despite preventive legislation, there has been a substantial growth in the crimes against women during the nineties. At the national level, the rate of crime against women (number of crimes per lakh of population) was 11.6 in 1995 and 13.8 in 1999, which implies that increase in crimes has outstripped the population growth. In 1999, the crime (against women) rate exceeded 20 in Rajasthan (24.5), Madhya Pradesh (21.7) and Tamilnadu (20.6). Nine other States (Maharashtra, Delhi, Mizoram, Andhra Pradesh, Haryana, Gujarat, Jammu & Kashmir, Kerala and Chandigarh) recorded a rate above the national average of 13.8.

Table 4.41: Crimes against Women in India (1991 -1999)

Crime	*Number of Cases Registered during the year*						
	1991	*1995*	*1996*	*1997*	*1998*	*1999*	*% increase 1991-99*
Rape	9,793	13,754	14,846	15,330	15,151	15,468	57.9
Kidnapping & abduction	12,300	14,063	14,877	15,617	16,351	15,962	29.8
Dowry deaths	5,157	5,092	5,513	6,006	6,975	6,699	29.9
Torture	15,949	31,127	35,246	36,592	41,376	43,823	174.8
Molestation	20,611	28,475	28,939	30,764	30,959	32,311	55.8
Sexual harassment	10,283	4,796	5,671	5,796	8,054	8,858	(–)13.9
Importation of girls	—	191	182	78	146	1	
Sati prevention	—	27	0	1	0	0	
Immoral traffic	—	8,447	7,706	8,323	8,695	9,363	10.8*
Indecent representation	—	339	96	73	190	222	(–)34.5*
Dowry prohibition	—	—	2,647	2,685	3,578	3,064	15.8**
All Crimes against women	74,093	1,06,471	1,15,723	1,21,265	1,31,475	1,35,771	83.2
Percent to all IPC crimes	4.4	6.4	6.8	6.4	6.7	7.0	

Source: Reports of National Crime Records Bureau, Ministry of Home Affairs, Govt. of India, 1995, 1996 and 1999.

* Percentage of 1999 over 1995; ** Percentage of 1999 over 1996.

> As opposed to 1999, the year (2000) saw an increase in crimes against women – like dowry deaths, rapes, sexual harassment and cruelty by husband and relatives. On the other hand, there was a decline in the number of burglaries, thefts and riots. Of the 1,078 cases reported from the 23 cities (which had a population of over one million in 1991), the highest, 34.7 per cent, were from Delhi. Among the 512 cases of dowry deaths from the 23 cities, the share of Delhi was 19.9 per cent. The maximum number of cases of molestation is from Delhi – 488 or 23.6 per cent of the total 2,066 cases.
>
> *Times of India, Delhi, 12 Sept. 2002*
> *based on data from National Crime Records Bureau*

The situation seems to have further deteriorated in the year 2000. The following 'snapshots' from the report of the Nationals Crime Records Bureau, 2000 speak for themselves:

- 4.1 per cent increase in crimes against women. Highest crime incidence in Uttar Pradesh (14.0%); highest crime rate in Rajasthan (24.0%) as compared to 14.1% at All-India
- 960 per cent increase in cases of buying of girls for prostitution, 49.2 per cent increase in foeticide cases over 1999
- 6.6 per cent increase in rape cases. (16,496 rapes in 2000, up from 15,468 in 1999). Every 54 minutes a woman is raped.
- 62.5 per cent of Importation of girls cases reported from Bihar state
- In 87.4 per cent of Rape cases, Offenders were known to the victims; 30 per cent of these were neighbours.

What is of greater concern is the fact that of the 77.8 per cent IPC *(Indian Penal Code)* cases that were investigated, 78 per cent were charge-sheeted, 15.8 per cent cases tried and of those, only 39.6 per cent resulted in convictions, these percentages compounding to an overall conviction rate of hardly 4 per cent of the registered cases. Another shameful aspect of the crime against women is the scant regard paid to the age of the victim. For example, girls below 10 years of age are as susceptible to rape as women above 60 years. Almost one-third of the rape victims in 1995 were below the age of 16 (see Chart 4.12). These statistics are only about the registered cases. For each registered case there are several that go unreported and unrecorded. Wife baiting, abusing and physical assault, though very common in many Indian households, are almost always pushed under the rug. The women just swallow all ill treatment, knowing the penalties for resistance. According to surveys by the International Centre for Research on Women (2003), about 60 per cent of all women face violence at some point in their married life and that "except for a few sensational cases, day to day physical abuse of women in their homes is largely hidden." What is astonishing is the fact that even well-to-do, highly qualified, employed and independent women are also victims of such violence.

Chart 4.12: Age Distribution of Rape Victims – 1995

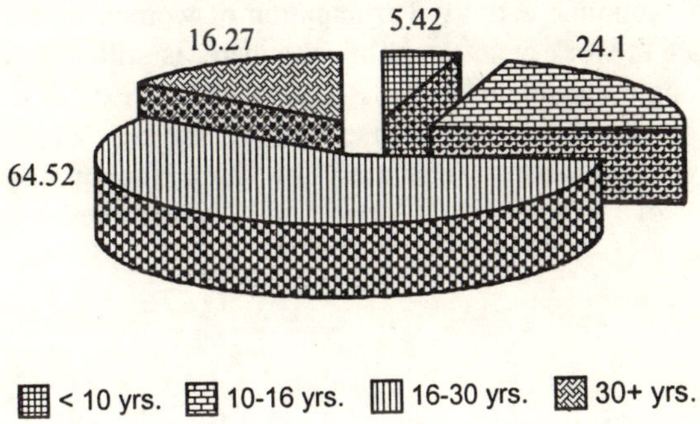

Source: Report of the National Crime Records Bureau, 1995

Summing Up

An attempt has been made in this Chapter to put together evidence that throws light on the status of women and the achievements in various aspects of their empowerment. The picture that emerges is one of promise and hope but also disappointing on some counts. On the positive side are the improved access for women to education and training, health care, increased entry into employment, diversification of occupational structure, narrowing down of gender differentials in remuneration, increased share in decision-making administrative positions, greater participation in local bodies and legislative organs of the state. There are areas of concern too. The most disturbing is the continued preference of people for male children, induced female foeticide notwithstanding the prohibitory legislation on pre-natal sex determination tests and the consequent fall in the sex ratio. What is more worrisome is that this lopsidedness in the sex ratio does not seem to get corrected with increased economic well-being of people. On the contrary, the available evidence for India suggests a positive correlation between economic prosperity and the practice of female foeticide. Secondly, even though enrolment of girls improved substantially over the years and the drop out rates at primary stage reduced, there are large areas of the country with very low female literacy and where universal enrolment is a very distant goal. Thirdly, women's economic contribution is not fully recognized and their participation in work is still considered secondary. Their work participation rates are low, particularly in the urban areas, belying the expectation that urbanization would induce more women into labour market. Considering the large proportion of educated women out of labour force, it would seem that acquisition of higher education too does not automatically guarantee its translation into economic activity. Participation of women in decision-making, whether in work or in the political sphere, is still at a nascent stage, even though several individuals have achieved excellence and climbed to top positions in diverse fields. Crimes of various hues against women continue unabated. In short, the approach to empowerment of women is slow and sometimes marked by retrogression.

Notes

1 In India the ratio is around 111 to 100 for reasons explored a little later

2 The rates for 1951, 1961 and 1971 relate to population aged 5+, while those for 1981, 1991, 2001 relate to population aged 7+

3 Gross enrolment ratio is the number of students enrolled at a particular stage of education as percentage of the number of children in the relevant age group, irrespective of whether they belong to the relevant age group or not. On the other hand net enrolment ratio takes into account only those enrolled students who are actually in the relevant age groups in the numerator.

4 According to Nursing Council of India, about 13,000 general nurses and midwives and 9,000 others like auxiliary nurses, midwives and health visitors were trained during 1998

5 The data on employment in the organized sector flows from the Employment Market Information programme of the Directorate General of Employment in the Ministry of Labour, Government of India. All establishments in the public sector irrespective of their size and private sector non-agricultural (excluding plantations) establishments employing 10 or more employees fall within the scope of this programme. Despite its limitations of completeness of coverage, this series of data is considered a useful 'barometer' of changes in the employment levels in the organized sector.

6 Informal sector, as defined in this Survey covers all un-incorporated proprietary and partnership enterprises and do not include enterprises run by cooperatives, trusts and private and public limited companies cot covered by the Annual Survey of Industries of the Central Statistical Organisation. The informal sector, therefore, is a subset of the unorganized sector as defined for the National Accounts.

7 According to the 50th Round (1993-94) survey of NSSO, the average wage rate for rural females who were literate but below middle, was only 52 per cent of the rate for the corresponding category of males. Further examination of the unexpected result in 1999-2000 survey showed that the aberration occurred only in the case of those engaged in communications, financial, education and health services which have a public sector bias. Sampling errors could be responsible.

8 Sexism and the Workplace Wars: report in Outlook 19 May 1999

9 Supreme Court of India:Visakha and Others vs. State of Rajasthan, 1997(6), SCC.

V

Social Orientation and Sex Segregation of Employment

The previous chapters have brought out ample evidence on the fact that generally women are lagging behind in every sphere of life as compared to men. It has also been seen that discrimination against women is not limited to developing countries only but is visible even in the developed world and in all the continents, though the degree of discrimination may vary. Some kind of gender bias appears to be prevalent globally as is evident from a proverb 'a home carries weight because of husband'. Explanations on the basis of physiological differences or, in other words, the natural differences are understandable up to a certain extent. Societies have characterised these natural differences as 'stronger' and 'weaker' according to the socio-cultural orientations. A negative interpretation of the biological characteristics of women has given birth to patriarchal structure of societies wherein females have been placed subordinate to males in the family hierarchy. Women have been conditioned in such a way that they submit to such notions and accept themselves as inferior to men. Even in the modern sections of the societies, where a number of individual women have succeeded in coming out of the traditional rut, as in case of professional and technical workers, they have still to accept their traditional roles at home, as males, in general, are not prepared to 'role-sharing'. Thus, male dominance continues, females accept their secondary status and continue to perform dual roles, often at the cost of their physical and mental health.

Society has given power and status to men. Industrial societies of the eighteenth and the nineteenth centuries expounded the idea of separation of gender-based segregation of arenas of work, where women were confined to domestic work and men to outside work. As Durkheim (1964) pointed out, today among cultivated people, the two great functions of the psychic life are dissociated in that one of the sexes takes care of the affective functions while the other the intellectual functions. The social anthropologists, believers in psycho dynamics of work and sociologists are united when they consider sex differences and say that there are socio-cultural and historic differences in males and females. Differences in construction may be seen in terms of differential valance of sexes (Heritier, 1996), sexual division of labour, and social differences (Kergoat 1998), but basically "there is a hierarchy of the sexes, with male supremacy" (Hirata and Kergoat 2000). Socialist feminist or gender theories also regard gender relations as 'sexual division of labour'. Social roles are bifurcated as 'domestic' for women and public and social for men. Lemert (1992) stated that "Feminists have challenged scientific - medical construction of women as biologically destined to be wives and mothers". The feminists also do not agree with the idea of naming the human beings as men and women as they consider both to be part of same identity *i.e.* mankind.

The gender-based division of functions mentioned above may be observed in world of occupations also. As mentioned in an earlier chapter, job markets have been segregated on the basis of sex and women have been found suitable for the occupations which match the roles they perform at home. Researchers have tried to classify the labour markets suitable for males and suitable for females on the basis of various factors. Openheimer (1968) classified the occupations as traditional and non traditional jobs for women. Traditional jobs were defined as those jobs that were always performed by women such as teaching, nursing, social work, etc... 'Care of human body in infancy and sickness' was one of the true professions of women according to him. The division of labour market has also been done on the basis of the proportion of the workforce in a particular occupation. Reubans and Reubans (1979) defined the non-traditional jobs for women as those jobs in which women workers form a considerably smaller proportion of the work force than their current share of the total employed population in all occupations. Bem's Gender Schema Theory (1980) of sex-typing of occupations suggests that not only men but also many women think that jobs in which women predominate are more appropriate for them. Women prefer to involve themselves in the jobs they have been doing for ages and where a sizeable number of women are working. For example, women made clothes for the family at home and did so outside. High occupational aspirations are not seen as promoting family welfare. This may be responsible for deterring women from going for higher studies or entering male dominated occupations. In 1977, two-thirds of women workers were in stereotypically female jobs (Barrett 1979).

Researchers have been trying to find out the factors that are responsible for such kind of bifurcation of the labour market. Oppenheimer found that some socio-economic factors such as "cheapness plus availability" and "cheapness plus skills" are responsible for this phenomenon. In other words, jobs with less pay, lower skills and ready supply of workers were female dominated. However, sociologists and anthropologists in recent times (Chaband and Rychter, 1998 and Heritier 1996) share the view that women's "incompetence" is socially constructed. Sehrank and Relay (1976) in their study on male and female labour markets found that the female labour force covers jobs that are clustered at the low level of prestige continuum. The Human Capital Theory believes that women are higher cost workers as compared to men because of higher absenteeism, requiring better facilities at the work place, less flexibility in the hours of work etc. For example, women may not be able to work late in the night or they may have to take more leave due to family responsibilities, etc. Barrett (1979) analysed the factors associated with sex labelling of occupations in psychological terms. He considered that women's work involves vicarious achievement – secretary achieves through manager, nurse through physician. Women's jobs also lack upward mobility. Turner and McCaffrey (1974) found that women who have internal locus of control have high career aspirations. Baruch (1972) found that women who have positive evaluation of their competence, excel in career. Women, in general, are said to be influenced by factors other than their own preferences in opting for a career based on sex-role-appropriateness of occupation. Such attitudes are formed in men and women since early childhood and continue to develop in adulthood during socialisation process (Sheperd and Hess, 1975 and Siegal, 1973).

Whatever may be the factors responsible, division of jobs encourages the development of two separate labour markets—male labour market *i.e.* the non-traditional labour market for women and the female labour market *i.e.* a traditional labour market for women. There is disagreement on the cut off point of such divisions. Hayes (1986) reviewed 30 studies in order to locate a norm for a systematic definition and measurement of gender concentrated occupations. He found that the cut off point for this bifurcation varies from 5 percent to 50 percent women working in an occupation. The researches of Tangri (1972) Brooks and Galligan (1985) suggest that, in general, researchers agree to about 30 percent as cut off point. Whatever the cut-off point may be, there is "a definite underlining of women's inferiority on the labour market" (Michon, 1997). "It is common knowledge that women earn less than men, are more often unemployed and are responsible for practically all domestic work, that employment policies are gendered at all levels, ranging from the higher sphere of the public sector to the labour contracts in small and medium firms. Everyone knows that women are held down by a glass ceiling and are quick to slide into the poverty trap" (Hirata and Kergoat, 2000).

Anker and Hein (1985 and 1986), who have done extensive work on the subject of occupational segregation, identified 13 typical female stereotypes that result in such occupational segregation by sex. Table 5.1 summarises their work.

Table 5.1: Common Stereotyped Characteristics of Women and their Expected Effect on Occupational Segregation by Sex

Common stereotyped characteristics of women[1]	*Effect on occupational segregation*	*Examples of typical occupations affected*[2]	*Comments*
(1)	*(2)*	*(3)*	*(4)*
Positive			
1. Caring nature	Helps qualify women for occupations where others are cared for, such as children, the ill, older people.	Nurse, Doctor, Ayah, Social worker, Midwife	Often felt to be biological (*i.e.* sex difference), because women are mainly responsible for child care in all societies. This is, however, a learned, gender-based difference. Note that occupations which require care but which also require greater authority, such as medical doctor, are often male-dominated.
2. Skill (and experience) at household-related work	Helps qualify women for occupations that are frequently done in the home (almost always by women), often as unpaid household work.	Maid, Housekeeper, Cleaner, Cook, Waiter, Launderer, Hairdresser, Spinner, Sewer, Weaver, Knitter, Tailor/ dressmaker	Skills easy to learn (therefore, women's greater experience before entering the labour market should not be very important).

Contd.

(1)	*(2)*	*(3)*	*(4)*
3. General manual dexterity (especially smaller, nimble fingers)	Helps qualify women for occupations where finger dexterity is important.	Sewer, Knitter, Spinner, Weaver, Tailor/ dressmaker	Belief is partly based on biological (sex) difference; and experience (gender) differences in house before joining the labour market (also see stereotype 2). Skill is easy to learn. Occupations often similar to those noted under household-related work activities (see stereo type 2).
4. Greater honesty	Helps qualify women for occupations where money is handled and/ or trust is important.	Cashier/ bookkeeper, Salesperson, Accountant	Higher paying and higher status occupations such as accountant which is a professional occupation) are often male dominated.
5. Physical appearance	Helps qualify women for occupations where physical appearance would help attract and/ or please customers.	Receptionist salespersons Shop assistant	This advantage is often thought to be combined with a more pleasant and accommodating personality of women (*e.g.* for receptionist or salesperson). Other times, sex appeal is used to attract male customers (*e.g.* barmaid or prostitute). In certain cultures and countries where public interaction between men and women is frowned upon, this characteristic disqualifies/ excludes women from certain occupations (*e.g.* salespersons in the Middle East).
Other			
6. Greater willingness to take orders Greater docility and less likeli-hood of	General characteristics which help qualify women for occupations and sectors of the economy where working	Note: These general characteristics (6,7,8) "qualify" women for many jobs which are low	These stereotypes have been combined because they are similar in that all imply a subservient nature. These are archetypal learned (gender-type) characteristics.

Contd.

(1)	(2)	(3)	(4)
Complaining about work or working conditions Less likelihood of joining trade unions Greater willingness to do monotonous / repetitive work	conditions are poor, labour laws are not applied (*e.g.* informal sector) and work is routinized.	paid, unskilled, unprotected and repetitious in nature.	
7. Greater willingness to accept lower wages Less need for income	General characteristics which help qualify women for low-paid occupations and sectors of the economy.		Often related to (and often justified by) belief that women are secondary earners (*i.e.* not main "breadwinner") This is despite: increase in incidence of female-headed households; and need of many families for multiple incomes. Often implies occupations which are highly competitive industries, where cost considerations are very important. This often includes export products such as textiles. Low-paid occupations may be partly low paid because they are highly feminized.
8. Greater interest in working at home	Helps qualify women for occupations and sectors of the economy where work is organized in a home-based "putting out" type of production system.		Home-based work is usually poorly remunerated and often based on piece-work. Home-based work is easy to combine with household/ child care. "Putting out" production system is often set up specifically to make use of the available cheap female labour. Home-based work is increasing in importance.[3]

Contd.

(1)	*(2)*	*(3)*	*(4)*
Negative			
9.Disinclination to supervise others	Helps disqualify women for all types of supervisory and managerial occupations.	Manager (general; production; trade, catering and lodging) Supervisor (clerical; sales; production) Government executive officer and administrator Legislative officials.	This is in many ways the opposite of willingness to take orders (see no. 6). This often affects vertical occupational segregation (with lower level jobs for women).
10. Less physical (muscular) strength	Helps disqualify women for occupations requiring heavy lifting and/or physical effort.	Construction worker Miner/quarrier Well driller	There is considerable overlap in the physical strength of individual women and men which means that many women are physically capable of doing this work. Becoming less and less important in today's economy.
11. Less able to do science and maths	Helps disqualify women for occupations where high levels of science and maths are required.	Physical scientist (chemist/ physicist) Architect Engineer Mathematician Statistics	Gender discrimination here begins in school where girls are discouraged from majoring in maths or science. Some believe that this is a biological (*i.e.* sex) difference. If so, it is a small average difference with a large overlap in the abilities of individual men and women.
12. Less willing to travel	Helps disqualify women for occupations where considerable travel is required.	Aircraft officer and worker transport equipment driver/ operator	Many women are willing to travel, as evidenced by, for example, airline stewardesses (who were originally sought for their physical appearance —see stereotype 5). Many drives do not travel overnight.

Contd.

(1)	*(2)*	*(3)*	*(4)*
13. Less willing to face physical danger and use physical force	Helps disqualify women for occupations where physical danger is relatively great.	Fire-fighter Police officer Security guard Minor/ Quarrier	This is a learned gender difference. Many women are willing to do these occupations.

Source: Observations of Anker. R (1998) and Anker and Hein (1985; 1986).

Anker opines that such occupational segregation affects basically the status of women in the society and works as a barrier in the process of women's empowerment. He also feels that this segregation could adversely affect the overall efficiency and functioning of labour markets as women workforce is kept out of certain jobs (where otherwise they could be very effective) and makes the market rigid. It is also responsible for male-female wage differentials.

Labour market climate, however, is gradually undergoing a significant change and women have been found excelling in typically male occupations all over the world. There are examples where women are getting better paid than men and are better trained. They have been able to cross the stereotype barriers to enter into the male domains. But such cases are only few and far between. The basic question is whether the attitudes in the society, in general, are changing and whether the women who gone beyond their stereotypic roles have been able to change their attitudes about the roles of women and men? In a quick survey conducted by the authors to examine this issue, a list of 33 jobs was given to 100 women who were asked to rank these as traditional jobs and non-traditional jobs for women. This sample of 100 included ten women from each of the following categories selected from Delhi.

1. Advocates
2. Journalists
3. Doctors
4. Administrators
5. Principals
6. Scientists
7. Nurses
8. Women Entrepreneurs
9. Social Workers
10. Writers

Each woman was to classify the list of occupations as traditional or non-traditional for women in the present context as per her own conviction and understanding of the concept. The frequency distribution of the responses is given in Table 5.2.

Table 5.2: Frequency of Women Classifying the Given Occupation as Traditional Job for Women

Sl. No.	*Occupation*	*Number out of 100 women classifying the occupation as traditional job*
1	Primary School Teacher	84
2	Secondary School Teacher	74
3	College Level Teacher	40
4	Head Mistress (Primary School)	76
5	Principal (Secondary School)	76
6	Principal (Degree College)	30
7	Nurse	80
8	Doctor	32
9	Technician	25
10	Engineer	06
11	Social Worker	56
12	Journalist	05
13	Office Administrator	15
14	Business Executive	05
15	Research Scientist (Natural Sciences)	05
16	Research Scientist (Social Sciences)	35
17	Stenographer	60
18	Telephone Operator	58
19	Actor	23
20	Programme Producer	19
21	Psychologist	15
22	Guidance Counsellor	15
23	Chartered Accountant	02
24	Advocate	10
25	Police Officer	03
26	Writer	49
27	Sales Representative	37
28	Air Hostess	07
29	Musician	38
30	Advertising Model	25
31	Artist	35
32	Editor	10
33	Agriculture worker	62

The table shows that most of the women consider the jobs of primary and secondary school teachers, principals, nurses, stenographers, musicians, artists, agriculture workers as traditional jobs for women and jobs like engineers, administrators, scientists, chartered accountants, police officers, business executives as non-traditional. Further probing revealed that women's entry into an occupation as well as the number of women employed therein are major factors that make an occupation traditional or non-traditional for women. This shows that women still believe in segregated labour markets and consider certain occupations as male dominated and appropriate for men only.

The unstructured interviews and informal interactions with the groups of women working as professionals, other educated and illiterates revealed that highly professionally qualified and working women wanted their girl children to be educated and opt a career as per their aptitudes and interests. It could be a non-traditional career or a traditional one. The other groups of educated women who were either housewives or working in traditional jobs generally opined that although education is necessary for girls, it is mainly for getting a suitable match for them. Marriage is the priority. Opting for a career depends on the choice of the husband or in-laws. This group of women also thought that their children should take up jobs compatible with the responsibilities of their married life. A totally non-traditional career could hinder smooth-going in the family. Many women preferred a teaching job for their female child or education which could have possibilities of starting something at home like that of beautician's work or opening a boutique or tuitions at home. Further probing revealed that these attitudes were consistent with the prevailing Indian social norms.

The thinking of illiterate women was, however, diversified. While a few of them wanted their daughters to be educated and working so that they might not have to face the calamities of life, some of them felt that only elementary education should be given to the girl child. Another group of illiterate women felt that education was not necessary They should learn to do the household work. Some had shown their inability to send their girl child to school due to family needs as adults had to go to work and the girl child had to look after the younger siblings and attend to other household chores. May be, if certain basic facilities, like crèches etc. are provided to these women, their thinking would change in favour of educating the girl child.

The results of the above study match with other researches conducted in various countries (Hungary, Bulgaria, Sri Lanka, India etc.) sponsored by the ILO. A survey in Hungary (1992-93), of a sample of employers showed that 90 per cent of the employers interviewed preferred men for certain occupations like repair work. In an Indian study conducted by Papola in Lucknow (1982), about 60 percent of employees stated that women were not suitable for certain jobs such as sales, production, supervisory occupations etc. It has also been seen that women's responsibility for housework and care for children is one of the important factor for such preferences. There are social restrictions due to cultural variations which also restrict women's entry in to certain occupations. For example, in Muslim culture interactions between men and women is restricted and so are the jobs for women where men are also working. On the other hand, sex segregation of jobs and female labour force participation have not been found significantly correlated in industrialised countries (Charles, 1992 and OECD, 1988). This also shows that socio-cultural factors are important for determining sex segregation of occupations. "There is a need to broaden women's limited choice of occupations by having women enter in greater numbers into non-traditional occupations for women (Anker, 1998).

The above discussion shows that even though certain amount of change in attitude is taking place in relation to gender segregation of work, it is very slow. Initiatives have to come from women themselves to make this change more pronounced and eventually eliminate segregation. A beginning has already been made with the advent of women in fields which so far had been male prerogatives. A certain amount of subconscious resentment, hesitation and resistance is understandable but to dismiss all the progress made by women just because of sex-typing of occupations is not justifiable. Various socio-economic and psychological causes are responsible for women's entry into the labour market but education is the most important factor that can change the mind-sets. It has been observed that many educated women have been able to change their attitudes towards work and are entering into the new and emerging fields. In near future, may be an integrated labour market would evolve, in which males and females could participate without any reservation or distinction. The journey has already started. As observed by Walby (1997), "In recent years there has been a major change in the gender regime. Overt attempts to restrict women's employment are now infrequent and illegal... As a consequence, barriers to women's entry to the public sphere have been reduced in arenas such as employment and education ..."

Personality Characteristics and Sex Segregation of Occupations

Another major factor that restricts women's entry into the world of work in a number of occupations, especially in higher level jobs involving management, administration, decision making, risk taking etc. and reduces women to a secondary status is attribution of certain characteristics differently to men and women. For instance, it is stated that "The model of the successful manager is a masculine one" (Douglas McGregar, 1967). Women are considered to be emotional, feminine, not good in decision making and dependent while men are considered to be dominating, independent, aggressive and competent. The very expression of emotion is widely viewed as feminine -- a trait that would interfere with being effective in top level jobs. These traits, when displayed by the appropriately designated gender are socially valued. Aggressiveness is valued when shown by men and denigrated if demonstrated by women. So strongly supported are these attitudes about the difference that both men and women would not hesitate to describe a woman 'unfeminine' if she displays certain aggressive behaviour. Thus, women are forced to learn and accept certain types of behaviour socially assigned to them as feminine. Gradually, stereotypic self-concept is developed in women. Most traditional attitudes define women in terms of and in relation to men. The standard is 'male' and women are compared against this standard. 'She thinks like a man', is an old 'compliment' given to women who show exceptional strength in decision making. Chodorow (1978) argued that women are more nurturant as compared to men. This is due to early childhood development. In the process of socialisation in the early childhood, boys are encouraged to develop traditional male behaviours like aggressiveness and competitiveness (Marini, 1988). Girls are encouraged to show emotions and nurturance and, therefore, become more suitable for such occupations that require these traits *e.g.* nursing or social work (Baines, Evans and Neysmith, 1991).

A number of studies on this and related issues show that the effects of external barriers are compounded by a number of closely related factors involving women's achievement-motivation, self-confidence, self-evaluations etc. which are viewed as being substantially different from those of men. Maccoby and Jackline (1974) reviewed 58 research studies and concluded that women, starting in their college years, have lower levels of self-confidence than men do. Even after actual performance, they give lower self-evaluations of it than their male counterparts in the same circumstances (Deaux, 1976a Deaux and Farris 1977, Deaux 1979). Crandall, (1969) after a series of studies found that females did not have good expectancies of their success even when their performance was good. Such low expectancies of success are likely to have debilitating effects on women's capacity to achieve (Feather, 1966).

Several other researches suggest that while dependency in boys is discouraged by parents, teachers, peers and the mass-media, it is acceptable in respect of girls (Kogam and Moss, 1962; Sears, Rau and Alpert, 1965). Parsons (1949, 1965) and Lynn (1962 and 1969) concluded that both males and females form their first attachment to the mother. As the child grows, the boy's separation from the mother is encouraged to learn male roles while girl is encouraged to maintain her identification with the mother which is less likely to establish an early and independent 'self'.

An additional factor affecting self-confidence is the way people assign causality to explain success and failure. Women tend to rely on external factors. Bartal and Frieze, 1977, Halperin and Abrams, 1978 showed that women consider luck as most important causal explanation for their good performance and show self-derogatory bias in response to failures (Nicholls, 1975). Thus, low expectations, low aspirations, high anxiety and self-derogatory attributions add upto lower confidence, an effective mechanism of self-discouragement and low achievement.

Sex-typing of occupations discussed earlier and personality traits also seem to be interrelated. There appears to be higher expectancies for success in tasks that are designated as sex-appropriate. Stein, Pohly & Mueller (1975), Deuax and Emswiller (1974) showed that males expect more success than females in 'masculine' tasks whereas the opposite would be true in case of 'feminine' tasks. Feedback of performance is also important to enhance self-confidence. When clear feedback is provided, there are no sex differences in reported levels of self-confidence (McMohan, 1973, Simon & Feather, 1973). House and Perney (1974), showed that women have higher self-confidence than men when performance feedback is provided. Flaherty and Dusek (1980), Bem (1977), Spence, Helmreich and Stapp (1975), used Bem Sex Role Inventory, operationalising sex-role orientation and found that lack of traditional sex role orientation in women is associated with greater psychological adjustment, better self-concept and higher self-esteem. It has also been seen that women with higher scores on 'Masculinity' display higher self-esteem. This is partly because the excessive compliance demanded by the female stereotype diminishes self-esteem.

While talking about empowerment and planning any empowerment programmes for women, these factors are to be kept in mind to develop positive self-concept; programmes need to be started from the early childhood. The view that certain personalities are suited only to certain jobs leads to conservative decisions regarding career choice. Jain (1980) found that parents and family environment play an important role in development of positive self-concept. It has also been seen that women who are highly educated and who excel in various fields, develop positive self-image and high self-esteem. Perhaps a positive self-image among women contrary to the traditional stereotypical social orientation of subordination status may make a sure and certain change in the direction of empowerment of women.

An investigative study conducted by the authors aimed at measuring the levels of self esteem among women working in traditional and non-traditional jobs. The sample consisted of a total of 200 women in Delhi -- 100 in traditional job and 100 in non-traditional job. Traditional job for women has been taken as Senior Secondary School Principals and non-traditional job as Research Scientists in Natural Sciences. Both the groups in the sample have been matched on education and income. To measure the self-esteem 'self-perception Inventory' (Adult Form) developed by Soares and Soares (1965, revised in 1975) was used. The inventory consists of five sub-scales. Two sub-scales of the Inventory *i.e.* Self-Concept Scale and Ideal Self-Concept were used to measure self-esteem. The discrepancy between the self-concept and ideal self provides a measure for self-esteem – low values of the measure indicating high levels of self-esteem and *vice versa*. The results of the study show that the selected sample of women, in general, have high self-esteem, the measure yielding a value of 2.89 on an average.

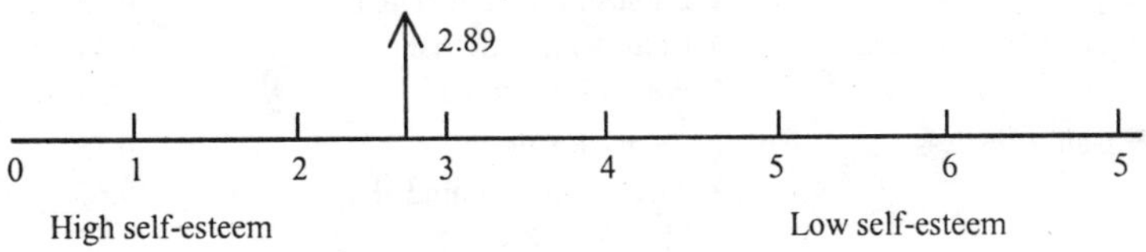

Mean = 2.89 and Standard Deviation 1.57

There are 36 bi-polar items in the instrument measuring self-esteem. The structure of self-esteem has been worked out applying Varimax Rotation Factor Analysis and 12 meaningful groups of self-esteem have been constituted as shown in Table 5.3. On the basis of these results, it is noted that in almost all factors the loadings are not systematic. In each factor there is one or two key items while other items are supportive, as their loadings are relatively low. Most of the factors have been named as per their highest loading on the scale.

Table 5.3: Factors, Items and their Loadings in Measurement of Self-esteem

Factors	*Items*	*Loadings of the Items*
1. Cheerful/Depressed	1. Cheerful - Depressed	0.71
	2. Contented - Worried	0.67
	3. Satisfied – Self-pitying	0.60
	4. Even tempered - Moody	0.45
2. Outgoing/Withdrawn	1. Outgoing - Withdrawn	0.65
	2. Sociable - Shy	0.62
	3. Relaxed - Nervous	0.57
	4. Optimistic - Pessimistic	0.50
	5. Self-confident - Insecure	0.45
	6. Persevering - Quitting	0.38
3. Ego-Strength	1. Well-adjusted – Poorly adjusted	0.69
	2. Worthy - Unworthy	0.66
	3. Mature - Immature	0.61
4 Self-controlled/Emotional	1 Self-controlled - Emotional	0.75
	2 Responsible - Frivolous	0.56
	3. Patient - Impatient	0.42
	4. Deliberate - Impulsive	0.34
5. Independent/Dependent	1. Independent - Dependent	0.63
	2. Tough - Sensitive	0.59
	3. Hopeful - Anxious	0.44
6. Good-natured/Critical	1. Good-natured - Critical	0.78
	2. Tolerant – fault-finding	0;47
7. Co-operative/Anti-social	1. Co-operative – Anti-social	0.75
	2. Enthusiastic - Indifferent	0.55
	3. Considerate - Selfish	0.54
	4. Poised - Ashamed	0.54
8. Calm/Restless	1. Calm - Restless	0.75
	2. Alert – Absent-minded	0;67
	3 Accepted - Rejected	0.52
9. Masculine/Feminine	1. Masculine - Feminine	0.77
	2. Trusting - Suspicious	0.62
10. Assertive/Submissive	1. Assertive - Submissive	0.82
	2. Self-sufficient – Easily influenced	0.63
11. Easy-going/Quick-tempered	1. Easy-going – Quick-tempered	0.81
12. Creative/Conforming	1. Creative - Conforming	0.73
	2. Adaptable - Rigid	0.52

To test the significance of the factor influences on the levels of self-esteem, two sub-samples of persons comprising the 30 per cent of the total sample of 200 (60 in number) with the highest and the 30 per cent (60 in number) with the lowest self-esteem have been taken as comprising the High and Low Self-esteem Groups and the differences in the sub-sample means for these two groups have been tested for each factor. The '*t*' values based on a total of 118 degrees of freedom are found significant at 1% level in the case of all factors other than Factor 9 (Masculine/Feminine), indicating that characteristics such as being cheerful, out-going, high ego-strength, self-control, independence, good-natured, cooperative, calm, assertive, easy-going and creativity characterize the high self-esteem group while the low self-esteem group appears to be less cheerful, less outgoing, having less ego-strength, less self-control, less independent, less good-natured, less cooperative, less calm, less assertive, less easy-going, and less creative. Interestingly, the masculine-feminine characteristics do not seem to bear any significant effect on self-esteem.

Table 5.4: Means/Standard Deviations of Real Self for High and Low Self-Esteem Groups

Factors	*High Self-esteem*		*Low-Self-esteem*		*t-value*
	Means	*SD*	*Mean*	*SD*	
1. Cheerful/Depressed	1.54	.52	0.74	.87	6.11
2. Outgoing/Withdrawn	1.47	.48	0.47	.89	7.69
3. Ego-Strength	1.78	.33	1.17	.83	5.30
4 Self-controlled/ Emotional	1.42	.54	0.42	.85	7.69
5. Independent/ Dependent	1.23	.62	0.005	.72	9.98
6. Good-natured/ Critical	1.63	.45	0.85	.87	6.16
7. Co-operative/Anti-social	1.77	.31	1.12	.69	6.70
8. Calm/Restless	1.65	.41	1.03	.80	5.34
9. Masculine/Feminine	1.23	.76	1.14	.73	0.66
10. Assertive/ Submissive	1.43	.57	0.42	1.04	6.60
11. Easy-going/Quick-tempered	1.30	.64	0.28	1.32	5.39
12. Creative/ Conforming	1.60	.44	0.74	.99	6.15

SD= Standard Deviation; t= Student's t value df = degrees of freedom.
The estimates are based on sub-samples of 60 each

Restricting to only the six factors of Outgoing/Withdrawn, Ego-strength, Self-control/Emotional, Independent/Dependent, Assertive/ Submissive and Creative/Conforming as more important factors, one finds that the significance of the '*t*' values in testing the differences between the two sub-sample means in respect of different factors improves further (Table 5.5).

Table 5.5: Means/Standard Deviations of Real Self for High and Low Self-Esteem groups on Restricted Number of Factors

Factor	*High Slef-esteem Group*		*Low Self-esteem Group*		*t*
	Mean	*SD*	*Mean*	*SD*	
2 Outgoing/ Withdrawn	1.44	.60	.29	.71	9.5
3 Ego-strength	1.82	.31	.97	.73	8.3
4 Self-control/ Emotional	1.49	.51	.48	.68	9.2
5 Independent/ Dependent	1.11	.62	.07	.82	7.8
10 Assertive/ Submissive	1.29	.74	.07	.87	8.3
12 Creative/ Conforming	1.57	.51	.49	.84	8.5

SD= Standard Deviation; *t* = Student's *t* value
The estimates are based on sub-samples of 60 each.

Tables 5.6 shows a comparative picture of the mean values of Real-Self and Ideal-Self, both for the High-Esteem and Low-Esteem groups, working in Traditional and Non-traditional Job in respect of various factors. No significant differences have been found in the levels of self-esteem of women working in traditional and non-traditional jobs.

Table 5.6: Mean Values of 'Real' and 'Ideal' Self of High and Low Self-Esteem Groups of Women in Traditional and Non-Traditional Job as Measured on Selected Factors

Factor	*High-Esteem Group*				*Low-Esteem Group*			
	Traditional Job		*Non-Traditional Job*		*Traditional Job*		*Non-Traditional Job*	
	Real Self	*Ideal Self*	*Real Self*	*Ideal Self*	*Real Self*	*Ideal Self*	*Real Self*	*Ideal Self*
Ego-Strength	1.82	1.88	1.82	1.89	0.81	1.73	1.08	1.78
Self-Control/ Emotional	1.55	1.76	1.31	1.72	0.61	1.42	0.33	1.61
Independent/Dependent	1.17	1.21	1.05	1.33	(-)0.06	1.49	0.08	1.50
Goodnatured/ Critical	1.57	1.82	1.54	1.71	0.77	1.22	0.72	1.69
Calm/Restless	1.68	1.80	1.76	1.87	0.89	1.67	0.67	1.74

However, variations have been observed in respect of three out of the twelve factors used for measurement of self-esteem, namely, Self-Control/Emotional, Good-natured/Critical and Calm/Restless. The significance of these variations has been tested in Tables 5.7 (i) to 5.7 (iii) below:

Table 5.7 (i): Self-Esteem in Women as Measured on Self-Control/ Emotional Component in Traditional and Non-Traditional Job

Type of Job	*Self-Control/Emotional*		*Total*
	High Self-Esteem	*Low Self-Esteem*	
Traditional	42 (37.76)	22 (33.23)	64
Non-traditional	18 (28.23)	38 (27.76)	56
Total	60	60	120

The Cell Values are the Observed Frequencies and the figures in brackets are Expected Frequencies.

Observed χ^2 =12.006. Tabulated χ^2 (with 1 degree of freedom) = 6.63 (.01 level).

Significant at 1 per cent level.

Table 5.7 (ii): Self-Esteem in Women As Measured on Good-natured/Critical Component In Traditional and Non-Traditional Job

Type of Job	*Good-natured/Critical*		*Total*
	High Self-Esteem	*Low Self-Esteem*	
Traditional	32 (26.5)	21 (26.5)	53
Non-traditional	28 (33.5)	39 (33.5)	67
Total	60	60	120

The Cell Values are the Observed Frequencies and the figures in brackets are Expected Frequencies.

Observed χ^2 = 4.08. Tabulated χ^2 (with 1 degree of freedom) = 6.63 (.01 level).

Tabulated χ^2 (with 1 degree of freedom) = 3.84 (.05 level).

Significant at 5 per cent level.

Table 5.7 (iii): Self-Esteem in Women as Measured on Calm/ Restless Component in Traditional and Non-Traditional Job

Type of Job	*Calm/Restless*		*Total*
	High Self-Esteem	*Low Self Esteem*	
Traditional	36 (30.24)	25 (30.24)	61
Non-traditional	24 (29.75)	35 (29.75)	59
Total	60	60	120

The Cell Values are the Observed Frequencies and the figures in brackets are Expected Frequencies.

Observed χ^2 = 4.42. Tabulated χ^2 (with 1 degree of freedom) = 6.63 (.01 level).

Tabulated χ^2 (with 1 degree of freedom) = 3.84 (.05 level).

Significant at 5 per cent level.

These tables indicate that women working in traditional job have high self-esteem as measured on self-control vs. emotional component while women working in non-traditional job have low self-esteem on this component. The same observation holds good, perhaps a little less strongly, in the case of the components—Good natured/Critical and Calm/Restless. On the other factors of self-esteem both the groups show similar patterns.

Findings of the study supporting the case that women have a fairly high level of self-esteem are somewhat contradictory to the results of the previous researches mentioned earlier in this chapter. The possible explanation is a positive relationship between amount of education and levels of self-esteem. High education facilitates in development of a positive self-concept and perceived high competence. Education broadens outlooks and helps in changing the mindsets. The respondents of the present study are highly educated. Moreover, the occupational choice of the respondents being in favour of top level jobs reflects their high self-esteem. Astin (1979) noted that self-concept plays an important role in career choice and suggested that high self-concept facilitates high career aspirations. Similarly, Richardson (1975) found that women were career-oriented if they had high self-esteem. As observed by Welch and Booth (1970), taking employment outside home itself is a correlate of high self-esteem in women. Researchers have also suggested that lack of traditional sex-role orientation in women is associated with positive self-concept and higher self esteem. The androgynous persons have high aspirations regarding their career. Thus, it may be logical to presume that respondents have a non-traditional or androgynous sex-role orientation and thereby have high self-esteem. The roles one plays also influence at least partially one's perceptions and evaluations. Individuals employed in relatively high level jobs are more likely to have positive self-evaluations. Family background also determines self-conception. Hennig and Jardin (1977) found that women remembered their parents as having valued and emphasized achievement and competence. Self-concept develops through such early childhood experiences and continues with adulthood.

No significant differences have been observed in the above study between type of job and levels of self-esteem. The findings support the results of the study of Banfield (1976). Here again, the role of higher education cannot be ignored as it has been indicated through a number of researches that high education facilitates the development of self-esteem. Researches also suggest that though women may choose either traditional or non-traditional job due to differences in their personality, but once they move up in the organisational hierarchy, they identify

their sub-samples into one group of students and one group of managers. Political, theoretical and economic values differed between male and female managers.

The Ohio State studies on leadership styles (Fleishman, 1957; Halpin & Winer, 1957) identified two dimensions on leadership styles, namely 'initiating structure' and 'consideration', which have become the basis for much subsequent research on leadership in general and sex differences and leadership in particular. 'Consideration' includes supervisory behaviour "indicative of friendship, mutual trust, respect and warmth, while 'initiating structure' includes behaviour in which "the supervisor organizes and defines group activities and his relation to the group" (Halpin & Winer, 1957). These differentiation parallels were made by Bales (1950) who proposed categories of leaders who have a greater socio-emotional orientation and those who are pre-dominantly task-oriented. Researches on leadership style suggest that the two leadership styles (*i.e.* Initiating structure and Consideration) are sex-linked. Women are concerned with interpersonal relationships while men are concerned with tasks (Bardwick, 1971). Eskilson & Wiley (1976) and Bartol & Butterfield (1976) found significant differences in leadership styles of students in laboratory experiments. Women scored high on consideration scores. Eskilson and Wiley (1976) employed a modified Bale's scoring technique to measure the leadership behaviour demonstrated in role-playing situations. Female leaders were less domineering than males when trying to assemble a geometric puzzle. In contrast, Helmich (1974) asked 550 company presidents to rate the least preferred co-worker. The evidence suggested that women are more task-oriented than men. Students were subjects in three other studies which also controlled leader's sex in role-playing situations. Bartol's findings (1974) indicated that factors other than sex play a role in determining leader behaviour. In the study of Lockheed and Hall (1976), there was no difference in male and female leadership style.

Bartol and Wortman (1976) and Petty, Odew, Bruning and Thomson (1977) conducted almost identical studies, in that both studies covered similar types of male and female supervisors and found that female leaders were not more 'consideration' oriented than their male counterparts. Like Helmich (op cit), Chapman (1975) had subjects rate their least preferred co-worker, but unlike Helmet's participants, who were top level managers, Chapman's participants were lower level supervisors. The lower level managers perceived no set differences in the managerial styles of men and women supervisors (Miner 1974). Bedian, Armenakis and Kemp (1976), and Roussell (1974) also found no sex-style differentiation. Miner asked lower, middle and higher level retail managers to fill out his Miner Sentence Completion test; and Bedian *et al* used the Schein-Ott Legitimacy of Organisational Influence Questionnaire. Similarly, Day and Stogdill's (1972) field study compared subordinate descriptions of 38 male and 38 female supervisors in the U.S. Air Force Logistics Command. They also found no significant sex differences on the 12 scales of LBDQ (Stogdill, Goode and Day 1962), *e.g.* structure, persuasiveness, consideration, production-emphasis and influence with supervisors.

Moderating effects of gender on leadership roles were examined in the contingency researches also. Researches which used students as subjects and researches which used managers as subjects were evenly divided to see as to whether gender was a moderating factor on leadership relationship. Over half of the studies on students and half of the managerial studies indicate sex as a significant contingency factor. A more in-depth study shows that the positive moderating relationship found in student studies substantiates the traditional female stereotype, whereas the positive moderating relationship found in the managerial studies is incongruent with the traditional female stereotype. Bartol (1974) and Cohen, Bunker, Burton, and McManus (1978) found no significant sex-moderating effects. Jacobson & Effertz's results (1974) indicate that male leaders are perceived as less effective than female leaders, although actual behaviour is the same. They conclude that a typical stereotyping phenomenon is taking place, namely expectations or standards are lowered for female leaders. Rosen and Jerdee's (1973) findings suggest that sex role stereotypes influence supervisory effectiveness for some but not all leadership styles *e.g.* reward style was rated high for men and friendly –dependent style rated high for women. Sashkin and Maier (1971) and Megargee (1969) found that under conditions of uncertainty female leaders are less likely to act on their own.

A major theme underlying much of the literature concerning discrimination against women in management is that females are ineffective leaders. Mark (1985) contends that recent research supports the belief that an ongoing process in organisation seems to reinforce the perception that effective management has a gender (*i.e.* male). It is suggested that male dominated corporations tend to recruit and promote women who fit a masculine profile that includes aggressiveness, competitiveness, forcefulness and a desire for responsibility and control.

A perusal of research evidence based on various theories leads to contradictory conclusions. Empirical evidence based on trait theory found a great deal of gender bias among both students and practising managers. Style studies show that practising managers overwhelmingly feel that there is no difference between male and female leadership styles, whereas students generally hold the opposite to be true. When sex was found to have a moderating effect on leadership roles, students supported the traditional female stereotype. In the case of practising managers, the moderating effects of sex were opposite of those one would expect from the typical stereotype female. A few studies have looked at male and female leaders from the power perspective. Hansen's (1974) analysis of a national survey, one of the few empirical pieces of research that compare male and female leaders on any dimensions of power *i.e.* autonomy, reports that female supervisors have significantly less autonomy and, in return, have smaller impact on the satisfaction of their subordinates. If the female supervisors do not themselves possess real power within the organisation, this puts a severe limitation on the extent to which they can mediate for their subordinates. This argument of limited powers is also consistent with the Goetz and Herman's (1976) explanation for their finding that groups with female supervisors are less satisfied with pay and promotions than those with male supervisors. This employee dissatisfaction may reflect the degree to which female supervisors have influence on their own superiors. Without real influence, women who hold formal titles of leadership cannot function as effectively as they are expected. Kreak, Bernhard, Nord Nüdiger, Dietlinde (1985) interviewed 96 women in low level to middle level jobs and their results indicate that women had lower expectations that they will be able to achieve independence and influence in the work-setting.

As women have been perceived as considerate and relationship oriented, their potential has been considered suitable for teaching, nursing, retailing as opposed to such occupations as construction, engineering and manufacturing (Agassi, 1977; Miner, 1974). Thus, there should be less sex discrimination and more effective leaders in typically female occupations. Data obtained from mental hospitals, civil service organisation and schools show no sex bias in leadership styles or leadership effectiveness.

Leadership effectiveness has also been correlated with various personality characteristics. Waetjin, Schuerger and Schwartz (1979) conducted a study to examine the relationships among self-concept as a manager, sex and supervisors' ratings of middle managers who were successful or unsuccessful. The personnel directors of the corporations were asked to identify a total of 14 men and 14 women middle managers as successful or unsuccessful. The unsuccessful female managers reported the highest self-concept. This asymmetry of findings has been explained in terms of their new entry in the managerial occupations. These women may function in a 'protected' environment in which they are given much encouragement in dealing with managerial tasks, and may not be given realistic feedback of their being ineffective. The result may be an unrealistic self-concept.

The changing cultural values concerning roles of women in society, coupled with legislations banning discrimination on the basis of sex in employment practices have opened many new opportunities for women in male dominated jobs. Studies support the view that women going for male-dominated *i.e.* non-traditional jobs are more task-oriented and achievement-concerned. Hennig & Jardim (1977) reported that the business women in the sample, as first-level technical specialist supervisors, emulated the masculine behaviour style and acted as little like a 'woman' as possible. He also revealed that women who advance in the business world move from a position of the highly structured technical specialist at the beginning levels to the more consideration or human relations type management behaviours as they move up the management hierarchy. A study by Sorrentino (1973) shows a positive relationship between achievement motivation and leadership position, *i.e.* the higher the management level, and the more non-traditional the work role, the higher the women scored on achievement dimension. Similarly, Moore and Rickel (1980) conducted a study taking a sample of 150 nurses as a traditional job. It was determined that women in non-traditional business roles were more achieving and emphasized production more than those in traditional jobs. They conclude that leadership behaviour of women does vary between organisational settings and across occupational levels in predictable ways.

Chusmir (1983) stated that psychologically masculine women choose non-traditional jobs. They demonstrate a need for achievement and have higher career commitment which differentiates these women from women in more traditional jobs and this masculinity has been associated with task-structured leadership pattern. On the other hand, Greenfield, Greiver, Larry & Wood, Marion (1980) studied 324 women working in male-dominated, female-dominated, and sex-ratio-balanced jobs. Women in female-dominated jobs rated the importance of task and the variables best predicting the results were their attitudes and background factors. Women in male-dominated jobs gave more importance to success in their feeling of well- being than women in female-dominated jobs.

Brad Chapman and Luthans (1975) conducted a study that shows it is neither the type of job nor sex of the manager that determines the leadership style. It is rather the favourability of the situation that matters. Leadership style of the manager varies according to the situation. They applied Fiedler's LPC instrument to practising males and females in a civilian and a military organisation as subjects. The military sample consisted of 146 males and 60 females and civilian sample 49 males and 28 females. The results of the study indicate that practising female managers do not have a significantly higher need for fostering good interpersonal relationships than do their male counterparts. Also of importance is the finding that the females studied are not significantly more task-oriented than males, although females might be expected to be task-oriented if they are to succeed in a traditionally male environment. In other words, the researches found no significant difference in male and female leadership style in situations where the degree of task-structure, position, power and leader-member relations were comparable.

Benedetti (1975) studied similarities and differences in the leadership styles of women in educational administration and women in business administration. The sample consisted of 150 administrators in each of the categories. Results show that women in educational administration scored higher on consideration dimension while women in business scored higher on initiating structure dimension. Banfield, (1976) conducted a study on women working in supervisory roles in public utilities services, school administration, private industry, banking, local government, media, college education and non-profit organisation. Most of the women agreed that human relations and public relations skills were top priorities for women entering management. A majority of subjects, regardless of type of occupation, characterised their leadership style as participative, a team approach and considered inter-personal human relation skills as their main strength. The study of Sadler (1970) also supports the view of participative style of leadership.

Self-Esteem and Leadership

The prevalent sex role stereotypes hamper the development of high self esteem in women which in turn obstruct their choice for managerial roles, their behaviour in these roles and the perception of their behaviour in these roles. It may be reiterated that males and females may perceive their beliefs about sexual inequality as accurate reflections of 'natural' social reality (Allport, 1954). In self-ratings as well as in evaluations by others, women rate stereotypically masculine characteristics as more socially desirable and significant than stereotypically feminine traits (Broverman *et al.*, 1970). This may indicate self-loathing among the women. It also reveals that in a patriarchy, males will be equipped with qualities necessary for leadership, *e.g.* innovation and dominance. These qualities will be deemed socially significant; and women, designated to play supporting roles, will be encouraged to develop the opposite – in this case, submissive qualities. Stake (1983) conducted a study on situation and person-centred approaches to promoting leadership behaviour in low performance self-esteem women. In each of 84 mixed sex pairs (dyads) of under-graduates, a low performance self-esteem woman was appointed to the role of the leader in the dyad's decision making task. When women were given information about the leader before hand, they behaved like a leader. Post-discussion self-ratings show a more obvious form of female discomfort with the leader role. Situation and person-centred approaches to promoting women's leadership behaviour were tested by providing information regarding the women's task relevant competence to one, both or neither dyad member prior to the day of the task.

The findings of studies on self-confidence show that girls, and particularly the bright ones, under-estimate their own ability. Difficult tasks are seen as challenging to men while females seek to avoid them (Veroff, 1969, McManic, 1969). Researches suggest that girls lack confidence in their own abilities and seek effectance through others (Crandall & Rabson 1960). Women give lower estimates of their abilities than men do. Even after actual performances, they give lower self-evaluations of their performance than males under the same circumstances. They attribute their success to luck rather than to their abilities (Bartal and Freize, 1977; Happerine and Adam, 1978; Deaux,1979). On the other hand, House & Perney (1974) showed that women have higher self-confidence when performance feedback is provided. Reld (1977) found that the positive self-concept is correlated with internal locus of control. While women have been seen possessing external locus of control, they tend to exaggerate the negative aspects of a task. They perceive themselves less skilled and as having even less control over the outcomes of their behaviour. Such 'external locus of control' orientation enhances women's feelings of helplessness and her avoidance of task oriented behaviour (Throop and McDonald, 1971; Deaux, 1976 Savage *et al*, 1979). Women, who are discouraged from developing both confidence and ambition, will learn to be dependent upon others which will result in developing their people oriented leadership pattern. The differences in leadership pattern among women themselves may be assumed with varying degrees of self-esteem.

Studies are cited that indicate that women, even while performing leadership roles implying high self-confidence and achievement, hold attitudes toward themselves as women having low self-esteem and expectations of negative consequences of managing – behaviour. Such negative attitudes make them relationship-oriented in their leadership patterns. In the context of Maslow's need hierarchy, women executives are more concerned with fulfilling a leadership responsibility through satisfaction of a social need. The behaviour of men is more closely related to esteem and self-actualisation.

Women do not want to threaten their femininity. They are aware of the 'feminine' responsibility of pleasing men. Consequently, most women who opt for male-dominated careers and hold non-traditional ideas about sex roles, also often exhibit behaviours which are known as feminine. Probably the removal of male support in work settings becomes devastating to them. The feminine style of exercising power decreases their self-esteem (Johnson & Goodschilds, 1976). In other words, on the one hand, self-esteem seems to determine the leadership style of a woman, and on the other hand, is determined by her leadership style. There is considerable amount of research evidence into the relationship between sex differences and self-concept showing that the higher a woman's feminity score on tests, the higher her anxiety and lower her self-esteem (Concentino and Heilburn, 1964; Gole, 1969; Sears, 1970; Spence and Helmreich, 1978); and the higher the masculinity score, the higher the self-esteem (Prager, 1983). Some other researches (Flaherty and Dusk, 1980; Bem, 1977; Spence, Helmreich and Stapp, 1975) also bring out that androgynous orientation in women is associated with better self-concept and higher self-esteem, while high self-esteem has been correlated with work achievement (Crook, Healy and O'Shea, 1984). McArther (1974) opines that women have a better aptitude for management than men. They are less emotional, more practical and are more skilled in the art of delegation, communication and decision making.

Type of Job, Self-esteem and Leadership Patterns

Recently, studies have appeared on the characteristics of effective women managers, their attitudes, leadership styles, their success in managerial roles and the dynamics of their work situation. Self-esteem is an important factor in taking up a job and exhibiting particular type of leadership pattern. In a study, Helmich and Erzen (1975) indicated that female respondents associate their behaviour of leadership with opportunity to develop close friendship. The reason lies in becoming concerned with fulfilling a leadership responsibility through satisfaction of a social need instead of esteem need. Due to this reason women are considered suitable for people-oriented occupations (traditional for women) so that they may fulfil their social needs.

A number of field studies have revealed significant differences in achievement motive responses across certain specific groups of women. In two studies (Baruch 1967; and Shelton, 1968), women functioning in professional careers had higher achievement motivation than housewives of comparable ability. In another study (Oliver, 1974) it was found that career-oriented women scored high on achievement and low on affiliation, while a study by Sorrentino (1973) shows a positive relationship between achievement motivation and leadership position, *i.e.*, the higher the management level and the more non-traditional the work role, the higher the women scored achievement dimension. Moore, Lorreta and Mary (1977) investigated characteristics which distinguish women who choose traditional versus non-traditional careers and function at different occupational levels. They found that women in non-traditional career such as business were more achieving and task-oriented. They viewed themselves as managers and men while women in traditional career *i.e.* nursing, were more 'female' like. Further, Moore and Rickel (1980) conducted a field study to investigate those characteristics which distinguish women who choose traditional as opposed to non-traditional careers and who function at different occupational levels. Subjects comprising the traditional sample were women in the nursing occupation employed in 13 hospitals and the sample of non-traditional group consisted of women employed in nine business and industrial organisations. The findings indicated that, compared to nurses, the business women as a group were more achieving, emphasized production more and saw themselves like managers and men not having characteristics that are not ascribed to these groups. The first supervisory level business women also were more job-involved and consideration-oriented than the first level supervisory (head) nurses. Conversely, at the non-supervisory level, the general duty nurses described themselves as more considerate than did the business women. When both organisational setting and occupational level were considered, both the non-traditional and those in higher occupational levels (a) had higher achievement motivation, (b) were more involved in their jobs (c) were more production oriented and (d) described themselves as having characteristics of managers and men. The results on consideration and structure scales were not significant.

Benedetti (1975) compared personal characteristics, leadership styles and women in educational administration and women in business administration. The study indicated that women in educational administration were more educated than women in business. They presented papers in seminars and professional meetings but were high on consideration leadership pattern while education is positively related with degrees of self-esteem. On the other hand women in business were high on structure dimension of leadership. Banfield (1976) conducted a study to see the relationship between competence as women manager and androgynous personality characteristics and self-concept. The study dealt with women managers' training, leadership style, personal and organisational limitations, and rewards problems. Subjects for the study were selected from public utilities organisations, district level school administration, private industry, banks, media, college-education and non-profit organisation. Results show that 93% of the subjects incorporated masculine characteristics into their personalities. The subjects were well integrated individuals with positive self-concepts. A majority indicated that on-the-job experience was valuable but human relation and public relation skills were top priorities. A majority of subjects characterised their leadership style as participative. Sacrificing femininity, fear of success and reluctance to assert themselves in domains of men were not viewed as limitations in the subjects' experience.

The Study

Very few studies have been conducted on women executives in India. A survey of 33 women executives was taken (Singh, 1980) to examine their attitudes toward their superiors, subordinates, job opportunities, positions etc. Responses supported the contention that women are suited to executive jobs and are as competent as male executives. Pereira (1978) showed that women with high levels of education had more favourable attitudes towards women in managerial positions. Chaturvedi (1985) says that many scholars and social scientists hold the view that women are able managers. They manage household with skill and so they can the office front. Feminine touch helps in managerial roles. Women magistrates are reported to deal better with cases of family disputes and other social offences (Gupta, 1960) and they also tend to administer with greater appeal and motivation. They possess the capability to get things done (Mishra, 1980). Tabb, Singhi and Bansal concluded that women administrators develop characteristics according to job requirement.

The author conducted a study on leadership styles of women managers and their effectiveness in terms of self-perception. The sample was the same as has been discussed in the previous chapter. Both groups *i.e.* Principals and Scientists were termed as middle level managers considering their occupational hierarchy and work functions.

To see the leadership patterns, Leadership Effectiveness and Adaptability Description (LEAD-self) by Hersey and Blanchard (1974) was used. The behaviour of the subjects is observed in this scale in terms of four quadrants based on different combinations of two types of leadership behaviours:

1. *Task Behaviour*: The extent to which leaders are likely to organise and define the roles of the members of their group (followers); to explain what activities each has to do and when, where and how tasks are to be accomplished; characterized by endeavouring to establish well defined patterns of organisation, channels of communication and ways of getting job accomplished.
2. *Relationship Behaviour*: The extent to which leaders are likely to maintain personal relationships between themselves and members of their group (followers) by opening up channels of communication, providing socio-emotional support 'psychological strokes' and facilitating behaviours.

On the basis of these two types of behaviours, the four quadrants are as follows:

(a) High task - Low relationship (HT-LR)

(b) High task - High relationship (HT-HR)

(c) High relationship - Low task (HR-LT)

(d) Low relationship - Low Task (LR-LT)

A leader follows the leadership style according to various situations and as per maturity of the followers. In one situation, one type of behaviour may be appropriate but in another situation, the same behaviour may not be. Thus, the questionnaire measures three aspects of leader behaviour Style, Style Range, and Style Adaptability. The basic leadership style is defined as the style or styles for which one has the maximum responses. If a person has 4 responses in Style 1, 5 responses in Style 2, and 3 responses in Style 3, his basic style would be Style 2 and others are supporting styles. But for supporting style, two or more responses are essential. Style Range is the extent to which one is able to vary one's leadership style. In the above example, the style range is Style 1, 2 & 3. The instrument also measures style adaptability which denotes effectiveness of the leader. Style Adaptability is the degree to which one is able to vary one's style appropriately to the demands of a given situation. Thus, this study is based on the situational model of leadership. Results of the study are presented below. Only Styles 1, 2 and 3 are considered as none in the sample exhibited Style 4.

Leadership Patterns

Sixty per cent of the 200 women managers covered in the study followed Style 2 of leadership which is a HighTask - High Relationship style and 28.5 per cent adopted Style 3, which is a High-Relationship – Low Task approach, while only 11.5 per cent adopted Style 1, High Task – Low Relationship style (Table 6.1). The observed data exhibit considerable deviations from the null hypothesis of evenness of the styles adopted. The χ^2 is found to be 72.67 which, with 2 degrees of freedom, is highly significant even at 1% level, supporting the conclusion that there are significant differences in leadership patterns of the sample of women managers studied. No significant differences in leadership behaviour were found in two types of occupations (Principals and Scientists).

Table 6.1: Leadership Patterns of Women Managers

Information	*Frequency of Leadership Patterns*			*Total*
	Style 1	*Style 2*	*Style 3*	
Observed Numbers	23	120	57	200
Expected Numbers	(66.66)	(66.66)	(66.66)	(200)

Observed χ^2 = 72.67.

Tabulated χ^2 (.01) with 2 degrees of freedom = 9.31.

Significant at 1 per cent level.

Self-Esteem and Leadership Patterns

The question whether the manager's style is related to her perception of self-esteem is examined next. Table 6.2 presents the observed frequencies in different cells and those expected under the hypothesis of independence.

Table 6.2: Leadership Patterns of Women Managers with High/Low Self-Esteem

Self-Esteem Level	*Leadership Patterns*			*Total*
	Style 1	*Style 2*	*Style 3*	
High Self Esteem	5 (7.5)	47 (35.5)	8 (17)	60
Low Self Esteem	10 (7.5)	24 (35.5)	26 (17)	60
Total	15	71	34	120

Figures in brackets are the expected frequencies

Observed χ^2 = 18.6

Tabulated χ^2 (.01) with 2 degrees of freedom = 9.31

Significant at 1 per cent Level.

The observed Chi Square is 18.6; is highly significant at 1% level with two degrees of freedom, and shows that perception of self-esteem is highly related with leadership patterns of women managers.

Three component factors of self-esteem *i.e.* ego-strength, independence/ dependence and assertive/ submissive seem to be significantly related with leadership patterns. Women managers who have high self-esteem as measured on ego-strength component of self-esteem follow HT-LR leadership pattern (Style 1), while low self-esteem women have HT-HR pattern (Style 2). Women who have high self-esteem on the other two components mentioned above have HT-HR pattern of leadership while women with low self-esteem on these factors have HR-LT pattern.

Type of Job, Self-esteem and Leadership Patterns

The data indicate significant interactions between type of job (traditional or non-traditional), self-esteem and leadership patterns. Table 6.3 gives the relevant statistical analysis.

Table 6.3: Type of job, self-esteem and leadership patterns of women managers

Type of Job	*High Self-Esteem (HSE) Leadership Patterns*			*Total HSE*	*Low Self-Esteem (LSE) Leadership Patterns*			*Total LSE*	*Total*
	Style 1	*Style 2*	*Style 3*		*Style 1*	*Style 2*	*Style 3*		
Traditional	3 (4.12) *(-).844*	27 (19.52) *3.23**	3 (9.35) *(-) 3.20**	33	8 (4.12) *2.99**	13 (19.52) *(-)2.45**	12 (9.35) *1.46*	33	66
Non-Traditional	2 (3.37) *(-)1.03*	20 (15.97) *1.74*	5 (7.65) *(-)1.34*	27	2 (3.37) *(-) 1.05*	11 (15.97) *(-)1.87*	14 (7.65) *3.5**	27	54
Total	5	47	8	60	10	24	26	60	120

Figures in brackets are the expected frequencies.

Figures in italics are the Residuals. The comparable value is 1.96

Observed $\chi^2 = 23.93$

Tabulated χ^2 (.01) with 7 degrees of freedom = 18.47

Significant at 1 per cent level

The observed Chi-Square is 23.93 which is highly significant showing that there are significant interactions in type of job, self-esteem and leadership patterns. Further analysis of the Residuals shows that there is a significant positive relationship between traditional job, high self-esteem and pattern 2 of leadership and a negative significant relationship in traditional job, high self-esteem and pattern 3 of leadership (res. values 3.23 and -3.2 respectively). On the other hand, low self-esteem is positively significantly related with pattern 1 of leadership and significantly negatively related to pattern 2 of leadership in traditional job (residual values 2.99 and -2.45 respectively). Non-traditional job, low self-esteem and pattern 3 of leadership are significantly positively related (residual value 3.5). In brief, women managers with high self-esteem working in traditional job follow leadership pattern 2 (*i.e.*, HT-HR) and women managers with low self-esteem in traditional job follow pattern 1 of leadership (*i.e.*, HT-LR). On the other hand, women managers working in non-traditional job with low self-esteem follow pattern 3 of leadership (*i.e.*, HR-LT).

Women Managers and Leadership Effectiveness

Results of the present study show that women managers, in general, are effective in their leadership behaviour (Effectiveness Mean = +5.77 and Standard Deviation = 4.89) (Fig. 6.1).

Figure 6.1 Measure of Effectiveness of Women Managers

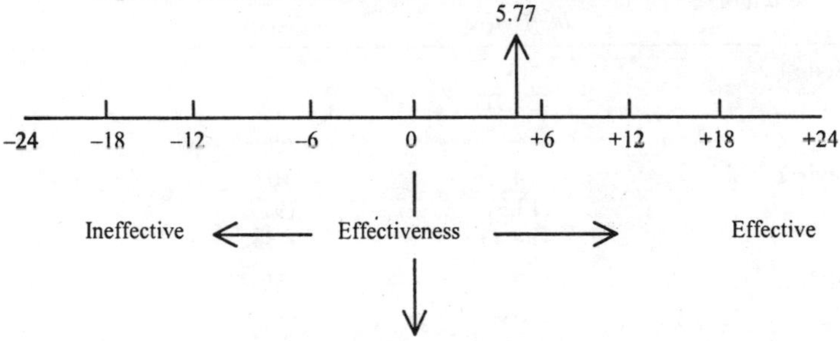

'0' indicates neither ineffective nor effective

Table 6.4 shows the frequency distribution of the sampled women managers by effectiveness score and type of job. In view of the smallness of frequencies in some of the cells, frequencies of -13 to -24 and -1 to -12 Effectiveness Score cells have been merged before further analysis. Data of cells +1 to +12 and +13 to +24 have also been similarly merged. Frequencies of '0' Effectiveness Score cell *i.e.* neither effective not ineffective have been ignored as there were only 9 frequencies - 8 in traditional job and only 1 in non-traditional job. Thus, there are only two categories of effectiveness for analysis *i.e.* Effective and Ineffective.

Table 6.4: Women Managers and Effectiveness by Type of Job

Type of Job	*Effectiveness Score*					*Total*
	−13 to −24	*−1 to −12*	*0*	*+1 to +12*	*+13 to +24*	
Traditional	0 (0)	17 (12)	8 (4.5)	66 (76)	9 (7.5)	100
Non-Traditional	0 (0)	7 (12)	1 (4.5)	86 (76)	6 (7.5)	100
Total	0	24	9	152	15	200

Leadership Patterns and Leadership Effectiveness

Table 6.5 studies the relationship between the leadership patterns of women managers and the effectiveness.

Table 6.5: Distribution of Women Managers by Leadership Patterns and Effectiveness

Leadership Pattern	*Effectiveness*		*Total*
	Ineffective	*Effective*	
Style 1	13 (2.89) *6.75**	10 (20) *(-) 6.59*	23
Style 2	4 (13.9) *(-) 4.43*	107 (97) *4.33*	11
Style 3	7 (7.16) *(-) 0.074*	50 (49.83) *0.01*	57
Total	24	167	191

Figures in brackets are the expected frequencies.

Figures in italics are the Residuals. The comparable value is 1.96

Observed $\chi^2 = 48.45$

Tabulated χ^2 (.01) with 2 degrees of freedom = 9.21

Significant at 1 per cent level.

The observedChi-Square (Table 6.5) is highly significant at 1 per cent level, which indicates that there are differences in leadership effectiveness of women managers following various leadership patterns as their basic patterns of leadership. Further analysis of Residuals shows that there is a significant negative relationship with leadership pattern 1 and effectiveness and a significant positive relationship between leadership pattern 1 and ineffectiveness (Residual values -6.59

and 6.75 respectively). On the other hand, there is a positive significant relationship between pattern 2 and effectiveness and a negative significant relationship between pattern 2 and ineffectiveness (Residual values 4.33 and -4.43 respectively being greater than comparable value 1.96). In other words, women managers following pattern 1 as their basic leadership pattern are ineffective while women managers following pattern 2 as their basic pattern of leadership behaviour are effective.

Type of Job and Effectiveness

Table 6.6 presents an analysis of the relationship between the leadership effectiveness of women managers studied and the type of job in which they are engaged.

Table 6.6: Leadership Effectiveness of Women Managers Working in Traditional/Non-traditional Job:

Type of Job	*Effectiveness*		*Total*
	Ineffective	*Effective*	
Traditional	17 (11.56) *2.37**	75 (80.43) *(-) 2.33**	92
Non-Traditional	7 (12.40) *(-) 2.36**	92 (86.56) *2.34**	99
Total	24	167	191

Figures in brackets are the expected frequencies.

Figures in italics are the Residuals. The comparable value is 1.96

Observed $\chi^2 = 5.62$

Tabulated χ^2 (.05) with 1 degrees of freedom = 3.84

Significant at 5 per cent level.

Table 6.6 shows that the observed value at 5.62 which is significant at 5% level supporting the conclusion that there are differences in leadership effectiveness of women managers depending upon the type of job. In other words, women managers in traditional and non-traditional jobs seem to differ in leadership effectiveness. Further, the data would suggest that there is a positive significant relationship between ineffectiveness and traditional nature of job and a significant positive relationship between effectiveness and non-traditional nature of job, with corresponding negative relationships between effectiveness and traditional job and between non-traditional job and ineffectiveness. Women managers working in traditional jobs seem to be ineffective in their leadership behaviour and women managers working in non-traditional job are effective.

Self Esteem and Effectiveness

Table 6.7 tries to establish the relationship between leadership effectiveness and the level of self-esteem of the women managers.

Table 6.7: Leadership Effectiveness of Women Managers with High/Low Self-Esteem

Self-Esteem	*Effectiveness*		*Total*
	Ineffective	*Effective*	
High Self-Esteem	3 (8.5) *(-) 2.90**	53 (47.5) *2.90**	56
Low Self-Esteem	14 (8.5) *2.90**	42 (47.5) *(-) 2.90*	56
Total	17	95	112

Figures in brackets are the expected frequencies.

Figures in italics are the Residuals. The comparable value is 1.96

Observed $\chi^2 = 8.39$

Tabulated χ^2 (.01) with 1 degrees of freedom = 6.63

Significant at 1 per cent level

The significance of the Chi-Square value suggests rejection of the view that leadership effectiveness is not related with levels of self-esteem. Further analysis shows that there is a significant negative relationship between high self-esteem and ineffectiveness and a positive significant relationship between high self-esteem and effectiveness. On the other hand, there is a significant negative relationship between low self-esteem and effectiveness and a positive significant relationship between low self-esteem and ineffectiveness. In other words, women managers with high self-esteem are effective in their leadership behaviour and women managers with low self-esteem are ineffective.

Type of Job, Self Esteem and Effectiveness

An additional variable, type of job, will now be introduced into the analysis of relationship between effectiveness and self-esteem. Table 6.8 presents the relevant data.

Table 6.8: Leadership Effectiveness of Women Managers with High/ Low Self-Esteem Working in Traditional/ Non-Traditional Job

Type of Job	*Self-Esteem*						
	High Self-Esteem			*Low Self-Esteem*			*Total*
	Ineffective	*Effective*	*Total*	*Ineffective*	*Effective*	*Total*	
Traditional	2 (4.47) *(-) 1.72*	27 (25.02) *0.79*	29	10 (4.47) *4.09**	20 (25.02) *(-) 1.85*	30	59
Non-Traditional	1 (4.02) *(-) 2.09**	26 (22.47) *1.40*	27	4 (4.02) *(-) 0.01*	22 (22.47) *(-) 0.15*	26	53
Total	3	53	56	14	42	56	112

Figures in brackets are the expected frequencies.

Figures in italics are the Residuals. The comparable value is 1.96

Observed $\chi^2 = 12.20$

Tabulated χ^2 (.05) with 4 degrees of freedom = 9.48

Significant at 5 per cent Level.

The analysis shows that there are significant interactions between type of job, self-esteem and leadership effectiveness. Further, there appears to be a significant positive relationship between traditional nature of job, low self esteem and ineffectiveness and a significant negative relationship between non-traditional nature of job, high self-esteem and ineffectiveness (residual values 4.09 and -2.09 respectively). In other words, women managers working in traditional job with low self-esteem are ineffective and women managers in non-traditional job with high self-esteem are not ineffective.

To sum up, some major findings of the author's research study are as follows –

- Women managers, in general follow pattern 2 (HT-HR) as their basic pattern of leadership. Their supportive patterns are patterns 1 and 3, *i.e.* LT-HR and HT-LR. They do not follow pattern 4 *i.e.* LT-LR pattern at all.
- Women managers with high self-esteem follow pattern 2, while low self-esteem women managers have pattern 3 as their basic leadership style.
- Types of job, levels of self-esteem and leadership patterns are significantly related. Women managers working as school principals (traditional job) with high self-esteem follow pattern 2 of leadership while low self-esteem women managers in this job

follow pattern 1. As research scientists (non-traditional job) those with low self-esteem follow pattern 3.

- In general, women managers are effective in their leadership behaviour.
- Women managers who follow pattern 2 as their basic leadership pattern are effective while those who follow pattern 1 as their basic pattern are ineffective.
- Type of job and effectiveness are significantly related.
- Women managers as school principals are ineffective while women managers working in non-traditional job are effective.
- Levels of self-esteem and effectiveness have been found to be significantly related. Women managers with high self-esteem are effective while those with low self-esteem are ineffective in their leadership behaviour.
- There is also a significant interaction between types of job, levels of self-esteem and leadership effectiveness. Women managers with low self-esteem in traditional jobs are ineffective while those with high self-esteem in non-traditional job are not ineffective.

Discussion of the Results of the Study

Results of present study do not support earlier theories that women are not task-oriented but believe in developing good relations at work place (Bardwick, 1971) or they are task-oriented (Helmich, 1974). The present study supports a combination of high-task-high-relationship behaviour. Bem's theory of androgyny helps us to explain women manager's high task-high relationship behaviour of leadership. It seems that women going for managerial roles tend to possess a combination of traits which makes them both 'expressive' and 'instrumental'. While men and women possess some distinct physiological differences, they may not necessarily be psychologically different. Aggressiveness, independence, self-esteem etc. are not biological traits unique to one gender. Distributions of these characteristics for men and women as groups overlap. Androgyny denotes the integration of both masculinity and femininity within a single individual (Bem, 1977). Androgynous individuals of both genders are able to engage in either instrumental (task-oriented) or expressive (relationship-oriented) behaviour, depending on situational demands.

High relationship behaviour of these women managers reflects their feminine traits. Women in general have been viewed as emotional, shirking from challenges, dependent, less decisive and people-oriented in their approach. High task behaviour on the part of these women managers suggests that once the horizon for women employment has extended to incorporate managerial roles also, the traits and behaviours considered to be appropriate for them seem to include those generally labelled as 'masculine' and the socialization practices also seem to change accordingly. Thus, women who are allowed to develop 'masculine' traits required for managerial roles show high task behaviour, a characteristic attributed to males, once they enter such roles. Further, to prove their competence as managers, they follow a pattern characterized by high task behaviour.

The complexities of the modern work organisations seem to be moving in directions away from the rugged individual. Increasingly, work has to be accomplished by team-work rather than by individuals working alone. In addition, there is a relatively new emphasis on introducing supportive elements into the work place with the push toward improvement in the quality of working life, job satisfaction and social gratification from work. Thus, certain attributes of the hard boiled 'he-man' may be dysfunctional and women's approach of a combination of high task and high relationship leadership behaviour seems to be more functional. The pursuit of organizational goals in an educational or a research organization involves team work, calling for concern both for the relationships and the task. Banfield (1976) also found that women managers working in educational, industrial, private organisations etc. perceived their leadership style as a team approach.

Sinha (1979) and Verma (1985) conclude in their studies that a combination of 'Nurturant' and 'Task' is workable and, therefore, executives attach greater values to both task and nurturance. They further explain that this leadership behaviour is justified in the Indian context where it is presumed that the national character incorporates some of the traits of authoritarianism and side by side relationship is considered as highly desirable in Indian managers. Evidence also brings out that Indian managers try to be more participative or nurturant just to compensate for their basic authoritarianism, so that they are not accused of their strict behaviour.

The results of the present study also show that along with a basic pattern of leadership, women managers follow some supportive patterns. Their supportive patterns are Style 3 *i.e.* high relationship – low task and Style 1 *i.e.* high task-low relationship. Results show that women managers understand demands of varying their leadership patterns from situation to situation. These results are congruent with the situational leadership theory which postulates that a leader must be flexible in the leadership roles and should change his/her leadership functioning pattern as per demands of the situations.

Women managers have not been found to follow Style 4 pattern of leadership, that is, low task-low relationship pattern. In terms of situational leadership model, leaders follow this pattern when they consider that followers have high maturity and are able to take initiative as well as take care of themselves on their own. It seems that the respondents of the present study do not consider their followers to have very high level of maturity which may adequately call for Style 4 of leadership.

Type of Job and Leadership Patterns

The results of the author's study indicate that there are no differences in leadership patterns of women managers on account of type of job. In other words, leadership patterns of women managers are similar in both traditional and non-traditional job. The results are in contrast with those from the previous studies (Henning and Jardim, 1977; Moore and Rickel, 1980; Chusmir, 1983; Benedetti, 1979 etc.) that women in non-traditional jobs are concerned with task and production while women in traditional jobs are concerned with relationships and so they are people-oriented. The results of present studies support the findings of Chapman (1975), Banfield (1976) that type of job has no significant effect on determining leadership patterns of women.

Numerous studies on career choice reviewed by Terborg (1977) indicate that young girls and women do differ with regard to sex-role concepts and that these orientations do affect their career choices. However, pressures from employment situation result in changes in attitudes and behaviours so that an interactive process appears to be involved. Chapman (1975) also concluded that it is not the type of job that determines the leadership pattern but it is rather the favourability of the situation that matters. He found no differences in female leadership style in situations where the degrees of task-structure, position-power and leader-member relations were comparable. When we observe the sample of our study, we note that in both types of jobs, managers are to deal with a group of professionals, their jobs demand innovation and creativity and they are placed in middle level management, therefore, their leadership patterns may also be similar.

Education plays an important role in determining one's behaviour. Women with similar education have basically identical scores on measures of psychological masculinity-femininity (Admns, Priest and Prince, 1985), which may lead them to exhibit similar patterns of behaviour. Since women managers in traditional and non-traditional job do not vary markedly regarding the level of their educational training, it is quite feasible that they exhibit similar leadership behaviour.

Self-Esteem and Leadership Patterns

Findings of the present study show that women with high self-esteem follow high task-high relationship leadership pattern while women with low self-esteem follow high relationship – low task leadership behaviour. An attempt to explain high task-high relationship behaviour of high self-esteem group again calls for a reference to Bem's theory of androgyny. Bem's (1977) multiple regression analysis indicates that self-esteem for males was significantly related to masculinity, but for females, self-esteem was significantly related to both masculinity and femininity. This integration of masculinity and femininity may lead women to exhibit high task and high relationship leader behaviour pattern. Banfield's study (1976) supports the view that women managers having a positive self-concept preferred a team approach in leadership functioning. It appears that high self-esteem women managers believe in team management approach which considers both task and human relationships as equally important aspects of leadership.

It may be added here that high self-esteem, in general, has been found to be correlated with task-oriented leadership behaviour. High self-esteem person has a sense of self-worth and evaluates him/herself as 'good enough' (Rosenberg, 1965). He/she is governed by internal locus of control, has high self-acceptance and high ego-strength. As Kelly and Worell (1977) indicated, these masculine valued traits are related to high level of self-esteem, which in turn lead to task behaviour of leadership. The results that women managers with high self-esteem follow task behaviour can be explained in this light.

On the other hand, women have been considered 'temperamentally' ill-suited for leadership positions. They have been considered to be lacking managerial characteristics. Researches show that in contrast to men, women have a negative self-concept and low self-esteem. They evaluate themselves as lacking in abilities. It may be reiterated that the person with low self-esteem is more likely to lack self-confidence, be dependent upon others, be shy and non-explorative (Rosenberg, 1965), be unimaginative and will value conformity (Linton and Graham, 1959). Due to these personality deficits one becomes relationship oriented. In case of women, it has been found that due to lack of self-confidence, they do not think themselves to be competent enough to attain certain goals they want to attain and try to get vicarious achievement. Therefore, they exhibit relationship behaviour instead of task behaviour (Bardwick, 1971; Bass, 1965). The respondents with low self-esteem are less independent, less assertive, low in ego-strength and less creative, thus, the high relationship behaviour and low task-behaviour of these respondents can be explained following the aforesaid arguments.

The findings may also be explained in terms of maturity in career attitudes. Crook (1984) suggests that self-esteem influences mature career attitudes and work achievement directly. High self-esteem persons adopt adult mores which orient people to effective career-management. Thus, women who have high self-esteem develop adult mores and consequently exhibit task-behaviour of leadership. On the other hand, women who have low self-esteem may not develop adult mores and may exhibit relationship behaviour of leadership.

Three components of self-esteem *i.e.* ego strength, independence/dependence and assertiveness/submissiveness are found to be significantly related to leadership patterns. It is interesting to note that except in the case of ego strength, the Low Self-Esteem (LSE) group on each component follows pattern 3 of leadership *i.e.* HR-LT pattern. But High Self-Esteem groups differ in basic style. The HSE group on independence/dependence and assertive/submissive components follows pattern 2 of leadership. The explanations given for the relationship between levels of self-esteem and a particular leadership pattern (for LSE and pattern 3, and HSE and pattern 2) can be extended to these relationships also.

In case of high self-esteem, as measured on ego-strength component, we see that this group follows pattern 1 of leadership *i.e.* high task-low relationship behaviour. The mean of real self on this component shows that high self-esteem group has higher level of ego-strength than low self-esteem group on this component. High ego-strength incorporates superiority feelings and higher maturity. It seems that such feelings make women managers become 'autocratic' in their leadership behaviour. Verma (1984) also indicated that high ego-strength person has positive association with authoritarianism. 'I' feeling is stronger in such a person.

The low self-esteem group on ego-strength component follows pattern 2 *i.e.* HT-HR pattern. The mean real self of this group shows that this group has relatively low ego-strength and characterized by relatively less maturity and lower level of superiority feeling which in turn make this group follow relationship behaviour as well as task behaviour.

In the light of three aspects of personality *i.e.* cognition, affection and conation which are related to thinking, feeling and behaviour respectively, we see that dimensions of self esteem which are related to affection dimension of personality do not affect leadership pattern, and factors of self-esteem that are related to cognitive dimension of personality affect the leadership pattern of women. In other words, the leadership behaviour of women in work-settings is not governed by their feelings or emotions; rather the cognitive component is predominant in determining behaviour in the work settings.

Type of Job and Self-Esteem

No significant differences have been found between type of job and levels of self-esteem of the respondents. Women managers in both traditional and non-traditional job have similar levels of self-esteem. The findings support the results of the study of Banfield (1976) and are in contrast with many other previous researches on the issue which show that women in non-traditional jobs have higher self-esteem than women in traditional jobs (Canter, 1979; Rezler, 1967). One of the reasons that no significant differences have been found in levels of self-esteem of women managers working in traditional and non-traditional job may be that the respondents of the present study in both traditional and non-traditional jobs are highly educated and while discussing the role of education in determining self-esteem, it has been observed that high education facilitates the development of self-esteem.

One's experience in the managerial role also influences, at least partially, the level of self-esteem. Researches suggest that though women may choose either traditional or non-traditional job due to the differences in their personality, but once they move up in the organizational hierarchy, they identify with the male model of managerial role and reject few traits they earlier endorsed (Henning and Jardim 1977; Schein, 1973). Terborg (1977) suggested that these orientations do affect their career choices but it has also been shown that pressures from employment situation result in changes in attitudes and behaviours. Besides, the traditional sex-role training that women receive within the society leaves women as a group to have the burden of convincing management that they are serious about their career. This may involve suppressing or eliminating attitudes and behaviours that would identify them as "typically female" (Moore and Rickel, 1980). This also explains why in both types of jobs, women in the middle managerial levels perceive themselves as having high self esteem – a masculine trait.

The components of self-esteem found to be significantly related with type of job were self-control/ emotional, good natured/ critical and calm/ restless. The results reveal that women managers in traditional job have high self esteem on these components. In other words, they perceive less discrepancy regarding the three aforesaid components of

manufacturing (Agassi, 1977; Miner, 1974). This suggests that females will be effective in typically female occupations. The results of the present study may be explained in the following way:

Pattern 2 of leadership, which was observed as the basic pattern in women managers in both traditional and non-traditional job, is effective in non-traditional job, while it is ineffective in traditional job. Since leadership patterns are effective or ineffective as per situational demands and followers maturity, it may be assumed that the task-maturity and psycho-social maturity of followers varies in degree in traditional and non-traditional job. Therefore, pattern 2 of leadership varies in its effectiveness also with the type of job.

Ineffectiveness on the part of women managers in traditional job also indicates that they are not able to vary their leadership patterns and their supporting styles appropriately as per demands of the situation. Researches have shown that while considering principal-teacher relations, it has been contended that in working with experienced faculty, pattern 4 (low relationship – low task pattern) characterized by decentralized organization structure and delegation of responsibility to individuals may be appropriate. The maturity of these people is often such that they do not need their Principals to initiate such 'structure', at times they resent authoritative behaviour. In addition some teachers desire or need only a limited amount of socio-emotional support. However, during early stages of a school year or curriculum change, some amount of 'structure' may be desired. A few inexperienced teachers may also welcome the same pattern to gain experience. Thus, pattern 4 as basic leadership pattern, at times supported by S_2 or S_1 may be desirable. The respondents of this study, on the other hand, do not at all include pattern 4 in their leader behaviour. This may be one reason for their being ineffective as leaders.

Self-Esteem and Effectiveness

The findings of the present study show that women managers with high self-esteem are effective in their leadership behaviour and women managers with low self-esteem have been found to be ineffective. Korman's theory (1970) implies that self-esteem facilitates acquisition of attitudes of successful adults, since from his postulates people seek to be consistent and that esteem derives from succeeding, it follows that high self-esteem people more than low esteem people are likely to hold attitudes similar to those of successful people. Super's theory implies that high-esteem persons would outperform low esteem people in work because high self-esteem facilitates perceiving one's career environment due to cognitive perceptual advantage.

Healy, Baily and Anderson (1973) and Barrett and Tinsley (1977) provided evidence that high self-esteem contributes to career progress by bolstering perceptiveness and work achievement. The findings of Crook (1984) suggest that high self-esteem helps in developing mature career attitudes which orient people to effective career management. Once their own career management is effective and is as per their attitudes, they are likely to be effective in their work environment also. These theories and research findings explain as to why high self-esteem women are effective in their managerial roles while low self-esteem women are ineffective.

Researches have also shown that high self-esteem women are androgynous and are thereby psychologically better adjusted. They have personal and behavioural flexibility and view themselves in a harmonious balance with their environment. It can, thus, be presumed that due to higher flexibility and better adjustment women managers with high self-esteem are effective in their leadership roles.

Type of Job, Self-Esteem and Effectiveness—Interactional Effects

Results of interaction effect of type of job and self-esteem on effectiveness show that women managers working in traditional jobs are more or less ineffective in their leadership behaviour irrespective of their levels of self-esteem and women managers working in non-traditional job are more or less effective irrespective of their levels of self-esteem. It shows that type of job plays an important role in determining leadership effectiveness of women managers.

Summing Up

The present study brings out that most of the women managers follow high task – high relationship pattern as their basic pattern of leadership and that there is no difference in the basic leadership pattern due to type of job. Though, women in general are said to be more concerned with maintaining relations instead of being concerned with attainment, present findings suggest that in order to prove themselves successful and competent for managerial roles, women managers combine high task behaviour with high relationship behaviour. The respondents who follow this pattern as their basic pattern of leadership have been found to be effective also. It appears that at middle level of management, a leader with human approach is more desirable in organisations than a 'hard boiled he-man' leader. Thus, leaders who focus on 'task' as well as 'relationship' are effective in their leadership roles.

It was also observed that pattern 3 and pattern 1 emerge as supportive patterns of these women managers. Pattern 4 is totally absent from their leadership behaviour. Probably, Indian managers hold the belief that subordinates do not possess maturity to the extent which is prerequisite for pattern 4. However, results lend support to situational leadership theory which states that leadership patterns vary from situation to situation and true leaders may not stick to any one pattern of leadership in all situations. The findings regarding leadership effectiveness of these women managers are also supportive of this contention. The mean effectiveness score of the respondents evidently indicates that they are capable of changing their leadership patterns appropriately as per demand of the situation. The findings thus reject the previous motion that women are ill suited for managerial roles.

Type of job does not influence the basic pattern of leadership of these women managers, but is related to their leadership effectiveness. Women managers in traditional job have been found to be ineffective while those in non-traditional job are effective in their leadership behaviour. It seems that woman managers in traditional job are unable to vary their leadership pattern appropriately in accordance with the demands of a particular situation while those in non-traditional job are able to vary their pattern appropriately.

Women managers in general have high self-esteem. Women are independent, outgoing, cheerful, having high ego-strength, self-controlled, cooperative, good-natured, assertive, creative, easy-going and calm. It is noteworthy that some of these characteristics *e.g.* independence, self-control, assertiveness, high ego-strength etc. are generally assigned to males and some characteristics *e.g.* outgoingness, cheerfulness, cooperativeness, good-nature etc. are generally assigned to females. Thus, the high self-esteem women managers may be labelled as androgynous.

Levels of self-esteem affect the leadership patterns of women managers. High self-esteem women managers follow pattern 2 of leadership while low self-esteem women managers follow pattern 3 of leadership as their basic pattern. In other words, high self-esteem in women managers leads them to have pattern of leadership that focuses on both the task and relationship leadership behaviour. As mentioned earlier, high esteem women have both 'male' and 'female' characteristics which are expressed in terms of patter 2, a combination of high task and high consideration behaviour of these women managers. On the other hand, women managers who have low self-esteem possess characteristics such as independence, assertiveness, self-control and ego-strength in a much less amount, thus becoming more dependent on others and expressing pattern 3, a high relationship behaviour along with low task-behaviour. These conclusions are further substantiated by findings regarding the relationship of leadership pattern with self-esteem as measured on independent/ dependent and assertive/submissive component. Outgoing/withdrawn and creative/ conforming components of self-esteem also show some probability of being related with leadership pattern in a similar manner. Results on relationship between self-esteem as measured on ego-strength and leadership pattern give a different picture. High self-esteem women managers on this component exhibit high task and low relationship behaviour (pattern 1), while self-esteem women managers on this component follow pattern 2 *i.e.* high task-high relationship behaviour. Means of real self on this component (see Tan;e 5.4 and 5.5) show high self-esteem. It may be inferred from this finding that women who have high ego-strength perceive themselves as superior than their followers and thereby become more 'autocratic' and directive than women managers with low ego-strength.

Levels of self-esteem influence the effectiveness of women managers also. To be specific, high self-esteem women managers are effective while low self-esteem women managers are ineffective in their leadership behaviour. High self-esteem facilitates better adjustment and flexibility to have a harmonious balance with the environment. Thus, women managers with high self-esteem become effective in their leadership behaviour.

Type of job and levels of self-esteem have not been found to be related. Though previous studies have shown that women who enter non-traditional jobs have higher self-esteem than those who enter traditional jobs, the present findings suggest that such differences in self-esteem disappear once they perform managerial roles in either traditional or non-traditional jobs.

Type of job and self-esteem taken together affect leadership patterns of women managers. High self-esteem women managers in traditional job follow pattern 2 while those in non-traditional job do not exhibit any definite pattern. Low self-esteem women managers in traditional job follow pattern 1 while those in non-traditional job follow pattern 3. It appears that low self-esteem women managers perceive the job competence and maturity of their ownselves and their subordinates somewhat differently in traditional and non-traditional jobs which, in turn, changes the basic pattern of low self esteem group from pattern 2 to pattern 1 in case of traditional job, and to pattern 3 in case of non-traditional job. Other factors underlying these differences in leadership patterns of low self esteem group—traditional job group and Low self esteem—non traditional job group may be difference in specific job demands and experience.

Results of interaction of type of job, self-esteem and effectiveness show that the effect of type of job is more prominent than effect of self-esteem as women managers in traditional job have been found to be ineffective irrespective of their levels of self-esteem and women managers in non-traditional job are effective irrespective of their levels of self-esteem.

In brief, women managers who mostly follow pattern 2 of leadership as their basic pattern, are effective in their leadership behaviour and have high self-esteem. Type of job does not affect either self-esteem or leadership patterns, but it influences leader effectiveness. Self-esteem influences both the basic leadership pattern and effectiveness. Type of job and self-esteem jointly influence basic leadership pattern as well as effectiveness. Thus, the findings of the present study suggest that an interactional approach combining trait and situational approach to leadership will help us to understand better the leadership in organizational settings. The traits of the manager seem to explain why a manager adopts a particular pattern of leadership and how effective one would be, while situational determinants, such as type of job, explain differences in leader effectiveness.

Implications of the Study

1. The study implies that entrance of women to managerial roles should be appreciated and encouraged as they possess the ability to diagnose situational demands and are able to vary their leadership patterns accordingly. In other words, they are effective as managers.
2. The study further indicates that a basic pattern of leadership that emphasizes goal attainment along with maintenance of the group is desirable in research organisations. On the other hand, educational institutions probably call for a different pattern, may be, pattern 4 of the leadership with more delegation of responsibility and authority to the followers. An autocratic pattern of leadership may be dysfunctional in both type of organisations and a 'feminine' touch in leadership behaviour is effective.
3. High self-esteem facilitates women managers to be effective in managerial roles. It indicates that socialization practices for women must follow a course leading to the development of high self-esteem in women so that they may be facilitated in entering non-traditional jobs and excelling in them.
4. The study is a breakthrough in showing that women are not deficit in characteristics that are considered to be necessary for managerial roles and non-traditional jobs. They must be encouraged to take up managerial positions and non-traditional jobs. The stereotypic attitudes about women must change.

VII

Towards Empowerment

An Alternative Paradigm

The past fifty years have seen a gradual transformation world wide in the approach towards gender equity and equality from one of welfare to empowerment. Over this period, international action on gender issues translated itself into a movement for the empowerment and mainstreaming of women as a necessary pre-requisite for the process of sustainable development itself and as matter of right of the women. The empowerment approach that emerged in the seventies takes into account, unlike the earlier approaches, the gender gaps in the existing power structure and views enhancement of women's role in decision-making in political, economic, social spheres at various levels as crucial for improving the status of women in the society. For some years now, multi-directional and multi-faceted programmes towards empowerment of women encompassing some or all of these aspects are in place through governmental and non-governmental initiatives, in the fields of health and nutrition, education and skill development, employment, social security and political process. Changes in Constitution through the 73rd and 74th Amendment Acts providing for reservation for women in Panchayats and municipal bodies, the initiatives of voluntary organizations in promoting awareness among and organizing women through self-help groups and co-operatives to improve their access to micro-credit and other inputs and thereby enhance productivity of their economic activities and incomes, and the positive response of the public agencies in the form of Rashtriya Mahila Kosh and support from financial institutions like NABARD to such initiatives, are among the significant direct efforts to empower women in recent decades.

That things have not improved to the extent desirable or to the extent justified by the resources spent on such programmes is well-known. The current profile of Indian women and the discussion of the empowerment programmes presented in two of the earlier Chapters support such a conclusion. Shortcomings in the visualization, conceptualization and implementation of the individual programmes, piecemeal approach and lack of synergy and convergence between programmes are often cited as the reasons, but it seems that there are certain conceptual issues relating to empowerment *per se* which require to be paid immediate attention. The fundamental question to be asked is whether economic, social and political empowerment can enable, separately or taken together, women to come out of their traditional stereotyped shells? Going by the available evidence, the answer does not seem to be very positive. A number of middle class women in India have access to higher education but their access to pursuit of gainful activities depends primarily on the whims and fancies of their husbands and elders of their families. Constitutional amendments have reserved decision-making positions in local bodies to women. Nonetheless they are not always allowed to be effectively in the driving seats and are remote-controlled by men-folk. Access to education and training, employment, role in decision making at home, in the society and the national affairs at large, etc. are all no doubt important means of achieving empowerment, but they do not by themselves constitute empowerment in its entirety. This brings us to the need to look at the concept of empowerment a little more closely.

Concept of Empowerment

The dictionary meaning of empowerment is the process of challenging existing power relations and of gaining greater control over the sources of power. The concept of empowerment of women as emerged in this country is in the context of the need to inject some change in the conditions of women and the focus of the effort has been on eradicating female poverty, improving their access to resources, and thereby strengthening their position in the family and the society at large. The Indian socio-cultural structure, as elsewhere, is made up of dichotomous power structures, namely, 'strongly powerful' and 'extremely weak'. This dichotomy operates at various levels in the social structures such as the patriarchal family system, within and between the religions, geographical or ethnic groups, political structures, etc. Cutting across all these socio-cultural structures is the gender-based dichotomy of 'dominating men' who are the most powerful and the 'dominated women' who are the 'extremely weak'. The concept of empowerment emerged against this background and with the aim of balancing the powers between the two halves of the humanity – the men and the women. Though presently used in the case of gender-based power structures, the concept can equally be applied to other structures including ideologies, communities and nations. Ratnaswamy (2000) defines empowerment as the process of enhancing the capacities of a "person, community, nation, institution, organization, concept, etc. in order to allow it to grow and sustain on its own empowered capacity. He argues that "Empowerment begins to empower where there is inadequacy; it builds additional capacity to expand; it adds power to enhance capacity building; it provides opportunity to evaluate its capacity to identify for future needs; it promotes the propensity to enrich its capacity consistently and continuously; it replenishes the stock, the ability to rebuild, and the capacity to rejuvenate; it is the equity, it ensures capital for future investment; it enriches itself in the process and it is the promise of future with a present on the basis of the past." In sociological terms, empowerment thus attacks the existing power structures of the society. Sen and Dreze (1996) define empowerment as a "transformation of the structure of subordination. It implies a process of redistribution of power within and between families/societies and a process aiming at social equality." Carr *et al* (1996) opine that "the goals of women's empowerment are to challenge patriarchal ideology ...to transform the structures and institutions that reinforce and perpetuate gender discrimination and social inequality... And to enable poor women to gain access to, and control of, both material and informational resources".

Thus, from one point of view the concept of empowerment implies the existence of individuals or sections of the society who are hitherto deprived of their legitimate power in some respect or other and the felt need to alter the power equations. There has to be a flow of powers from one to another, either naturally through an approach of 'give and take' or that the powers are to be snatched away from those wielding them now and given to those perceived as the deprived. It could be a family, a section of the populace, the society at large or an organization, and such intervention may be at the level of an individual, family, group, society or nation as a whole. Several pertinent issues emerge. Will such a transformation of power structures be smooth, acceptable and sustainable? Will the snatching away of power from some lead to over-tilting the balance in such a way that the 'stronger' become the weaker? What will be the equilibrium point where the process will stop? It is also argued that the effect of any intervention to disturb the existing power structures that have been stabilized and imbedded in the societies through ages may be devastating and may lead to destabilization and disintegration of the societies. If that is the case, will the 'weaker' be always in subordination to the 'stronger'? These women's empowerment and incorporated "the building of a positive self-image, developing ability to think critically, building up group cohesion and fostering decision-making, ensuring equal participation in the process of bringing about social change and providing the wherewithal for economic independence" as important ingredients of empowerment of women.

In its broadest sense, therefore, empowerment implies an approach towards a state in which a person has the means of making the fullest use of his/her potential for realizing oneself. Empowerment, therefore, "is a holistic concept. It is multi-dimensional in its approach and involves a basic realisation and awareness of one's powers and potentialities, capabilities and competencies and of one's rights and opportunities for development in important spheres of life... Women's empowerment, therefore, may normally be described as a process by which women become able to develop their confidence and increase their inner strength and self-reliance to decide and determine their important choices in life" (Das and Mishra, 2002). Economic empowerment, improved access to education and various social services, share in political power and in decision-making positions and legislative support against exploitation, each of which addresses the issue only partially, provide an enabling environment and help in attaining the true state of empowerment. Roy (2001) described the nature of empowerment as a thing or object which "has to be cultivated through transforming the self submerged in helplessness and passivity into the self that is vibrant with hope and activeness" and advocates psychological mobilization to bring about a mental state in which one is confident, independent and has self-belief and conviction to raise voice for one's rights. While such a state of mind has to come from within one-self, it has to be supported by an enabling environment providing positive inducements to give it a practical effect.

While embarking on any venture, it is obviously wise to assess the resources at one's disposal. A mistake usually committed at this stage is to take account of external resources like finance, marketing facilities, etc. and ignore the internal resources that constitute one's self. Development of 'self' presupposes this awareness of one's traits, potentials, capabilities and abilities on the one hand and one's negative characteristics on the other. Empowerment, therefore, is giving power to self first by first realising the self, its potential, its adequacy and acknowledging its inadequacies. Once the inadequacies and shortcomings are realized and accepted, these may be overcome by overall personality development through appropriate training inputs. Thus, in our opinion, empowerment is a self-development process, which is continuous. External measures towards social, economic and political empowerment could provide only supplementary inducements and an enabling environment to speed up the process, but without self-development, the effect of such an environment would be minimal. This does not mean that self-development can come about in isolation independently of social, economic and political participation. It has to be interrelated with the processes of acquiring knowledge and skills, positive social attitudes and social participation, and ability to cope with barriers. Self-empowerment comes from within with proper social orientation and cognitive development and gets catalyzed through proper awareness generation, motivation and training inputs.

There are reasons to believe in the potential strength of the above approach to empowerment. For decades, efforts are being made both at national and international levels to empower women through creating favourable conditions for their participation on equal terms with men in social, economic and political activities, discussed at length in the earlier chapters. While these efforts have no doubt made some positive impact on the process of empowerment, the results have not been commensurate with the effort in the absence of adequate attention to the central area of self-development. Education and economic well-being have not wiped out the preference of parents to a male child. Nor have they invariably contributed to a perceptibly improved participation of women in economic and income-earning activities of their choice. The efforts externally forced through legislation to give them a role in the political process at the level of local bodies have not always borne the desired fruit. There have no doubt been many success stories in the area of women's economic empowerment through organisation, whether in the form of unionisation, co-operatives or self-help groups, but the element of success in these instances can be traced once again to the raised levels of self-belief brought about through organisational strength.

Process of Empowerment

Our argument, therefore, is that creation of an enabling environment by improving access to various types of social services, educational development, various constitutional safeguards and legislations facilitating human rights to and protection of women against crimes and injustice, by itself would not automatically lead to empowerment of women in the absence of a change in the mind-sets of the people, men and women alike, and their attitudes towards issues of gender equality in different spheres of life. Even if it does, the process would be painfully slow. If empowerment of women is defined as the process of transformation from a passive state of dependence on men in all decision-making to an active state in which women themselves, individually and collectively, decide on all matters concerning them and at all stages of life, the basic thrust towards empowerment has to come from among women themselves. They have to move from a state of mind of self-belief which modifies their personal assessment from "I cannot" to "I can" through a process of self-development. It must be stated immediately that self-belief, in the absence of opportunities to develop oneself, could lead to frustration, though many a time a person believing in her own abilities could create the necessary opportunities to flourish. What is required is, therefore, a process of self-development of women aided and supported by an enabling environment providing the necessary opportunities, with an emphasis on the former.

Such a process would be self-sustaining and self-catalysing, with greater self-belief resulting in greater ability to avail of the available opportunities, which in turn would augment confidence in self to higher levels. The transition from a state of "I cannot" to one of "I can" would make oneself believe in one's ability to pursue education, acquire vocational skills, take up wage or self-employment, gain control of incomes and assets, make own decisions in matters relating self, family, society and eventually in the political spheres. Each level of achievement in any of these spheres would be accompanied by further additions to the levels of self-belief, if necessary through appropriate personality development inputs. The main difference between this approach and that currently adopted in most programmes for empowerment of women lies in the fact that in the latter the self-development input is minimal while in the approach proposed it is accorded pride of place in the entire scheme of things. In the traditional approach, it is generally taken for granted that once facilities for education, health, skill development and employment are provided and various protective safeguards are put in place, self-development is an automatic concomitant of general development. There are, however, a few exceptions such as the programmes for promotion of self-employment activities where an element of entrepreneurship development is sometimes thrown in with beneficial results. In contrast, self-development through appropriate personality development programmes is the key element in the proposed approach. While in the normal approach, self-development is usually an implicitly expected outcome of various programmes for social, educational and political empowerment of women, what we suggest is an explicit inclusion of self-development and a linkage between personality development and other development programmes. A schematic representation of the two approaches is shown in the following diagram.

Figure 7.1: Existing Empowerment Strategy

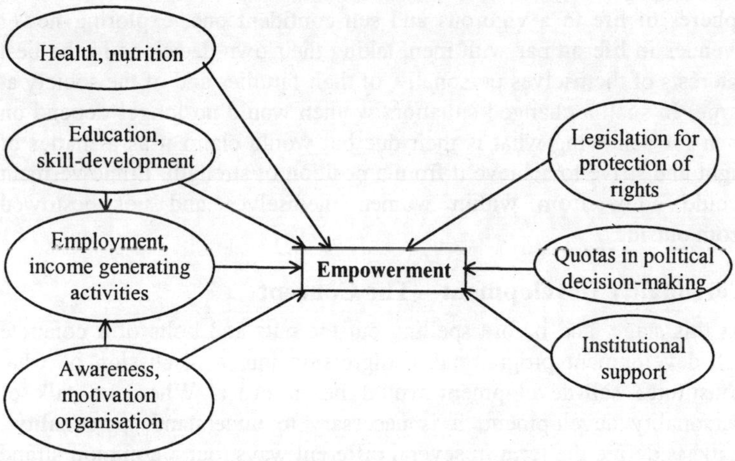

Figure 7.2 Proposed Strategy

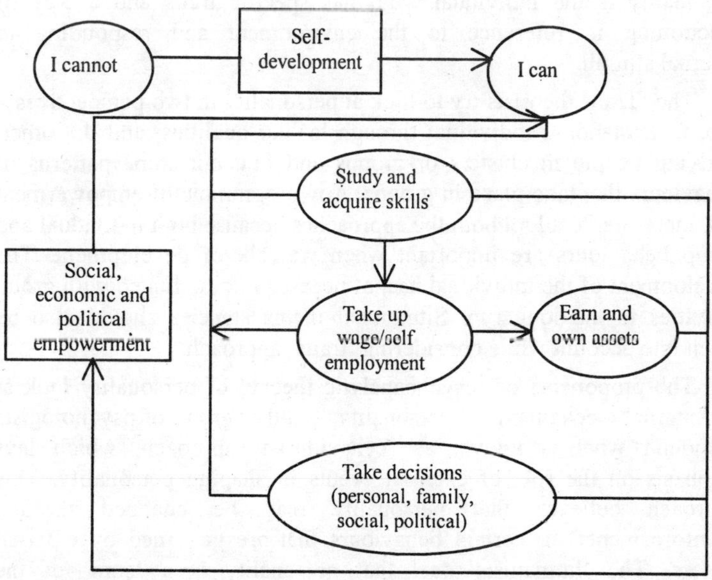

In short, the proposed strategy envisages empowerment as bringing about a change in the mind-set of women from one of diffidence and bound by those age-old traditions that have restricted women to limited spheres of life to a vigorous and self-confident one, exploring newer avenues in life on par with men, taking their own decisions in the best interests of themselves personally, of their families and of the society at large. In such a changed situation, women would no longer depend on men for achieving what is their due but would claim it as a matter of right and strive to achieve it from a position of strength. Empowerment would come from within women themselves and not bestowed from outside.

Personality Development—The Concept

At this stage, and before spelling out the nuts and bolts of a concrete self-development programme, a digression into a discussion of what constitutes self-development would be in order. When we talk of personality development, it is necessary to understand 'personality'. Experts define the term in several different ways, but a common strand running through all the definitions is that "personality usually refers to the distinctive patterns of behaviour, including thoughts and emotions) that characterize each individual's adaptation to the situations of his/her life" (Mischel, 1986). It shows that at the centre of the concept of personality is the individual, who has specific traits and a way of functioning in reference to the environment and responding to external stimuli.

The 'Trait' theorists try to look at personality in two perspectives – one, understanding individual through his/her qualities, and the other, studying people in clusters or groups and find out some patterns of behaviours that take place in groups. Any programme of empowerment has, therefore, to adopt both the approaches because both individual and group behaviours are important when we talk of development. The development of the individual has, of necessity, to be linked with group activities in the long run. Situational inconsistencies should also be taken into account while considering 'traits' approach.

The proponents of 'psychoanalytic theory' of personality look at the internal mechanisms of personality. Another group of psychologists propound what is known as 'behaviourist' approach, which lays emphasis on the role of external events in shaping personality. This approach believes that personality may be changed through 'reinforcements' to certain behaviours that are governed by external factors. The 'humanists' feel that personality is a 'sum' of the individual's personal understanding of the world, which includes his/her attitudes, beliefs, feelings, etc. Thus, this theory lays emphasis on 'self', which is a by-product of the above 'sum', and a positive sense of self leads to personality growth.

All the approaches explain personality in terms of the individual, the group and the environment. There are different methods of assessment of personality depending on the approach adopted, which include behavioural observation, interview technique, rating scales, personality inventories (like Cattel's 16 Factor Personality Test, known as 16PF), Minnesota Multiphasic Personality Inventory called MMPI, California Psychological Inventory known as CPI, etc.), and questionnaires. Another popular technique to observe inner thoughts and feelings is projective tests technique like Rorschach Ink-Blot Test and Thematic Apperception Test. There are many other verbal and non-verbal tests that measure intelligence, attitudes, aptitudes and several aspects of personality, and have been standardized in various situations and for various groups of individuals. Specially trained personnel can use these techniques and instruments.

The first stage of personality development process involves assessment, in the manner described above, of the individual's fortes and foibles, and the individual is made to realize these strengths and weaknesses. In the second stage, the attempt would be to help the individual improve in areas where he/she is good at and overcome the weaknesses to the extent possible. This would be possible, as mentioned above, through 'reinforcements' to certain behaviours that are governed by external factors. If one is dealing with groups of individuals, it would be possible, in addition, to so form the groups that the individual weaknesses and strengths balance out and the group as a whole exhibits improved personality characteristics.

A Programme of Action

What is required is a concrete plan of action to translate the above strategy into a workable system, whose objective should be to facilitate empowerment of women through appropriate programmes of self-development so that they are able to make effective contribution to decision-making on personal, family, social, economic and political issues, as a step towards full realization of the benefits of various programmes for development. It should, however, be noted that such self-development programmes are not to be visualized independently of the on-going development programmes in different sectors but have to be integrated with them to ensure higher levels of achievement of the desired goals, as otherwise the likely gap between expectations and reality could acerbate frustrations. There are, no doubt, some personality development and entrepreneur development programmes in operation but they touch only a fringe of the female population, and that too a relatively well-off fringe. In the case of poorer women, the emphasis generally has been on economic empowerment through facilitating micro-credit and relatively less, if at all, on essential self-assessment that should ideally precede. There are also, for example, some non-government organisations helping women before, during and after elections to Panchayat Raj Institutions such as Young India Project (Suvarchala, 1999) and Sanghamitra (Sivaji, 1999) in Andhra Pradesh, PRAXIS (Tuscano, 1999) in Karnataka and SHARE (Murugesan, 1999) in Tamilnadu. Again, the training agenda of only some of them includes a modicum of effort at self-development covering subjects such as confidence-building, leadership and managerial skills, with the main thrust being on providing information about aspects such as Panchayat Raj Act and administration, role of local bodies, women's rights, reservations and benefits, problems and malpractices in elections, resources of local bodies and their utilisation, etc.

Several aspects have to be considered while designing such an integrated self-development programme, namely, the population for which it is meant, its content, institutional mechanism to organise the programme and linkages with various development programmes.

Target Group

Obviously, the intended programme has to take into account the diverse needs of different sections of the female population. It has, therefore, to be a target group oriented one and there will be several target groups, such as the in-school girls, out of school girls, adult women out of labour force for various reasons, the unemployed, those employed in informal sector and those in the organised sector, women likely to join the political streams, etc. keeping in view the importance of organization of programmes for small homogeneous groups of women from the point of view of logistics, interaction within the group and with the organizers, costs and effectiveness of delivery of the service. Self-development programmes relevant to the target group have to be designed, taking into consideration the existing level of motivation within the group, level of self-confidence, strengths, weaknesses and, opportunities and threats within the relevant development programmes —educational, skill development, wage employment, self-employment, participation in political process, etc. This linkage with on-going development programmes is important for reaping quick benefits of enhanced state of self-belief likely to prevail after the process of self-development. The programme should aim at assessing the personality characteristics, strengths and weaknesses of the target group by administering appropriate psychological tests, helping the participants in developing their overall personality, providing counselling services, generating awareness about the development programme to which the personality development programme is linked and impart necessary motivation. The approach should be to provide assistance to women in a sequential manner as per the perceived needs and to equip them to negotiate their way towards their autonomy. Table 7.1 indicates the possible target groups, their developmental needs and the type of interventions needed. The target groups can be further homogenised, breaking them down by income levels and the rural-urban divide.

The quantum of effort needed to organise such a self-development programme covering all the sections of female population is immense. It would, therefore, be necessary to think of some order of priority in covering different categories of target groups. Obviously, the poor rural women have a claim for the highest priority. Also, a number of developmental programmes and poverty alleviation programmes, like the Integrated Child Development Programme, rural wage and self-employment programmes, micro-credit programmes, etc. are already directed towards this section of the population and are organised on a group basis. Further, non-government organisations are associated with their implementation. Awareness generation and motivation are often part of these programmes. The additional cost in incorporating an initial module of self-development would be minimal. Finally, rural women below poverty line constitute a substantial chunk of the female population. All these factors combine to make the category of women below poverty line in the rural areas as the ideal target group to start the programme of self-development.

Institutional Mechanism

As regards the issue of suitable institutional mechanisms for the delivery of the programme, the choice is between institutions of the state and non-governmental and voluntary organisations. While in the past most of the development programmes in the country tended to be operated by the state institutions, there is today a greater reliance on private efforts, supported and funded partly or fully by the state through the medium of non-governmental organisations. Whether it is awareness generation programmes, welfare programmes for various categories of beneficiaries, making available micro-credit to self-help groups for embarking on or enhancing the productivity of micro-enterprises, or organizing women to fight for their rights, it is the non-government organizations that have been proving effective. Enough evidence has accumulated by now to repose faith on this means of service delivery, notwithstanding occasional black sheep among such

Table 7.1: Target Groups of Women and their Development Needs

Target Group	*Development Need*
(1)	*(2)*
I. Presently out of Labour Force	
(a) girl children in school	Continuation of general/vocational education or technical training leading to productive employment/self-employment
(b) girl children not in school	Formal/non-formal education to bring them into the regular educational streams; vocational education or technical training leading to productive employment/self-employment; self-development
(c) adult females (not educated), neither working nor seeking work	Adult education and functional literacy; awareness generation; self-development; motivation to work, employment counseling; technical training leading to productive employment/self-employment;
(d) adult females (educated), neither working nor seeking work	Awareness generation; motivation to work, counseling; self-development; technical training leading to productive employment/self-employment;
II. Presently in Labour Force, Unemployed	
(a) uneducated, without skills	Functional literacy; self-development; short-term employment-oriented skill training as per market needs to improve employability; organisation into SHGs where necessary for income-generating activities; credit and related services
(b) uneducated with skills	Functional literacy; self-development; short-term employment-oriented skill training as per market needs to upgrade skills and improve employability; organisation into SHGs where necessary for income-generating activities; credit and related services
(c) educated without skills	Employment counselling; technical training (institutional or on-the-job); soft skills like communication and inter-personal relations; self-development; entrepreneurial development; organisation into SHGs where necessary for income generating activities; credit and related services
(d) educated with skills	Employment counselling; up-gradation of skills to suit market demand; soft skills; self-development; entrepreneurial development; organisation into SHGs where necessary for income generating activities; credit and related services

Contd.

(1)	*(2)*
III. Presently Employed in Unorganised Sector	
(a) uneducated, without skills	Functional literacy; self-development to enhance aspirations; short duration training in simple skills and soft skills to improve productivity
(b) uneducated with skills	Functional literacy; self-development to enhance aspirations; retraining to update skills and training in supplementary skills to improve productivity; motivation to take up income-generating activities
(c) educated without skills	Self-development to enhance aspirations; short duration training to impart vocational/technical skills; soft skills; entrepreneurial development to promote self-employment
(d) educated with skills	Self-development to enhance aspirations; retraining to update skills and training in supplementary skills to improve productivity; soft skills; entrepreneurial development to promote self-employment
IV. Presently Employed in Organised Sector	
(a) uneducated, without skills	Functional literacy; awareness generation; self-development; short duration training in simple skills and soft skills to enhance productivity
(b) uneducated with skills	Functional literacy; awareness generation; self-development; retraining to update skills and training in supplementary skills to improve productivity; motivation to take up income-genrating activities
(c) educated without skills	Self-development to enhance aspirations; short duration training to impart vocational/technical skills; soft skills; entrepreneurial development to promote self-employment
(d) educated with skills	Self-development to enhance aspirations, retraining to update skills and training in supplementary skills to improve productivity; soft skills; entrepreneurial development to promote self-employment
V Groups like elected representatives of local bodies or those contesting elections	Personality development, social skills, office administration, knowledge of development programmes

organisations. There are today between ten to twenty thousand NGOs operating country-wide in diverse development sectors with proven capabilities. It would, therefore, be best to integrate the proposed self-development activities into the on-going programmes for promotion of education, skill formation, employment, micro-credit and general awareness and counseling programme.

Experienced though the NGOs are in service delivery, many of them would be new to providing training in self-assessment using various psychological tests and personality development techniques, which is a highly skilled and professional job. Entrusting the self-development programme to them should be preceded by a comprehensive training of trainers chosen from such NGOs. It requires prior identification of reputed training institutes engaged in personality development in different parts of the country, each of which in its turn needs to identify resourceful and committed NGOs in its area and then competent and committed trainers from each of them to be imparted necessary training.

It must be recognized that self-development is not a one-time affair but needs to be pursued on a continuous basis, periodically evaluating the impact of the programme on the levels of self-confidence attained and achievements in raising the aspirations and on the behavioural patterns of the target groups. The impact on the trainers also should be similarly evaluated and the inputs they bring from their field experiences should help in further refining the training programmes. Such periodical evaluations should also be conducted by the training institutes identified above.

Linkage with Skill-Development and Income-Generation

As pointed out earlier, self-development programmes, to be attractive and successful, need to be interwoven with other developmental programmes that would bring in tangible benefits to the target group. Better employment and improved incomes would be the most tangible and satisfying results and imparting new skills or improving existing skills to make them more productive is the obvious means to achieve that. There is ample evidence to suggest that even a small increment in the skill input would enhance significantly the earning capacity. Readily marketable skills at local levels have to be identified on an area to area basis through area skill surveys and an efficient and dynamic labour market information system capturing signals of changes in demand for and supply of various skills from time to time. Such training programmes have to be very flexible to enable modifications and short notice. This is of crucial importance in the present times of changing labour markets due to the processes of globalisation and fast pace of technological innovations (Agrawal and Naqvi, 2002).

Operational Process of Empowerment Programme

A schematic representation of the essentials of implementation of self-development is shown in the diagram given below. The core elements of the process are indicated as personality development linked to income generating activities. Income generating activities have been chosen as they are the most relevant in the case of a majority of women, particularly of the poor women. Quite obviously, there are other areas that can be linked to personality development. For example, in the case of women contesting elections or the elected Sarpanches of local bodies, personality development programme has to be linked to training in office administration, social skills, budgeting, developmental needs, etc.

Figure 7.3: Operational Process of Empowerment Programme

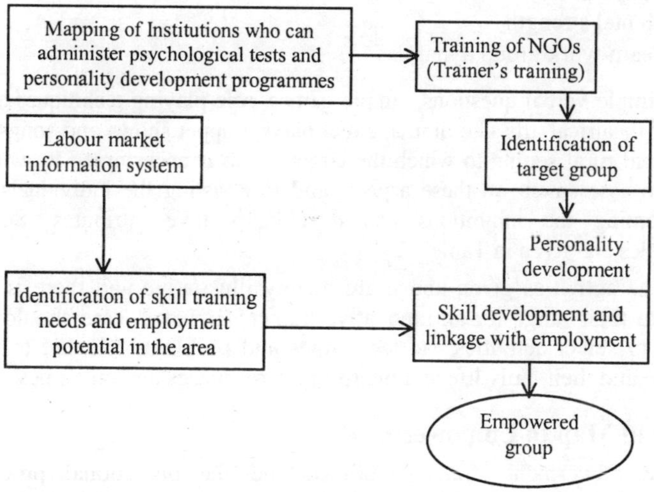

An Illustrative Programme for Personality Development

A variety of tools and techniques are readily available in published form for personality assessment and subsequent self-development in the case of educated clients. On the other hand, it requires certain amount of skillful improvisation in the case of illiterates and semi-literates who constitute the bulk of the poor women in the rural areas, the target group that should receive the highest priority. It may, therefore, be useful to explore, in terms of content, how the proposed self-development programme could be operated in their case.

Some of the essential traits that are to be looked at while undertaking personality assessment in relation to self-development are:

- Confidence
- Responsibility and reliability
- Leadership
- Self-awareness
- Risk taking ability
- Social skills
- Creativity
- Orderliness/Organisation of tasks
- Inhibition
- Calmness/tolerance to stress
- Ambition
- Orientation toward future
- Outward orientation
- Helpful attitude
- Adaptability
- Mental strength
- Team-work/group dynamics

Simple verbal questions, simple games, role-playing techniques and use of theatrical arts like drama, street plays, puppet shows and songs in the usual rural setting to which the target group is accustomed to would help in assessment on these aspects and in assisting the individuals in overcoming the inhibitions and develop positive attributes. Some examples are given in Table 7.2.

The activities given above are merely illustrative and there is no limit to their range for an innovative trainer. However, care should be taken to select activities, stories, games and problems relevant to the village and their daily life and interpret the responses and outcomes

A Road Map to Empowerment

The empowerment strategy outlined and the operational process indicated above suggest the following roadmap towards empowerment centred round development of self.

- Identification of specialist institutions in the area of personality development as core group of trainers
- Mapping of grass root level organisations that can be involved in the programme
- Training of carefully selected personnel of local level organisations by the core group trainers in personality assessment and development
- Identification of target groups based on classification by education and skill levels and activity status and assessing their needs.

- Assessment of personality characteristics, strengths and weaknesses of the target group and its members through personality tests and observations
- Designing and organising appropriate personality development programmes, taking into account the strengths and weaknesses assessed
- Providing individual or group counselling wherever required
- Exploration of the potential for income generating activities through area-specific approach and identification of specific viable activities
- Matching the identified activities with the target groups taking into account the strengths and weaknesses of the group and the requirements of the activities
- Creation of general awareness about the world of work, emerging fields of occupations, their requirements, etc.
- Motivating women to take up income generating activities, individually or collectively as a group
- Imparting specific skills needed to pursue the identified activities
- Establishing linkages with credit and marketing facilities
- Providing the group technical and operational guidance in pursuing the activity
- In case the needs of the group are non-employment related, linking self-development with the appropriate needs
- Monitoring the progress and making mid-course corrections where necessary

A national plan for personality development of women needs to be put in motion, implementation of which may be taken up in a phased manner, with special focus on the most needy women.

Conclusion

To conclude, the process of empowerment, as visualised here, is a movement towards a state of self-belief among women enabling them to decide for themselves in matters relating to them, their families and the community at large in various fields and in an environment of opportunities at par with men. Development programmes in education, health, employment and other areas increasingly provide that environment in which women with self-confidence can avail of the opportunities that present themselves effectively and advance towards equality with men in all spheres of life. Gender parity so brought about in the main by women acting for themselves and evolving from inner strengths is likely to be more effective, self-sustaining and satisfying.

Table 7.2: Personality Assessment and Development of Rural Uneducated – Some Examples

Objectives	*Technique*	*Outcomes and Inferences*
(1)	*(2)*	*(3)*
(a) Self-awareness	*Ask the individuals to* - Mention five good points about yourself - Mention five negative points about yourself - Name five activities you can perform well - Name two activities you cannot perform - Tell five things you like most *If they are not able to tell, assist them in the process.* *Give them tasks like putting thread in the needle and tell the persons completing quickly that they could do it* *Give an exercise like* - Name five colours you can see immediately. *The tendency is to look outside to locate the colours and not towards themselves and mention the colours of their dresses*	Indicates level of self-belief of the individual
(b) Awareness of others	*Ask the individuals to* - Tell about the strengths of each of the other members of the group	Indicates the perception of the individual about others

Contd.

(1)	(2)	(3)
(c) Problem solving and getting along with others	*Give an exercise like* - Comb hair without taking your hands behind yourself - Distribute among yourselves these matchsticks/flowers/stones/any other item (keep the total number indivisible by the number of persons in the group and observe how they distribute.	It is expected that they would comb hair of each other indicating ability to think of a solution to the problem and inclination for mutual cooperation In the second exercise, if after even distribution, the remaining are kept apart, it may be used to introduce concept of saving
(d) Risk taking	*Ask the individuals to play* - <u>Ring toss game</u>: *Place several objects in front of the individual at gradually increasing distances and ask the individual to throw a ring around one of the objects, with appropriate costs and rewards depending on the distance to which the ring is aimed at and successfully thrown* - <u>Paper Boats game</u>: *Teach the group how to make paper boats and ask them to make as many boats as possible within a specified time. The number of boats a person can make within the time limit should be announced in advance by the individual. Successful completion will earn rewards*	Indicates the extent to which the individual can commit himself to goals in the face of risks involved
(e) Leadership	*Ask the group to* - Discuss about the problems of the village - Perform a group task relating to the village *Show how a leader emerges during the discussion*	Indicates extent of shyness, leadership qualities, initiative, public speaking

Contd.

(1)	*(2)*	*(3)*
(f) Development of creative thinking	*Give an exercise like* - A lion, a goat and a bundle of grass have to be taken across a river in the only boat available by a boatman. Only one of the three can be taken at a time. The lion eats goat and the goat eats grass, if left alone by the boatman. (The lion does not eat the boatman!). How can they cross?	Indicates creative thinking in solving problems
(g) Development of positive thinking	*Ask the individuals to prepare a story from words like* - Snake, child and pot	Some possible stories are a) the child went to the pot to take out rice from it. There was a snake nearby which attacked and killed the child; b) The child saw a snake near the pot and called out to a man who caught hold of the snake and left it in the forest. The stories may be analysed to attitudes. The first story indicates a negative attitude while the second a positive attitude.
(h) Business skills	*Ask the individuals to* - Solve a simple profit and loss problem - Select a venture prevalent in the village, list activities involved and indicate how to organise *Guide them with suggestions*	Indicates entrepreneurial skills
(i) Development of social skills and overcoming shyness	*Ask the individuals to* - Tell about the strengths of the other members of the group - Role-play one as the leader of the group presenting their problems/credit needs to the other as Sarpanch/ bank officer.	Observe how the Sarpanch refuses to listen or the bank manager refuses to give loan and how the leader tries to convince.

Contd.

(1)	(2)	(3)
	The exercise may be made more interesting by putting a turban on the person playing Sarpanch. The roles can be reversed in the second attempt. *Ask them to play the game* - Pass a ring or any suitable object to the neighbour while music goes on. As soon as the music stops the person who has an object has to do what she is told to do – sing, dance, laugh loudly, act like someone, etc. Ask the group to come one by one to the dais, and - Speak on a specific problem of the village or any subject of her choice	

It does not, however, mean that empowerment of women does not depend on what happens to the male half of the society and can be brought about irrespective of the attitudes and responses of the men. It has already been said that the objective of empowerment is to bring about gender parity through a process characterised by mutual respect among men and women for each other's capabilities and giving each other the fullest opportunity to develop and exploit these capabilities for the benefit of the family, community and the country. No empowerment of women will be easy, if at all possible, without a realisation among the men of the inequities and inequalities that characterise the present society in relation to women's rights. Traditional attitudes of men in relation to themselves and of women have to change, as much as those of women. The difficulty in passing the bill to reserve parliamentary seats for women is an example of the fact that they have not changed yet to the desired degree. In fact, if right attitudes prevail and if women increasingly believe in themselves, there would not be any need for such reservations in any sphere of activity. Empowerment, then, would be a spontaneous and self-sustaining process, needing no external interventions or stimuli.

The approach towards empowerment of women, therefore, needs to be a holistic one, with self-development taking the centre-stage. The educational system has to be geared towards the objective of promoting attitudinal changes in the society as to how it views the role of women. Its objective should be to build up personality, equally among men and women, which is characterised by self-confidence and by a scientific spirit that does not allow one to accept traditions without questioning their validity and being satisfied about it. Government's programmes—legislative and developmental—play an important part in the interim. Non-governmental agencies, in particular organisations working for the betterment of women, have to be the agents of the social change, by spreading awareness, by promoting right attitudes and, of course, by implementing developmental programmes. All the social partners have their own important role to play in bringing about a harmonious transition to a gender-egalitarian environment. It may sound too idealistic but worth aspiring for.

We conclude with the words of the Nobel Laureate Amartya Sen, "The elimination of needless inequalities in opportunities must be seen as objectives that are valued for their own sake."

Annexures

Annexure 1

Women's Access to the Rights to Vote and to Stand for Elections: World Chronology

Period	*Countries Granting Rights*
(1)	*(2)*
Before 1900	United States (to stand for election) (1788); New Zealand (to vote) (1893)
1900 - 1924	Australia* (1902); Finland (1906); Norway (to stand for election)* (1907); Norway *(1913); Denmark (1915); Iceland (1915); Canada (to vote)* (1917); Netherlands (to stand for election) (1917); Austria (1918); Canada (to vote) H (1918); Estonia (1918); Georgia* (1918); Germany (1918); Ireland * (1918); Kyrgystan (1918); Latvia (1918); Poland (1918); Russian Federation (1918); United Kingdom* (1918); Belarus (1919); Belgium(to vote)* (1919); Luxembourg (1919); Netherlands (to vote) (1919); New Zealand (to stand for4 election) (1919); Sweden* (1919);, Ukraine (1919); Albania (1920); Canada (to stand for election) (1920), Czech Republic (1920); Slovakia (1920); United States (to vote); Armenia (1921); Azerbaijan (1921); Belgium (to stand for election) (1921); Georgia** (1921); Lithuania (1921); Sweden* (1921); Kazakstan* (1924); Mongolia (1924); Saint Lucia (1924); Tajikistan (1924)
1925 - 1949	Turkmenistan (1927); Ireland** (1928; United Kingdom** (1928); Ecuador H (1929); Romania (1929); South Africa (whites) (1930); Turkey (to vote) (1930); Chile* (1931); Portugal* (1931); Spain (1931); Sri Lanka (1931); Maldives (1932); Thailand (1932); Uruguay (1932); Brazil (1934); Cuba (1934); Portugal* (1934); Turkey (to stand for election) (1934); Myanmar (to vote) (1935); Philippines (1937); Bolivia* (1938); Uzbekistan (1938); El Salvador (to vote) (1939); Panama* (1941); Dominican Republic (1942); Bulgaria (1944); France (1944); Jamaica (1944); Croatia (1945); Guyana (to stand for election) (1945); Indonesia (1945); Italy (1945); Japan* (1945); Senegal (1945); Slovenia (1945); Togo (1945); Cameroon (1946); Democratic Peoples' Republic of Korea (1946); Djibouti

Contd.

(1)	*(2)*
	(to vote) (1946); Guatemala (1946); Liberia (1946); Myanmar (to stand for election) (1946); Panama** (1946); Romania** (1946); Macedonia (1946); Trinidad and Tobago (1946); Venezuela (1946); Vietnam (1946); Yugoslavia (1946); Argentina (1947); Japan** (1947); Malta (1947); Mexico (to vote) (1947); Pakistan (1947); Singapore (1947); Belgium** (1948); Israel (1948); Niger (1948); Republic of Korea (1948); Seychelles (1948); Suriname (1948); Bosnia and Herzegovina (1949); Chile** (1949); China (1949); Costa Rica (1949); Syrian Arab Republic (to vote) (1949)
1950- 1974	Barbados (1950); Canada** (to vote) (1950); Haiti (1950); India (1950); Antigua and Barbuda (1951); Dominica (1951); Grenada (1951); Nepal (1951); Saint Kitts and Nevis (1951); Saint Vincent and the Grenadines (1951); Bolivia* (1952); Cote d'Ivoire (1952); Greece (1952); Lebanon (1952); Bhutan 91953); Guyana (to vote) (1953); Hungary (to vote) (1953); Mexico (to stand for election) (1953); Syrian Arab Republic 88 (1953); Belize (1954); Colombia (1954); Ghana (1954); Cambodia (1955); Eritrea (1955); Ethiopia (1955); Honduras (1955); Nicaragua (1955); Peru (1955); Benin (1956); Comoros (1956); Egypt (1956); Gabon (1956); Mali (1956); Mauritius (1956); Somalia (1956); Malaysia (1957); Zimbabwe (to vote) (1957); Burkina Faso (1958); Chad (1958); Guinea (1958); Hungary (to stand for election) (1958); Lao Peoples Democratic Republic (1958); Nigeria (1958); Madagascar (1959); San Marino (to vote) (1959); Tunisia (1959); United Republic of Tanzania (1959); Canada (to stand for election) (1960); Cyprus (1960); Gambia (1960); Tonga (1960); Bahamas* (1961); Burundi (1961); El Salvador (to stand for election) (1961); Malawi (1961); Mauritania (1961): Paraguay (1961); Rwanda (1961); Sierra Leone (1961); Algeria (1962); Australia** (1962), Monaco (1962); Uganda (1962); Zambia (1962); Congo (1963); Equatorial Guinea (1963); Fiji (1963); Iran (Islamic Republic of) (1963); Kenya (1963); Moro0cco (1963); Papua New Guinea (to stand for election) (1963); Bahamas** (1964); Libyan Arab Jamahiriya (1964); Papua New Guinea (to vote) (1964); Sudan (1964); Afghanistan (1965); Botswana (1965); Lesotho (1965); Ecuador** (1967); Kiribati (1967): Tuvalu (1967): Yemen (People's Democratic Republic of) (1967); Democratic Republic of Congo (to vote) (1967); Nauru (1968); Swaziland (1968); Andorra (to vote) (1970); Yemen (Arab Republic) (1970); Democratic Republic of Congo (to stand for election) (1970); Switzerland (1971); Bangladesh (1972); Andorra (to stand for election) (1973); Bahrain (1973); San Marino (to stand for election) (1973); Jordan 91974); Solomon Islands (1974)

Contd.

(1)	*(2)*
1975-1994	Angola 91975); Cape Verde 91975); Mozambique (1975); Sao Tome' and Principe (1975); Vanuatu (1975); Portugal** (1976); Guinea Bissau (1977); Republic of Moldova * (1978); Zimbabwe (to stand for election) (1978); Marshall Islands (1979); Micronesia (Fed. States) (1979); Palau (1979); Iraq (1980); Vanuatu** (1980); Liechtenstein (1984); South Africa (coloureds + Indians) (1984); Central African Republic (1986); Djibouti (to stand for election) (1986); Namibia (1989); Samoa (1990); Kazakstan (1994); Republic of Moldova* (1994); South Africa (blacks) (1994)
Yet to recognize women's right to vote and to stand for election	Kuwait and United Arab Emirates

Source: Inter-Parliamentary Union Study No. 28, 1997; "Men and Women in Politics: Democracy Still in the Making" cited in www.idea.int/women/parl/ch6. table8.htm

* Right subject to conditions or restrictions ** Restrictions or conditions lifted

Annexure 2

Women in Parliament (1945 – 1995)—Global Picture

Year	*No. of parliaments*	*Percentage of women members*	*Percentage of women senators*
1945	26	3.0	2.2
1955	61	7.5	7.7
1965	94	8.1	9.3
1975	115	10.9	10.5
1985	136	12.0	12.7
1995	176	11.6	9.4

Source: Inter-Parliamentary Union Study No. 28, 1997; "Men and Women in Politics: Democracy Still in the Making" cited in www.idea.int/women/parl/ch6_table9.htm

of their marital status, on a basis of equality of men and women, of human rights and fundamental freedoms in the political, economic, social, cultural, civil or any other field.

Article 2

States Parties condemn discrimination against women in all its forms, agree to pursue by all appropriate means and without delay a policy of eliminating discrimination against women and, to this end, undertake:

To embody the principle of the equality of men and women in their national constitutions or other appropriate legislation if not yet incorporated therein and to ensure, through law and other appropriate means, the practical realization of this principle;

To adopt appropriate legislative and other measures, including sanctions where appropriate, prohibiting all discrimination against women;

To establish legal protection of the rights of women on an equal basis with men and to ensure through competent national tribunals and other public institutions the effective protection of women against any act of discrimination;

To refrain from engaging in any act or practice of discrimination against women and to ensure that public authorities and institutions shall act in conformity with this obligation;

To take all appropriate measures to eliminate discrimination against women by any person, organization or enterprise;

To take all appropriate measures, including legislation, to modify or abolish existing laws, regulations, customs and practices which constitute discrimination against women;

To repeal all national penal provisions which constitute discrimination against women.

Article 3

States Parties shall take in all fields, in particular in the political, social, economic and cultural fields, all appropriate measures, including legislation, to ensure the full development and advancement of women, for the purpose of guaranteeing them the exercise and enjoyment of human rights and fundamental freedoms on a basis of equality with men.

Article 4

1. Adoption by States Parties of temporary special measures aimed at accelerating de facto equality between men and women shall not be considered discrimination as defined in the present Convention, but shall in no way entail as a consequence the maintenance of unequal or separate standards; these measures shall be discontinued when

the objectives of equality of opportunity and treatment have been achieved.

2. Adoption by States Parties of special measures, including those measures contained in the present Convention, aimed at protecting maternity shall not be considered discriminatory.

Article 5

States Parties shall take all appropriate measures:

To modify the social and cultural patterns of conduct of men and women, with a view to achieving the elimination of prejudices and customary and all other practices which are based on the idea of the inferiority or the superiority of either of the sexes or on stereotyped roles for men and women;

To ensure that family education includes a proper understanding of maternity as a social function and the recognition of the common responsibility of men and women in the upbringing and development of their children, it being understood that the interest of the children is the primordial consideration in all cases.

Article 6

States Parties shall take all appropriate measures, including legislation, to suppress all forms of traffic in women and exploitation or prostitution of women.

Part II

Article 7

States Parties shall take all appropriate measures to eliminate discrimination against women in the political and public life of the country and, in particular, shall ensure to women, on equal terms with men, the right:

1. To vote in all elections and public referenda and to be eligible for election to all publicly elected bodies;
2. To participate in the formulation of government policy and the implementation thereof and to hold public office and perform all public functions at all levels of government;
3. To participate in non-governmental organizations and associations concerned with the public and political life of the country.

Article 8

States Parties shall take all appropriate measures to ensure to women, on equal terms with men and without any discrimination, the opportunity to represent their Governments at the international level and to participate in the work of international organizations.

(d) To provide special protection to women during pregnancy in types of work proved to be harmful to them.

3. Protective legislation relating to matters covered in this article shall be reviewed periodically in the light of scientific and technological knowledge and shall be revised, repealed or extended as necessary.

Article 12

1. States Parties shall take all appropriate measures to eliminate discrimination against women in the field of health care in order to ensure, on a basis of equality of men and women, access to health care services, including those related to family planning.
2. Notwithstanding the provisions of paragraph 1 of this article, States Parties shall ensure to women appropriate services in connexion with pregnancy, confinement and the post-natal period, granting free services where necessary, as well as adequate nutrition during pregnancy and lactation.

Article 13

States Parties shall take all appropriate measures to eliminate discrimination against women in other areas of economic and social life in order to ensure, on a basis of equality of men and women, the same rights, in particular:

The right to family benefits;

The right to bank loans, mortgages and other forms of financial credit;

The right to participate in recreational activities, sports and all aspects of cultural life.

Article 14

1. States Parties shall take into account the particular problems faced by rural women and the significant roles which rural women play in the economic survival of their families, including their work in the non-monetized sectors of the economy, and shall take all appropriate measures to ensure the application of the provisions of this Convention to women in rural areas.
2. States Parties shall take all appropriate measures to eliminate discrimination against women in rural areas in order to ensure, on a basis of equality of men and women, that they participate in and benefit from rural development and, in particular, shall ensure to such women the right:

   (a) To participate in the elaboration and implementation of development planning at all levels;

(b) To have access to adequate health care facilities, including information, counselling and services in family planning;

(c) To benefit directly from social security programmes;

(d) To obtain all types of training and education, formal and non-formal, including that relating to functional literacy, as well as, *inter alia*, the benefit of all community and extension services, in order to increase their technical proficiency;

(e) To organize self-help groups and co-operatives in order to obtain equal access to economic opportunities through employment or self-employment;

(f) To participate in all community activities;

(g) To have access to agricultural credit and loans, marketing facilities, appropriate technology and equal treatment in land and agrarian reform as well as in land resettlement schemes;

(h) To enjoy adequate living conditions, particularly in relation to housing, sanitation, electricity and water supply, transport and communications.

Part IV

Article 15

1. States Parties shall accord to women equality with men before the law.
2. States Parties shall accord to women, in civil matters, a legal capacity identical to that of men and the same opportunities to exercise that capacity. In particular, they shall give women equal rights to conclude contracts and to administer property and shall treat them equally in all stages of procedure in courts and tribunals.
3. States Parties agree that all contracts and all other private instruments of any kind with a legal effect which is directed at restricting the legal capacity of women shall be deemed null and void.
4. States Parties shall accord to men and women the same rights with regard to the law relating to the movement of persons and the freedom to choose their residence and domicile.

Article 16

1. States Parties shall take all appropriate measures to eliminate discrimination against women in all matters relating to marriage and family relations and in particular shall ensure, on a basis of equality of men and women:

   (a) The same right to enter into marriage;

(b) The same right freely to choose a spouse and to enter into marriage only with their free and full consent;

(c) The same rights and responsibilities during marriage and at its dissolution;

(d) The same rights and responsibilities as parents, irrespective of their marital status, in matters relating to their children; in all cases the interests of the children shall be paramount;

(e) The same rights to decide freely and responsibly on the number and spacing of their children and to have access to the information, education and means to enable them to exercise these rights;

(f) The same rights and responsibilities with regard to guardianship, wardship, trusteeship and adoption of children, or similar institutions where these concepts exist in national legislation; in all cases the interests of the children shall be paramount;

(g) The same personal rights as husband and wife, including the right to choose a family name, a profession and an occupation;

(h) The same rights for both spouses in respect of the ownership, acquisition, management, administration, enjoyment and disposition of property, whether free of charge or for a valuable consideration.

2. The betrothal and the marriage of a child shall have no legal effect, and all necessary action, including legislation, shall be taken to specify a minimum age for marriage and to make the registration of marriages in an official registry compulsory.

Part V

Article 17

1. For the purpose of considering the progress made in the implementation of the present Convention, there shall be established a Committee on the Elimination of Discrimination against Women (hereinafter referred to as the Committee) consisting, at the time of entry into force of the Convention, of eighteen and, after ratification of or accession to the Convention by the thirty-fifth State Party, of twenty-three experts of high moral standing and competence in the field covered by the Convention. The experts shall be elected by States Parties from among their nationals and shall serve in their personal capacity, consideration being given to equitable geographical distribution and to the representation of the different forms of civilization as well as the principal legal systems.

2. The members of the Committee shall be elected by secret ballot from a list of persons nominated by States Parties. Each State Party may nominate one person from among its own nationals.
3. The initial election shall be held six months after the date of the entry into force of the present Convention. At least three months before the date of each election the Secretary-General of the United Nations shall address a letter to the States Parties inviting them to submit their nominations within two months. The Secretary-General shall prepare a list in alphabetical order of all persons thus nominated, indicating the States Parties which have nominated them, and shall submit it to the States Parties.
4. Elections of the members of the Committee shall be held at a meeting of States Parties convened by the Secretary-General at United Nations Headquarters. At that meeting, for which two thirds of the States Parties shall constitute a quorum, the persons elected to the Committee shall be those nominees who obtain the largest number of votes and an absolute majority of the votes of the representatives of States Parties present and voting.
5. The members of the Committee shall be elected for a term of four years. However, the terms of nine of the members elected at the first election shall expire at the end of two years; immediately after the first election the names of these nine members shall be chosen by lot by the Chairman of the Committee.
6. The election of the five additional members of the Committee shall be held in accordance with the provisions of paragraphs 2, 3 and 4 of this article, following the thirty-fifth ratification or accession. The terms of two of the additional members elected on this occasion shall expire at the end of two years, the names of these two members having been chosen by lot by the Chairman of the Committee.
7. For the filling of casual vacancies, the State Party whose expert has ceased to function as a member of the Committee shall appoint another expert from among its nationals, subject to the approval of the Committee.
8. The members of the Committee shall, with the approval of the General Assembly, receive emoluments from United Nations resources on such terms and conditions as the Assembly may decide, having regard to the importance of the Committee's responsibilities.
9. The Secretary-General of the United Nations shall provide the necessary staff and facilities for the effective performance of the functions of the Committee under the present Convention.

Article 18

1. States Parties undertake to submit to the Secretary-General of the United Nations, for consideration by the Committee, a report on the legislative, judicial, administrative or other measures which they have adopted to give effect to he provisions of the present Convention and on the progress made in this respect:
   (a) Within one year after the entry into force for the State concerned; and
   (b) Thereafter at least every four years and further whenever the Committee so requests.
2. Reports may indicate factors and difficulties affecting the degree of fulfilment of obligations under the present Convention.

Article 19

1. The Committee shall adopt its own rules of procedure.
2. The Committee shall elect its officers for a term of two years.

Article 20

1. The Committee shall normally meet for a period of not more than two weeks annually in order to consider the reports submitted in accordance with article 18 of the present Convention.
2. The meetings of the Committee shall normally be held at United Nations Headquarters or at any other convenient place as determined by the Committee.

Article 21

1. The Committee shall, through the Economic and Social Council, report annually to the General Assembly of the United Nations on its activities and may make suggestions and general recommendations based on the examination of reports and information received from the States Parties. Such suggestions and general recommendations shall be included in the report of the Committee together with comments, if any, from States Parties.
2. The Secretary-General shall transmit the reports of the Committee to the Commission on the Status of Women for its information.

Article 22

The specialized agencies shall be entitled to be represented at the consideration of the implementation of such provisions of the present Convention as fall within the scope of their activities. The Committee may invite the specialized agencies to submit reports on the implementation of the Convention in areas falling within the scope of their activities.

Part VI

Article 23

Nothing in this Convention shall affect any provisions that are more conducive to the achievement of equality between men and women which may be contained:

In the legislation of a State Party; or

In any other international convention, treaty or agreement in force for that State.

Article 24

States Parties undertake to adopt all necessary measures at the national level aimed at achieving the full realization of the rights recognized in the present Convention.

Article 25

1. The present Convention shall be open for signature by all States.
2. The Secretary-General of the United Nations is designated as the depositary of the present Convention.
3. The present Convention is subject to ratification. Instruments of ratification shall be deposited with the Secretary-General of the United Nations.
4. The present Convention shall be open to accession by all States. Accession shall be effected by the deposit of an instrument of accession with the Secretary-General of the United Nations.

Article 26

1. A request for the revision of the present Convention may be made at any time by any State Party by means of a notification in writing addressed to the Secretary-General of the United Nations.
2. The General Assembly of the United Nations shall decide upon the steps, if any, to be taken in respect of such a request.

Article 27

1. The present Convention shall enter into force on the thirtieth day after the date of deposit with the Secretary-General of the United Nations of the twentieth instrument of ratification or accession.
2. For each State ratifying the present Convention or acceding to it after the deposit of the twentieth instrument of ratification or accession, the Convention shall enter into force on the thirtieth day after the date of the deposit of its own instrument of ratification or accession.

Article 28

1. The Secretary-General of the United Nations shall receive and circulate to all States the text of reservations made by States at the time of ratification or accession.
2. A reservation incompatible with the object and purpose of the present Convention shall not be permitted.
3. Reservations may be withdrawn at any time by notification to this effect addressed to the Secretary-General of the United Nations, who shall then inform all States thereof. Such notification shall take effect on the date on which it is received.

Article 29

1. Any dispute between two or more States Parties concerning the interpretation or application of the present Convention which is not settled by negotiation shall, at the request of one of them, be submitted to arbitration. If within six months from the date of the request for arbitration the parties are unable to agree on the organization of the arbitration, any one of those parties may refer the dispute to the International Court of Justice by request in conformity with the Statute of the Court.
2. Each State Party may at the time of signature or ratification of this Convention or accession thereto declare that it does not consider itself bound by paragraph 1 of this article. The other States Parties shall not be bound by that paragraph with respect to any State Party which has made such a reservation.
3. Any State Party which has made a reservation in accordance with paragraph 2 of this article may at any time withdraw that reservation by notification to the Secretary-General of the United Nations.

Article 30

The present Convention, the Arabic, Chinese, English, French, Russian and Spanish texts of which are equally authentic, shall be deposited with the Secretary-General of the United Nations.

In witness whereof the undersigned, duly authorized, have signed the present Convention.

Annexure 4

National Policy for The Empowerment of Women—2001

Introduction

1.1 The principle of gender equality is enshrined in the Indian Constitution in its Preamble, Fundamental Rights, Fundamental Duties and Directive Principles. The Constitution not only grants equality to women, but also empowers the State to adopt measures of positive discrimination in favour of women.

1.2 Within the framework of a democratic polity, our laws, development policies, Plans and programmes have aimed at women's advancement in different spheres. From the Fifth Five Year Plan (1974-78) onwards there has been a marked shift in the approach to women's issues from welfare to development. In recent years, the empowerment of women has been recognized as the central issue in determining the status of women. The National Commission for Women was set up by an Act of Parliament in 1990 to safeguard the rights and legal entitlements of women. The 73rd and 74th Amendments (1993) to the Constitution of India have provided for reservation of seats in the local bodies of Panchayats and Municipalities for women, laying a strong foundation for their participation in decision making at the local levels.

1.3 India has also ratified various international conventions and human rights instruments committed to secure equal rights of women. Key among them is the ratification of the Convention on Elimination of All Forms of Discrimination Against Women (CEDAW) in 1993.

1.4 The Mexico Plan of Action (1975), the Nairobi Forward Looking Strategies (1985), the Beijing Declaration as well as the Platform for Action (1995) and the Outcome Document adopted by the UNGA Session on Gender Equality and Development & Peace for the 21st century, titled "Further actions and initiatives to implement the Beijing Declaration and the Platform for Action" have been unreservedly endorsed by India for appropriate follow up.

1.5 The Policy also takes note of the commitments of the Ninth Five Year Plan and the other Sectoral Policies relating to empowerment of women.

1.6 The women's movement and a wide-spread network of non-Government Organisations which have strong grass-roots presence and deep insight into women's concerns have contributed in inspiring initiatives for the empowerment of women.

1.7 However, there still exists a wide gap between the goals enunciated in the Constitution, legislation, policies, plans, programmes, and related mechanisms on the one hand and the situational reality of the status of women in India, on the other. This has been analyzed extensively in the Report of the Committee on the Status of Women in India, "Towards Equality", 1974 and highlighted in the National Perspective Plan for Women, 1988-2000, the Shramshakti Report, 1988 and the "Platform for Action, Five Years After- An assessment"

1.8 Gender disparity manifests itself in various forms, the most obvious being the trend of continuously declining female ratio in the population in the last few decades. Social stereotyping and violence at the domestic and societal levels are some of the other manifestations. Discrimination against girl children, adolescent girls and women persists in parts of the country.

1.9 The underlying causes of gender inequality are related to social and economic structure, which is based on informal and formal norms, and practices.

1.10 Consequently, the access of women, particularly those belonging to weaker sections, including Scheduled Castes/Scheduled Tribes/ Other Backward Classes and minorities, majority of whom are in the rural areas and in the informal, unorganized sector to education, health and productive resources, among others, is inadequate. Therefore, they remain largely marginalized, poor and socially excluded.

Goal and Objectives

1.11 The goal of this Policy is to bring about the advancement, development and empowerment of women. The Policy will be widely disseminated so as to encourage active participation of all stakeholders for achieving its goals. Specifically, the objectives of this Policy include:

(a) Creating an environment through positive economic and social policies for full development of women to enable them to realize their full potential.

(b) The de-jure and de-facto enjoyment of all human rights and fundamental freedom by women on equal basis with men in all spheres – political, economic, social, cultural and civil.

(c) Equal access to participation and decision making of women in social, political and economic life of the nation.

(d) Equal access to women to health care, quality education at all levels, career and vocational guidance, employment, equal remuneration, occupational health and safety, social security and public office etc.

(e) Strengthening legal systems aimed at elimination of all forms of discrimination against women.

(f) Changing societal attitudes and community practices by active participation and involvement of both men and women.

(g) Mainstreaming a gender perspective in the development process.

(h) Elimination of discrimination and all forms of violence against women and the girl child; and

(i) Building and strengthening partnerships with civil society, particularly women's organizations.

Policy Prescriptions

Judicial Legal Systems

2.1 Legal-judicial system will be made more responsive and gender sensitive to women's needs, especially in cases of domestic violence and personal assault. New laws will be enacted and existing laws reviewed to ensure that justice is quick and the punishment meted out to the culprits is commensurate with the severity of the offence.

2.2 At the initiative of and with the full participation of all stakeholders including community and religious leaders, the Policy would aim to encourage changes in personal laws such as those related to marriage, divorce, maintenance and guardianship so as to eliminate discrimination against women.

2.3 The evolution of property rights in a patriarchal system has contributed to the subordinate status of women. The Policy would aim to encourage changes in laws relating to ownership of property and inheritance by evolving consensus in order to make them gender just.

Decision Making

3.1 Women's equality in power sharing and active participation in decision making, including decision making in political process at all levels will be ensured for the achievement of the goals of empowerment. All measures will be taken to guarantee women equal access to and full participation in decision making bodies at every level, including the legislative, executive, judicial, corporate, statutory bodies, as also the advisory Commissions, Committees, Boards, Trusts etc. Affirmative action such as reservations/quotas, including in higher legislative bodies, will be considered whenever necessary on a time bound. basis. Women–friendly personnel policies will also be drawn up to encourage women to participate effectively in the developmental process.

Mainstreaming a Gender Perspective in the Development Process

4.1 Policies, programmes and systems will be established to ensure mainstreaming of women's perspectives in all developmental processes, as catalysts, participants and recipients. Wherever there are gaps in policies and programmes, women specific interventions would be undertaken to bridge these. Coordinating and monitoring mechanisms will also be devised to assess from time to time the progress of such mainstreaming mechanisms. Women's issues and concerns as a result will specially be addressed and reflected in all concerned laws, sectoral policies, plans and programmes of action.

Economic Empowerment of Women

Poverty Eradication

5.1 Since women comprise the majority of the population below the poverty line and are very often in situations of extreme poverty, given the harsh realities of intra-household and social discrimination, macro economic policies and poverty eradication programmes will specifically address the needs and problems of such women. There will be improved implementation of programmes which are already women oriented with special targets for women. Steps will be taken for mobilization of poor women and convergence of services, by offering them a range of economic and social options, along with necessary support measures to enhance their capabilities.

Micro Credit

5.2 In order to enhance women's access to credit for consumption and production, the establishment of new, and strengthening of existing micro-credit mechanisms and micro-finance institution will be undertaken so that the outreach of credit is enhanced. Other supportive measures would be taken to ensure adequate flow of credit through extant financial institutions and banks, so that all women below poverty line have easy access to credit.

Women and Economy

5.3 Women's perspectives will be included in designing and implementing macro-economic and social policies by institutionalizing their participation in such processes. Their contribution to socio-economic development as producers and workers will be recognized in the formal and informal sectors (including home based workers) and appropriate policies relating to employment and to her working conditions will be drawn up. Such measures could include:

(a) Reinterpretation and redefinition of conventional concepts of work wherever necessary *e.g.* in the Census records, to reflect women's contribution as producers and workers.

(b) Preparation of satellite and national accounts.

(c) Development of appropriate methodologies for undertaking (i) and (ii) above.

Globalization

5.4 Globalization has presented new challenges for the realization of the goal of women's equality, the gender impact of which has not been systematically evaluated fully. However, from the micro-level studies that were commissioned by the Department of Women and Child Development, it is evident that there is a need for re-framing policies for access to employment and quality of employment. Benefits of the growing global economy have been unevenly distributed leading to wider economic disparities, the feminization of poverty, increased gender inequality through often deteriorating working conditions and unsafe working environment, especially in the informal economy and rural areas. Strategies will be designed to enhance the capacity of women and empower them to meet the negative social and economic impacts, which may flow from the globalization process.

Women and Agriculture

5.5 In view of the critical role of women in the agriculture and allied sectors, as producers, concentrated efforts will be made to ensure that benefits of training, extension and various programmes will reach them in proportion to their numbers. The programmes for training women in soil conservation, social forestry, dairy development and other occupations allied to agriculture like horticulture, livestock including small animal husbandry, poultry, fisheries etc. will be expanded to benefit women workers in the agriculture sector.

Women and Industry

5.6 The important role played by women in electronics, information technology and food processing and agro industry and textiles has been crucial to the development of these sectors. They would be given comprehensive support in terms of labour legislation, social security and other support services to participate in various industrial sectors.

5.7 Women at present cannot work in night shift in factories even if they wish to. Suitable measures will be taken to enable women to work on the night shift in factories. This will be accompanied with support services for security, transportation etc.

Support Services

5.8 The provision of support services for women, like child care facilities, including crèches at work places and educational institutions, homes for the aged and the disabled will be expanded and improved to create an enabling environment and to ensure their full cooperation in social, political and economic life. Women-friendly personnel policies will also be drawn up to encourage women to participate effectively in the developmental process.

Social Empowerment of Women

Education

6.1 Equal access to education for women and girls will be ensured. Special measures will be taken to eliminate discrimination, universalize education, eradicate illiteracy, create a gender-sensitive educational system, increase enrolment and retention rates of girls and improve the quality of education to facilitate life-long learning as well as development of occupation/vocation/technical skills by women. Reducing the gender gap in secondary and higher education would be a focus area. Sectoral time targets in existing policies will be achieved, with a special focus on girls and women, particularly those belonging to weaker sections including the Scheduled Castes/Scheduled Tribes/Other Backward Classes/ Minorities. Gender sensitive curricula would be developed at all levels of educational system in order to address sex stereotyping as one of the causes of gender discrimination.

Health

6.2 A holistic approach to women's health which includes both nutrition and health services will be adopted and special attention will be given to the needs of women and girls at all stages of the life cycle. The reduction of infant mortality and maternal mortality, which are sensitive indicators of human development, is a priority concern. This policy reiterates the national demographic goals for Infant Mortality Rate (IMR), Maternal Mortality Rate (MMR), set out in the National Population Policy 2000. Women should have access to comprehensive, affordable and quality health care. Measures will be adopted that take into account the reproductive rights of women to enable them to exercise informed choices, their vulnerability to sexual and health problems together with endemic, infectious and communicable diseases such as malaria, TB, and water borne diseases as well as hypertension and cardio-pulmonary diseases. The social, developmental and health consequences of HIV/AIDS and other sexually transmitted diseases will be tackled from a gender perspective.

6.3 To effectively meet problems of infant and maternal mortality, and early marriage, the availability of good and accurate data at micro level on deaths, birth and marriages is required. Strict implementation of registration of births and deaths would be ensured and registration of marriages would be made compulsory.

6.4 In accordance with the commitment of the National Population Policy (2000) to population stabilization, this Policy recognizes the critical need of men and women to have access to safe, effective and affordable methods of family planning of their choice and the need to suitably address the issues of early marriages and spacing of children. Interventions such as spread of education, compulsory registration of marriage and special programmes like BSY should impact on delaying the age of marriage so that by 2010 child marriages are eliminated.

6.5 Women's traditional knowledge about health care and nutrition will be recognized through proper documentation and its use will be encouraged. The use of Indian and alternative systems of medicine will be enhanced within the framework of overall health infrastructure available for women.

will link up with Women's Studies Centres and other research and academic institutions through suitable information networking systems.

11.4 While institutions at the district level will be strengthened at the grass roots, women will be helped by Government through its programmes to organize and strengthen into Self-Help Groups (SHGs) at the Anganwadi/Village/Town level. The women's groups will be helped to institutionalize themselves into registered societies and to federate at the Panchyat/Municipal level. These societies will bring about synergistic implementation of all the social and economic development programmes by drawing resources made available through Government and Non-Government channels, including banks and financial institutions and by establishing a close Interface with the Panchayats/ Municipalities.

Resource Management

12.1 Availability of adequate financial, human and market resources to implement the Policy will be managed by concerned Departments, financial credit institutions and banks, private sector, civil society and other connected institutions. This process will include:

(a) Assessment of benefits flowing to women and resource allocation to the relating programmes relating to them through an exercise of gender budgeting. Appropriate changes in policies will be made to optimize benefits to women under these schemes.

(b) Adequate resource allocation to develop and promote the policy outlined earlier based on the above by concerned Departments.

(c) Developing synergy between personnel of Health, Rural Development, Education and Women & Child Development Department at field level and other village level functionaries.

(d) Meeting credit needs by banks and financial credit institutions through suitable policy initiatives and development of new institutions in coordination with the Department of Women & Child Development.

12.2 The strategy of Women's Component Plan adopted in the Ninth Plan, ensuring that not less than 30% of benefits/funds flow to women from all Ministries and Departments, will be implemented effectively so that the needs and interests of women and girls are addressed by all concerned sectors. The Department of Women and

Child Development, being the nodal Ministry, will monitor and review the progress of the implementation of the Component Plan from time to time, in terms of both quality and quantity in collaboration with the Planning Commission.

12.3 Efforts will be made to channelize private sector investments too, to support programmes and projects for advancement of women.

Legislation

13.1 The existing legislative structure will be reviewed and additional legislative measures taken by identified departments to implement the Policy. This will also involve a review of all existing laws including personal, customary and tribal laws, subordinate legislation, related rules as well as executive and administrative regulations to eliminate all gender discriminatory references. The process will be planned over a time period. The specific measures required would be evolved through a consultation process involving civil society, National Commission for Women and Department of Women and Child Development. In appropriate cases the consultation process would be widened to include other stakeholders too.

13.2 Effective implementation of legislation would be promoted by involving civil society and community. Appropriate changes in legislation will be undertaken, if necessary.

13.3 In addition, following other specific measures will be taken to implement the legislation effectively:

(a) Strict enforcement of all relevant legal provisions and speedy redressal of grievances will be ensured, with a special focus on violence and gender related atrocities.

(b) Measures to prevent and punish sexual harassment at the place of work, protection for women workers in the organized/ unorganized sector and strict enforcement of relevant laws such as Equal Remuneration Act and Minimum Wages Act will be undertaken.

(c) Crimes against women, their incidence, prevention, investigation, detection and prosecution will be regularly reviewed at all Crime Review fora and Conferences at the Central, State and District levels. Recognised, local, voluntary organizations will be authorized to lodge Complaints and facilitate registration, investigations and legal proceedings related to violence and atrocities against girls and women.

(d) Women's Cells in Police Stations, Women Police Stations, Family Courts, Mahila Courts, Counselling Centers, Legal Aid Centers and Nyaya Panchayats will be strengthened and expanded to eliminate violence and atrocities against women.

(e) Widespread dissemination of information on all aspects of legal rights, human rights and other entitlements of women, through specially designed legal literacy programmes and rights information programmes will be done.

Gender Sensitization

14.1 Training of personnel of executive, legislative and judicial wings of the State, with a special focus on policy and programme framers, implementation and development agencies, law enforcement machinery and the judiciary, as well as non-governmental organizations will be undertaken. Other measures will include:

(a) Promoting societal awareness to gender issues and women's human rights.

(b) Review of curriculum and educational materials to include gender education and human rights issues.

(c) Removal of all references derogatory to the dignity of women from all public documents and legal instruments.

(d) Use of different forms of mass media to communicate social messages relating to women's equality and empowerment.

Panchayati Raj Institutions

15.1 The 73rd and 74th Amendments (1993) to the Indian Constitution have served as a breakthrough towards ensuring equal access and increased participation in political power structure for women. The PRIs will play a central role in the process of enhancing women's participation in public life. The PRIs and the local self Governments will be actively involved in the implementation and execution of the National Policy for Women at the grassroots level.

Partnership with the Voluntary Sector Organizations

16.1 The involvement of voluntary organizations, associations, federations, trade unions, non-governmental organizations, women's organizations, as well as institutions dealing with education, training and research will be ensured in the formulation, implementation, monitoring and review of all policies and programmes affecting women. Towards this end, they will be provided with appropriate support related to resources and capacity building and facilitated to participate actively in the process of the empowerment of women.

International Cooperation

17.1 The Policy will aim at implementation of international obligations/ commitments in all sectors on empowerment of women such as the Convention on All Forms of Discrimination Against Women (CEDAW), Convention on the Rights of the Child (CRC), International Conference on Population and Development (ICPD+5) and other such instruments. International, regional and sub-regional cooperation towards the empowerment of women will continue to be encouraged through sharing of experiences, exchange of ideas and technology, networking with institutions and organizations and through bilateral and multi-lateral partnerships.

Bibliography

1. Acharya, Sarthi (1996). "The Equal Remuneration Act of 1976: An Assessment Based on Views of Unions and Officials", The Indian Journal of Labour Economics, Vol. 39, No.1.
2. Adams, J. Priest, R.F., & Prince, H.T. II (in press). Achievement motive: Analyzing the validity of the wofo. Psychology of Women Quarterly.
3. Adi Sankaracharya, *Saundaryalahari.*
4. Adi Sankaracharya, *Vivekachudamani.*
5. Agassi, J.B. (1977). The quality of working life. In Jewell, D.O. (Ed.), Women and management: An expanding role. Atlants, Ga.: Georgia State University.
6. Agrawal, Rashmi and Naqvi, Talmeez Fatima (2002): "Skill Development in the Changing Global Context", Indian Journal of Labour Economics, Vol. 45, No. 4, October – December 2002.
7. Agrawal, Sarita (1993). Gender Discrimination in the Labour Market: A Review of Literature, The Indian Journal of Labour Economics, Vol.36, No.2.
8. Ahooja-Patel, Krishna (1993). Gender Distance Among Countries, Economic and Political Weekly, Mumbai, 13 February, 1993.
9. Allport, G. (1935). Attitudes, in C. Murchison (ed.) A Handbook of Social Psychology, Worcester, Mass.: Clark University Press, pp. 798-844.
10. Almquist, E.M. (1974). Sex stereotypes in occupational choice. The case for college women. Journal of Vocational Behaviour, 5, 13-21.
11. —, and Angrist, S.S. (1971). Role model influence on college women's career aspirations, Merrill-Palmer Quarterly, 17, 263-279.
12. Altman, S.L., & Grossman, F.K. (1977). Women's career plans and maternal employment. Psychology of Women Quarterly, 1, 365-376.
13. Altrochi, J., O. Parsons and H. Dickoff (1960). Changes in self-ideal discrepancy in repressors and sensitizers. Journal of Abnormal and Social Psychology 61: 67-72.
14. Anastasi, A. (1961). Psychological Testing, New York; Macmillan.
15. Anker, M, Hein, C. (1985). Why Third World urban employers usually prefer men, International Labour Review (Geneva); ILO, Vol.124, No.1 pp.73-90.
16. Anker, R. (1998). Gender and Jobs: Sex Segregation of Occupations in the World, ILO, Geneva.
17. —, (1937). Personality: A Psychological Interpretation, New York: Henry Hold.
18. —, (1943). The Ego in Contemporary Psychology. Psychological Review 50: 451-479.

19. Arora, K.K. (Miss), Bhattacharya and others (1963). Women and Career, A Group Project Report submitted to the Tata Institute of Social Sciences (Bombay) for Post-Graduate Diploma in Social Service Administration with Specialization in Family and Child Welfare.
20. Arya, Anita. (2001) Indian Women. Vols. 1,2,3. Gyan Pub. New Delhi.
21. Astin, H. (1967). Factors associated with the participation of the woman doctorate in the labor force. Personnel Guidance Journal, 45, 240-246.
22. Avasthi, Abha and Srivastava, A.K. (2001). Modernity, Feminism and Women Empowerment, Rawat Publication, Jaipur and New Delhi.
23. Bachtold, L.M. (1976). Personality Characteristics of Women of Distinction. Psychology of Women Quarterly, 1, 70-78.
24. Bailyn, L. (1959). Mass Media and children. A study of exposure habits and cognitive habits. Psychological Monographs, 73, (no.471).
25. Baines, Carol, Patriwa Evans and Sheila, Neysmith (eds.) (1991). Women Caring: Feminist Perspective on Social Welfare, Toronto, Ontario, McClelland and Steward.
26. Baker, E.F. (1964). Technology and women's work. New York: Columbia University Press.
27. Bales, R. (1950). Interaction process analysis: A method for the study of small groups. Cambridge, Mass.: Addison Wesley.
28. Banfield, E.E. (1976). Women in Middle Management Positions: characteristics, training, leadership style, limitation, rewards and problems: Dissertation Abstract International, 37(4-8), 1952-1953.
29. Bardwick, J.M., & Donvan, E. (1972). Ambivalence: The socialization of women. In J.M. Bardwick (Ed.), Readings on the psychology of women, New York: Harper & Row.
30. Barnett. R.C. (1971). Personality correlates of vocational planning. Genetic Psychology Monographs, 83, 349-356.
31. Barrett, N.S. (1979). Women in the job market: Occupations, earnings, and career opportunities. In R.E. Smith (Ed.), The subtle revolution. Washington, D.C.: The Urban Institute.
32. Barrett, T.C. & Tinsley, H.E.A. (1977), Vocational self-concept crystallization and vocational indecision. Journal of Counseling Psychology, 24, 301-307.
33. Bartal, D., & Frieze, I.H. (1977). Achievement motivation for males and females as a determinant of attributions for success and failure. Sex Roles, 3, 301- 314.
34. Bartol, K.M. (1974). Male versus female leaders: The effect of leader need for dominance on follower satisfaction. Academy of Management Journal, 17(2), 225-233.
35. —, and Butterfield, D.A. (1976). Sex effects in evaluating leaders. Journal of Applied Psychology, 61(4), 446-545.
36. —, and Wortman, M.S. (1975). Male versus female leaders: Effects on perceived leader behaviour and satisfaction in a hospital. Personnel Psychology, 28, 533-547.
37. Baruch, G.K. (1972). Maternal influence upon college women's attitudes toward women and work. Developmental Psychology, 6(1), 32-37.
38. Baruch, R. (1967). The achievement motive in women: Implications for career development. Journal of Personality and Social Psychology, 5, 260-267.

39. Bass, B., Krusall, J., & Alexander, R.A. (1971). Male managers' attitudes toward working women. American Behavioral Scientist, 15(2), 221-236.

40. Bass, B.M. (1960). Leadership psychology and organizational behaviour. NewYork: Harper & Row.

41. Bedeian, A.G., Armenakis, A.A., & Kemp, B.W. (1976). Relation of sex to perceived legitimacy of organizational influence. The Journal of Psychology, 94, 93-99.

42. Bem, S.L. (1974). The measurement of psychological androgyny. Journal of Consulting and Clinical Psychology, 42, 155-162.

43. —, (1975). Sex role adaptability: One consequence of psychological androgyny. Journal of Personality and Social Psychology, 21, 634-643.

44. —, (1977). On the utility of alternative procedures for assessing psychological androgyny. Journal of Consulting and Clinical Psychology, 45, 196-205.

45. —, (1980). Gender schema theory: A cognitive account of sex-typing. Psychological Review.

46. Benedetti, C.R., (1975). Similarities and differences in the leadership styles and personal characteristics of women in educational administration and women in business administration. Dissertation Abstract International, 36 (3-A), 1188-1189.

47. Berger, E.M. (1952). The relation between expressed acceptance of self and expressed acceptance of others. Journal of Abnormal and Social Psychology 47: 778-782.

48. —, (1955).Relationships among acceptance of self, acceptance of others, and MMPI scores. Journal of Counseling Psychology 2: 279-283.

49. Bhomik, S. K. 2001, "Worker cooperatives and Empowerment of the Marginalized" in Roy, Debalk Singher, Social Development and the Empowerment of Marginalized Groups: Perspective and Strategies, Sage Publications, New Delhi.

50. Bieri, J. (1960). Parental identification, acceptance of authority and differences in cognitive behaviour. Journal of Abnormal & Social Psychology, 6, 76-79.

51. Blake, R.R. and Mouton, J.S. (1964). The Managerial Grid, Houston: Texas, Gulf Publication.

52. Boshier, R. (1969). A study of the relationship between self-concept and conservatism. Journal of Social Psychology 77: 139-140. .

53. Bowman G.W., Worthy, N.B., & Greyser, S.A. (1965). Are women executives people? Harvard Business Review, 43, 14-17.

54. Brooks, L., & Galligan, M. (1985). The effects of a non-traditional role-modeling interventics on sex-typing of occupational preferences and career salience in adolescent females. Journal of Vocational Behaviour, 26, 264-276.

55. Broverman, I.K., Broverman, D.M., Clarkson, F.E., Rosenkrantz, P.S., & Vogel, S.R. (1970). Sex-role stereotypes and clinical judgments of mental health. Journal of Counseling and Clinical Psychology, 34 (1), 1-7.

56. Brownfain, J. (1952). Stability of the self-concept as a dimension of personality. Journal of Abnormal and Social Psychology 47: 596-606.

57. Bryce, R.A, (1970). Characteristics of women holding executive, managerial, and other high level positions in four areas of business. Dissertation Abstracts International, 30, 4216A-4217A. .

58. Canter, R. (1979). Achievement-related expectations and aspirations in college women. Sex Roles, 5(4), 453-470.
59. Carr, Marylin et al.(1996), Speaking out Women's Economic Empowerment in South Asia, Vistaar Publications, New Delhi.
60. Cash, T.F., Gillen, B., & Burns, D.S. (1977). Sexism and "beautyism" in personnel consultant decision-making. Journal of Applied Psychology, 62, 301-310.
61. Cecil, E.A., Paul, R.J., & Olins, R.A. (1973). Perceived importance of selected variables used to evaluate male and female job applicants. Personnel Psychology, 26, 397-404.
62. CEDAW (1997). Convention on Elimination of all Forms of Discrimination Against Women, India's First Report, Government of India.
63. Chapman, J.B. (1975). Comparison of male and female leadership styles. Academy of Management Journal, 18, (3), 645-650.
64. Charles, M.; Cross-national variation in occupational sex segregation, American Sociological Review, N.Y., 1992. Vol.57, pp.483-502.
65. Chaturvedi, G. (1985). Women Administrators of India, Anuj Printers.
66. Chodorow, N.; (1978). The Reproduction of Mothering, Berbelly University of California Press.
67. Chusmir, L.H. (1983). Characteristics and Predictive Dimension of Women who make non-traditional vocational choices. Personnel & Guidance Journal, 62(1), 43-47.
68. Clark, E.T. (1967). Influence of sex and social class on occupational preference and perception. Personnel and Guidance Journal, 45,440-441.
69. Cohen, A. (1959). Some implications of self-esteem for social influence, pp. 102-120 in C. Hovland and I. Janis (eds.) Personality and Persuasibility. New Haven: Yale University Press.
70. Cohen, S.L., Bunker, K.A., Burton, C.A., & McManus, P.D. (1978). Reactions to sex-role congruency of immediate supervision. Sex Roles, 4(2), 297-311.
71. Consentino, F. and Heibrun, A.B. (1964). Anxiety Co-relates of Sex-Role. Identity in College Students. Psychological Reports, 14, 729-730.
72. Cooley, C.H. (1902). Human Nature and the Social Order. New York: Charles Scribner's Sons.
73. Coopersmity, S. (1959). A method for determining types of self-esteem. Journal of Abnormal and Social Psychology, 59: 87-94.
74. —, (1967). The Antecedents of Self-Esteem. San Francisco: W.H. Freeman.
75. Cottle, T.J. (1965). Self concept, ego ideal and the response to action. Sociology and Social Research, 50: 78-88.
76. Crandall, R. (1973). The measurement of self-esteem and related constructs, pp. 45-158 in J. Robinson and P. Shaver, Measures of Social Psychological Attitudes. Ann Arbor, Mich.: Institute of Social Research..
77. Crandall, V.C. (1969). Sex differences in expectancy of intellectual and academic reinforcement. In C.P. Smith (Ed.), Achievement-related motives in children, New York: Russell Sage Foundation, 1969.
78. Crandall, V.J., & Rabson, A.L. (1960), Children's repetition choices in an intellectual achievement situation following success and failure. Journal of Genetic Psychology, 97, 161-168.

79. —, Katkovsky, W., & Preston, A. (1962). Motivational and ability determinants of young children's intellectual achievement behaviours. Child Development, 33, 643-661.

80. Crook, R.H., Healy, C.C. & O'shea, D.W. (1984). The linkage of work achievement to self-esteem, career maturity and college achievement, Journal of Vocational Behaviour, 3, 25, 70-79.

81. Das, Deenbandhu and.Mishra, B.N(2002), "Economic Empowerment of Women: Dimensions of Participation and Progress in Orissa State" in Women Work Participation and Empowerment: Problems and Prospects, ed. S. Murty and K.D. Gaur RBSA Pub., Jaipur.

82. Day, D.R., & Stogdill, R.M. (1972). Leader behaviour of male and female supervisors: A comparative study. Personnel Psychology, 25, 353-360.

83. Dayal, I. (1976). Workers Involvement in the organisation. (Monograph) New Delhi: Shri Ram Centre for Industrial Relations and Human Resources.

84. Deaux, K. (1976a). The behaviour of women and men. Monterey, Calif.: Brooks/Cole.

85. —, (1979). Self-evaluations of male and female managers. Sex Roles, 5(5), 571-580.

86. —, and Emswiller, T. (1974). Explanations of successful performance on sex-linked tasks: What is skill for the male is luck for the female. Journal of Personality and Social Psychology, 29, 80-85.

87. —, and Farris, E. (1977). Attributing causes for one's own performance: The effects of sex, norms and outcome. Journal of Research in Personality, 11, 59-72.

88. Denmark, F.L., & Diggory, J.C. (1966). Sex differences in attitudes toward leaders' display of authoritarian behaviour. Psychological Reports, 18, 863-872.

89. Devadas, Rajammal P.,(1999). Introduction in Education and Women's Empowerment, Association of Indian University. Delhi.

90. Dhingra, O.P. (1972). Women in Employment, Report of Field Investigation into the Problems of Professionally Trained Employed Women in India, Shri Ram Centre for Industrial Relations and Human Resources, New Delhi.

91. Diggory, J.C. (1966). Self-Evaluation: Concepts and Studies, New York: John Wiley.

92. Duncan, O.D., & Duncan, B. (1955). A methodological analysis of segregation indexes. American Sociological Review, 29, 210-217.

93. Duraiswamy, Malathy and Duraiswamy, P. (1999). Women in the Professional and Technical Labour Market in India: Gender Discrimination in Education, Employment and Earnings, The Indian Journal of Labour Economics, Vol.42, No. 4. .

94. Durkheim. E. (1964). The Division of Labour in Society, New York. Free Press, 1964.

95. Dweck, C.S. (1975). The role of expectations and attributions in the alleviation of learned helplessness. Journal o f Personality and Social Psychology, 31, 674-685

96. Eskilson, A., & Wiley, M.G. (1976). Sex composition and leadership in small groups. Sociometry, 39(3), 183-194.

97. Etaugh, C., & Brown, B. (1975). Perceiving the causes of success and failure of male and female performers. Developmental Psychology, 11, 103.

98. Everitt, B.S. (1977). The Analysis of Contingency Tables. A Halsted Press Book, New York.

99. Feather, N.T. (1966). Effects of prior success and failure on expectations of success and failure. Journal of Personality and Social Psychology, 3, 287-298.

100. —, (1969). Attribution of responsibility and valence of success and failure in relation to initial confidence and task performance. Journal of Personality and Social Psychology, 13, 129-144.

101. —, and Simon, J.G. (1973). Fear of success and casual attribution of outcomes. Journal of Personality, 41, 525-542. .

102. —, and Simon, J.G. (1975). Reactions to male and female success and failure in sex-linked occupations: Impressions of personality, causal attribution, and perceived likelihood of different consequences. Journal of Personality and Social Psychology, 31, 20-31.

103. Feldman, S.D. (1974). Escape from the doll's house: Women in graduate and professional school education. A report prepared for the Carnegie Commission on Higher Education. New York: McGraw-Hill, 208 pp.

104. Feldman-Summers, S., & Kiesler, S.B. (1974). Those who are number two try harder: The effect of sex on attributions of causality. Journal of Personality and Social Psychology, 30, 846-855.

105. Fiedler, F.E., (1958). Leader Attitudes and Group Effectiveness. Urbana: University of Illinois Press.

106. —, (1961). Leadership and Leadership Effectiveness Traits: A Re-conceptualization of the Leadership Trait Problem. Leadership and Inter-personal Behaviour, Luigi Petrullo and Bernard M. Bass, eds. New York: Holt, Rinehart & Winston, Inc.

107. —, (1965). Engineer the Job to fit the Manager, Harvard Business Review, 51, 115-122.

108. —, (1967). A Theory of Leadership Effectiveness. New York: McGraw-Hill Book Company.

109. Fish, B. and S. Karabenick (1971). Relationship between self-esteem and locus of control. Psychological Reports 29: 784.

110. Fitts, W. (1965). Tennessee Self-Concept Scale Manual. Nashville, Tenn.: Counselor Recordings and Tests.

111. —, (1970), Interpersonal Competence: The Wheel Model, Nashville, Tenn.: Counselor Recordings and Tests.

112. —, (1972a). The Self-Concept and Psycho-pathology, Nashville, Tenn.: Counselor Recordings and Tests.

113. —, (1972b). The Self Concept and Performances. Nashville, Tenn.: Counselor Recordings and Tests.

114. —, (1972c). The Self Concept and Behavior: Overview and Supplement. Nashville, Tenn.: Counselor Recordings and Tests.

115. —, and W. Hamner (1969). The Self Concept and Delinquency, Nashville, Tenn.: Counselor Recordings and Tests.

116. —, J. Adams, F. Radford, W.Richard, B. Thomas, M. Thomas and W. Thompson (1971). The Self-Concept and Self-Actualization. Nashville, Tenn.: Counselor Recordings and Tests.

117. Flaherty, J.F., Dusek, J.B. (1980). An investigation of the relationship between psychological androgyny and components of self-concept. Journal of Personality and Social Psychology, 38, 6, 984-992.
118. Fleishman, E.A. (1957). A leader behavior description for industry. In R.M. Stogdill and A.E. Coons (Eds.), Leader behavior: Its description and measurement. Columbus: Ohio State University, Bureau of Business Research, Monograph No.88, 103-119.
119. Fogarty, M.P., Rapoport, R., & Rapoport, R.N. (1971).Career, sex and family. London: Allen and Unwin.
120. Frieze, I.H., McHugh, M.C., Fisher, J., & Valle, V.A.(1975). Attributing the causes of success and failure: Internal and external barriers to achievement in women. Paper presented at the APA-NIMH Conference on New Directions for Research on Women, Madison.
121. Fromm, E. (1939). Selfishness and self-love. Psychiatry: Journal for the Study of Interpersonal Processes 2: 507-523.
122. —, (1955). The Sane Society. Greenwich, Conn.: Fawcett.
123. Gall, M.D. (1969). The Relationship between Masulinity- Femininity and Manifest Anxiety. Journal of Clinical Psychology, 25, 294-295.
124. Garrett, H.E. and Woodworth, R.S. (1965). Statistics in Psychology and Education. Vakils, Feffer and Simons Pvt. Ltd., Bombay.
125. Gecas, V. (1972). Parental behavior and contextual variations in adolescent self- esteem. Sociometry, 35: 332-345.
126. Gergen, K. (1971). The concept of self. New York: Holt, Rinehart & Winston.
127. —, and R. Bauer (1967). Interactive effects of self-esteem and task difficulty on social conformity. Journal of Personality and Social Psychology, 6: 16-22.
128. —, and S. Morse (1967). Self-consistency: measurement and validation. Proceedings of the 75th American Psychological Association Convention 2: 207-208.
129. Ghosh, Bahnishikha (1990), The Indian Population Problem, Sage Publications.
130. Gibb, C.A. (1969). Leadership. In G. Lindzey & E. Aronson (Eds.), Handbook of Social Psychology, Reading, Mass.: Addison-Wesley, 4, 205-282.
131. Gilmer, B. (1961). Industrial psychology. New York: McGraw-Hill.
132. Goetz, T.E., & Herman, J.B. (1976). Effects of supervisors' and subordinates' sex on productivity and morals. Paper presented at the American Psychological Association 84th Annual convention, Washington, D.C.
133. GOI (1969). Report of National Commission on Labour, Chapter 27.
134. GOI (1974). Report of the Committee on the Status of Women in India.
135. GOI (1986). National Policy on Education (1986).
136. GOI (1987). "Shram Shakti": Report of the Commission on Self-employed Women, 1987 .
137. GOI (1997). Convention on Elimination of all Forms of Discrimination against Women, India's First Report.
138. GOI (1998). Nursing Council of India for the year 1998.
139. GOI (1999). National Family Health Survey (NHFS)-II, 1998-99.
140. GOI (2000). Central Statistical Organisation: Report of the Time Use Survey.
141. GOI (2002). Census 2001 (Electronic data) reproduced in The Indian Journal of Labour Economics, Vol. 45 No.1.

142. GOI, Annual Employment Reviews 1981-80 and 1990-91 and Quarterly Employment Review 2000-2001, Ministry of Labour.

143. GOI, Annual Report, Department of Woman & Child Development, Ministry of HRD, New Delhi.

144. GOI, Census of India 1981.

145. GOI, Central Statistical Organisation, System of National Accounts.

146. GOI, Education for All (2000). Ministry of Human Resource Development, New Delhi.

147. GOI, Indian Labour Year Books, 1989, 1991, 1999, Labour Bureau, Ministry of Labour.

148. GOI, National Policy on Education, 1992.

149. GOI, National Sample Survey Organisation: Report on Employment and Unemployment, 55th Round (July 1999 to June 2000), 2000.

150. GOI, National Sample Survey Organisation: Sarvekshana Vol. 23, No. 3, 82nd Issue, January-March 2000.

151. GOI, National Sample Survey, Report on 52nd Round, July 1995 – June 1996.

152. GOI, Planning Commission: The First Five Year Plan.

153. GOI, Planning Commission: The Second Five Year Plan.

154. GOI, Planning Commission: The Third Five Year Plan.

155. GOI, Planning Commission: The Fourth Five Year Plan.

156. GOI, Planning Commission: The Fifth Five Year Plan.

157. GOI, Planning Commission: The Sixth Five Year Plan.

158. GOI, Planning Commission: The Seventh Five Year Plan.

159. GOI, Planning Commission: The Eighth Five Year Plan.

160. GOI, Planning Commission: The Ninth Five Year Plan.

161. GOI, Planning Commission: The Tenth Five Year Plan.

162. GOI, Registrar General of India, Sample Registration System .

163. GOI, Registrar General of India: 2001 Census, Paper No. 1, Final Population Count, 2001.

164. GOI, Report of The Committee on the Status of Women in India, 1974.

165. GOI, Shram-Shakti, The Report of the National Commission on Self-employed Women, 1987.

166. Goldstein, R. (1972). Indian Women in transition - A Bangalore Case Study. Metuchen, N.J. Scarecrow Press.

167. Greene, C.N. (1975). Principal nature of influence between leader and subordinates, Journal of Applied Psychology, 60(2), 187-193.

168. Greenfeld, S., Grainer, Larry & Wood, Marion M. (1980). The "Feminine Mystique" in male dominated jobs: A comparison of attitudes and background factors of women in male dominated vs. female dominated jobs. Journal of Vocational Behaviour, 17(3), 291-309.

169. Haberman, S.J. (1973). The analysis of residuals in cross-classified tables, biometrics, 29, 205-220.

170. Hall, D.T. (1976). Careers in organisations. Pacific Palisades, Calif.: Goodyear Publications.

171. Halperin, M.S., & Abrams, D.L. (1978). Sex differences in predicting final examination grades: The influence of past performance, attributions and achievement motivation. Journal of Educational Psychology, 70, 763-771.

214. Karmakar, K.G., (1999), Micro-Finance Needs and Concepts in India, Sage Publications, New Delhi.

215. Karnik, V.B. (1973). Status of Women-Economic and Employment Aspects, Paper read in a Seminar on the "Status of Women," held in Bombay.

216. Kelly, J.A., & Worell, J. (1977). New formulations of sex roles and androgyny: A critical review. Journal of Counselling and Clinical Psychology, 45, 1101-1115.

217. Kerlinger, F.N. (1978). Foundations of Behavioural Research, Surjeet Publications, Delhi.

218. Khan, Sakina Yusuf, (2003) "Look who's beating their wives" in The Times of India, February 16, .

219. King, Angela E.V. (2000). United Nations Assistant Secretary General and Special Advisor on Gender Issues and Advancement of Women, in her Keynote speech on "The Global Perspective: Outcomes of Beijing + 5 Gender Equality, Development and Peace" at the Panel Discussion on "Progress for Women in the New Millennium: the Way Forward" organized by The Commonwealth Secretariat and The United Nations Information Center, London, 4 December 2000.

220. Kirchner, B.P. and Vondracek, S.I. (1973). What do you want to be when you grow up? Vocational choice in children aged three to six. Paper presented at biennial meeting of the Society for Research in Child Development. Philadelphia.

221. Koontz, Harold, and Cyril O'Donnell (1968). Principles of Management (4th edn.). New York: McGraw-Hill Book Company.

222. Korman, A. (1968). Self-esteem, social influence, and task performance: some tests of a theory, Proceedings of the 76th American Psychological Association Convention 3: 567-568.

223. Kornreich, L.B., Straka, J. and Kane, A. (1968). Meaning of self-image disparity as measured by the Q sort. Journal of Consulting and Clinical Psychology, 32: 728-730.

224. Kraak, Bernhard & Nord Nudigler (1985). Dietlinde - Die berufliche Motivation Von Frauen (Women Career Motivation), Germ Psychologie and Praxis, 29(4), 153-161.

225. Kriger, S.F. (1972). Nach and perceived parental child-rearing: Attitudes of career women and homemakers. Journal of Vocational Behavior, 2, 419-432.

226. Laws, J.L. (1979). The second X: Sex role and social role. New York: Elsevier.

227. Lemert, Charles (1992). General Social Theory. Irony, Post Modernism in Seidman & Wagner, Blackwell, U.K. .

228. Lenny, E. (1977). Women's self-confidence in achievement settings. Psychological Bulletin, 84, 1.13.

229. Lewis, E.O. (1968). Developing women's potential. Ames: Iowa State University Press.

230. Linton, H. and Graham, E. (1959). Personality correlates of persuasibility, pp.69-101 in C. Hovland and I. Janis (eds.) Personality and Persuasibility. New Haven: Yale University Press.

231. Lipman-Blumen, J. (1972). How ideology shapes women's lives. Scientific American, 226, 34-42.

232. Lockhead, M., & Hall, K. (1976). Conceptualizing sex as a status characteristic: Applications to leadership training strategies. Journal of Social Issues, 32(3), 111-124.

233. Looft, W. R. (1971a). Sex differences in the expression of vocational aspirations by elementary school children. Developmental Psychology, 5(2), 366-372.

234. —, (1971b).Vocational aspirations of second-grade girls. Psychological Reports, 28, 241-242.

235. Lynn, D.B. (1962). Sex-role and parental identification. Child Development, 33, 555-564.

236. —, (1969). Parental identification and sex role, Berkeley: Mc Cutchan.

237. Maccoby, E. and Jacklin, C. (1974). The Psychology of Sex Differences. Stanford, Calif.: Stanford University Press.

238. Majumdar, Vina. (2001). Peasant Woman Organise for Empowerment: The Bankura Experiment, in Singh Roy, Debal K., (Ed) Social Development and the Empowerment of Marginalised Groups, Sage, New Delhi.

239. Mann, R.D. (1959). A review of the relationships between personality and performance in small groups. Psychological Bulletin, 56, 241-270.

240. Manpower Profile India Year Book 2001, Institute of Applied Manpower Research (IAMR).

241. Marini, Margaret Mooney (1988). Sociology of Gender in the Future of Sociology, ed. by E.F. Borgatta and K.S. Cook, Beverly Hills, C.A. Sage.

242. Mark, L. (1985). Masculinity in management: Type A behaviour and the corporation. Organaisation Development Journal, 3(1), 6-9.

243. Maslow, A.H. (1954). Motivation and Personality. Harper and Row Publishers, New York. .

244. Mayo, Elton, (1933). The Human Problems of an Industrial Civilization. New York: The Macmillan Company.

245. —, (1945). The Social Problems of an Industrial Civilization. New York: The Macmillan Company.

246. —, (1945). The Social Problems of an Industrial Civilization, Boston: Harvard Business School.

247. McArthur, J., (1974). Why are not there more women managers? Canadian Business, 47(12).

248. McGregor, Douglas, (1944). Conditions of effective leadership in industrial organisation, Journ al of Consulting Psychologists, 8, 56-63.

249. —, (1960). The Human Side of Enterprise, New York: McGraw-Hill Book Company.

250. —, (1966). Leadership and Motivation. Boston: MIT Press.

251. —, (1967). Professional Manager. New York: McGraw-Hill Book Company.

252. McMahon, F.D., (1973). Relationships between causal attributions and expectancy of success. Journal of Personality and Social Psychology, 28, 108-114.

253. McManis, D.L. (1965). Pursuit-rotor performance of normal and retarded children in four verbal incentive conditions, Child Development, 36, 667-583.

254. Mead, G.H. (1934). Mind, Self, and Society, Chicago: University of Chicago Press.

255. —, (1956). The Social Psychology of George Herbert Mead. (A. St rauss, ed.) Chicago: University of Chicago Press.

256. Megargee, E.I. (1969). Influence of sex roles on the manifestation of leadership. Journal of Applied Psychology, 53(5), 377-382.

257. Michon, F., 1997, "Reorganisation des temps de travail et division sexuee du travail: quells change ments? Les cahiers du mage, no. 2 pp. 93-97 in Jenson J., Lanfer J. and Marvani M., (eds.) The Gendering of Inequalities: Women, Men & Work, Ashgate Publishing Limited, England, 2000.

258. Milton, G.A. (1957). The effects of sex-role identification upon problem solving skill. Journal of Abnormal and Social Psychology, 55, 208-212.

259. Miner, J.B. (1974). Motivation to manage among women: Studies of business managers and educational administrators. Journal of Vocational Behavior, 5, 197-208.

260. Mischel, Walter (1986). "Introduction to Personality" (4th ed.), Holt, Rinehart and Winston, New York .

261. Mishra, L.N. (1996). Women Labour in India, V.V. Giri National Labour Institute.

262. Mishra, R. (1980). A study of role clarity, efficiency and job satisfaction. Ph.D. thesis, Patna University, Patna.

263. Montemeyor,R. (1972). Children's performance on and attraction to an activity as a function of masculine, feminine or neutral lables and sex-role preferences. Paper presented at EPA.

264. Moore, L.M. and Rickel, A.U. (1980). Characteristics of women in traditional and non-traditional managerial roles, Personnel Psychology, 33, 317-333.

265. Morrison, R.A. & Sebald (1974). Personal characteristics differentiating female executives from female non-executive personnel. Journal of Applied Psychology, 59, 656-659.

266. Moser, Caroline O.N. (1989). Gender Planning in the Third World, Meeting Practical and Strategic Gender Needs, World Development, Vol. 17,No. 11, 1989.

267. Murugesan, K. (1999). 'Experiences of SHARE in its Attempt at Ensuring Participation of Women in the Election to Local Administration', in Decentralised Government and NGOs, Issues, Strategies and Ways Forward, ed. D. Rajasekhar, 1999, Concept Publishing Co., New Delhi .

268. Myrdal Gunnar, (1968) Asian Drama – An Enquiry into the Poverty of Nations, Oxford University Press.

269. Narula, U.N. (1967). Career failure among women, Social Welfare, pp.4-5.

270. NCW, Study to Assess the Harassment of Women at Work in Organised and Unorganised Sectors, Santek Consultants (prepared for the National Commission for Women).

271. Nelson, R.C. (1963). Knowledge and interests concerning sixteen occupations among elementary and secondary school students. Educational and Psychological Measurement, 23(4), 741-754.

272. Nicholls, J.G. (1975). Causal attribution and other achievement-related cognitions: Effects of task outcome, attainment value, and sex. Journal of Personality and Social Psychology, 31, 379-389.

273. Nieva, V.F. and Gutek, B.A. (1981). Women and Work - A Psychological Perspective, Praeger Publishers, USA.

274. O'Hara, R.P. (1962). The roots of careers. Elementary School Journal, 62, 277-280.

275. OECD (1988). Women's activity, employment and earnings; A review of recent developments in OECD Employment Outlook (Paris) Sep.

276. OECD (2001). Employment Outlook 2000 cited in International Labour Office: World Employment Report.

277. Oetzel, R .M. (1961). The relationship between sex-role acceptance and cognitive abilities. Unpublished master's thesis, Stanford University. In Mednick et al, Women and Achievement - social and motivational analyses (1975).

278. Oliver, L.W. (1974). Achievement and affiliation motivation in career-oriented and homemaking-oriented college women. Journal of Vocational Behaviour, 4, 275.281.

279. Oppenheimer, V. (1968). The sex-labeling of jobs. Industrial Relations, 7, 219-234.

280. —, (1973). Demographic influence on female employment and the status of women. American Journal of Sociology, 79, 946-961.

281. Orcutt, M.A. & Walsh, W.B. (1979). Traditionality and congruence of career aspirations for college women. Journal of Vocational Behavior, 14, 1-11.

282. Osgood, C.E., Suci, G.J. and Tannenbaum, P.H. (1957). The Measurement of Meaning, University of Illinois Press, Urbana.

283. Outlook (1999). Sexism and the Workplace Wars, Report on 19 May 1999.

284. Pahwa, A. (1980). A study of the self-concept and self-esteem of institutionalised and non-institutionalised boys and girls, Delhi University, Delhi.

285. Papola, T.S. (1986). Women Workers in the formal sector of Lucknow. India in R. Anber and C.Hein (eds.): Sex inequalities in urban employment in the Third World (London: Mac Millan).

286. Parson, T. (1940). An Analytical approach to the theory of social stratification, American Journal of Sociology, Vol. VI, p.850.

287. —, (1949). Essays in sociological theory pure and applied. Glencoe, Illinois: Free Press.

288. —, (1969). Family structure and the socialization of the child. In T. Parsons and R.F. Bales (Eds.), Family socialization and interaction process, Glencoe, Illinois: Free Press.

289. Patel, Mahesh (1999). 'Gender Sensitive Measures of Development and Discrimination' in 'Women and Development' ed. Krishna-Ahooja Patel, S. Uma Devi and G.A. Tadas. .

290. Peters L.H., Terborg, J.R. & Jacobs, J. (1974). Women As Managers Scale (WAMS): a measure of attitudes toward women in management positions. JSAS Catalog of Selected Documents in Psychology. No.585.

291. Petty, M.M., Odewahn, C.A., Bruning, N.S., & Thomason, T.L. (1977). An examination of the moderating effects of supervisor sex and subordinate sex upon the relationships between supervisory behavior and subordinate outcomes in mental health organizations. Academy of Management Proceedings, 37th Annual Meeting, Orlando, Fla, August 14-17. pp 408-412.

292. Piore, M. (1970). The dual labor market: Theory and Implications. Reprinted from M.J. Piore, Jobs and training, in Beer and Barringer (Eds.), The state and the poor. New York: Winthrop.
293. Platt, J., Eisenman, R. and Darbes, M. (1970). Self-esteem and Internal-External control: a validation study. Psychological Reports 26: 162.
294. Power, M., (1975). Women's work is never done - by men: A socio-economic model of sex-typing in occupations. Journal of Industrial Relations, 17, 225-240.
295. Priest, R.F., Rice, R.W., & Prince, H.T., II (1980). Effects of rater attitudes and attributes on female and male leader's effectiveness. Paper presented at the 1980 Biannual ANEDI Psychology Symposium, Washington.
296. Ramanamma, Angara (1969). Position of Women in India (With Special Reference to Poona), Ph.D. Thesis in Sociology, University of Poona, Poona.
297. Rao, B.V.L.N. (2001). Women in Financial Services – Present Status and Prospects, a paper prepared for the Group on Women Workers and Child Labour, the National Commission on Labour. .
298. Rao, P. Vasudeva and Prasad, L.S.N. (2002). 'Changing Status of Women in Panchayat Raj in Guntur District' in Empowerment of Women and Ecological Development, ed. Dr. A. Ranga Reddy, Serial Publications, New Delhi.
299. Razvi,S.(1992), Agrarian Change: A Comparative Study in South Eastern Iran, D.Phil. Dessertation, St. Antony"s College, Oxford Univ. .
300. Reddin, W.J. (1967). The 3-D Management Style Theory, Training and Development Journal, 8-17.
301. —, (1970). Managerial Effectiveness. New York: Mc Graw-Hill Book Company.
302. —, (1971). Effective Management by Objectives: The 3-D Method of MBO. New York: McGraw-Hill Book Company.
303. Registrar General of India, Census 2001, Paper No. 1, Final Population Count. The rates for 1951, 1961 and 1971 relate to population aged 5+, while those for 1981, 1991, 2001 relate to population aged 7+.
304. Reld, D.W. (1977). Locus of desired control and positive self-concept of the elderly. Journal of Gerontology 32(4), 441-450.
305. Rezler, A.G. (1967). Characteristics of high school girls choosing traditional or pioneer vocations. Personnel and Guidance Journal, 45, 659-665.
306. Richardson, M.S. (1975). Self-concepts and role concepts in the career orientation of college women. Journal of Counseling Psychology, 22(2), 122-126.
307. Roe, A. (1957). Early determinants of vocational choice. Journal of Counseling Psychology, 4, 212-217.
308. Rogers, C. (1950). The significance of the self-regarding attitudes and perceptions, pp.374-382 in M.L. Reymert (ed.) Feeling and Emotion: The Mooseheart Symposium. New York: McGraw-Hill.
309. —, (1951). Client-Centered Therapy. Boston: Houghton Mifflin.
310. Rosen, B., & Jerdee, T.H. (1973). The influence of sex-role stereotypes on evaluations of male and female supervisory behavior. Journal of Applied Psychology, 57(1), 44-48.
311. Rosenberg, M., (1964). Parental interest and children's self-conceptions. Sociometry 26: 35-49.

312. —, (1965). Society and the Adolescent Self-Image. Princeton, N.J. Princeton University Press.

313. —, (1967). Psychological selectivity in self-esteem formation, pp.26-50 in C. Sherif and M. Sherif (eds.) Attitude, Ego-Involvement and Change. New York: John Wiley.

314. and Simmons, R.(1971). Black and White Self-Esteem: The Urban School Child. Washington, D.C.: American Sociological Association.

315. Rossi, A.S., (1965a). Barriers to career choice of engineering medicine or science among American Women. In J.A. Mattfeld et al. (eds.), Women and the Scientific Professions. Cambridge, Mass.: MIT Press .

316. Rothboeck, Sandra and Acharya, Sarthi (1999). Gender-based Segregation in the Indian Labour Market, The Indian Jou8rnal of Labour Economics, Vol.44, No.4. .

317. Roussell, C. (1974). Relationship of sex of department head to department climate. Administrative Science Quarterly, 19(2), 211-220.

318. Rychlak, B., & Ecker, J.N. (1962). The effects of anxiety, delay and reinforcement on generalized expectancies. Journal of Personality and Social Psychology, 30, 123-134.

319. Sadler, P.J. (1970). Leadership style, confidence in management, and job satisfaction. Journal of Applied Behavioral Science, 6, 3-19.

320. Sakina, Yusuf Khan (2003). Look who's beating their wives, in The Times of India, February 16, 2003.

321. Santek Consultants: Study to Assess the Harassment of Women at Work in Organised and Unorganised Sectors, (prepared for the National Commission for Women).

322. Sarason, I.G. (1963). Test Anxiety and intellectual performance. Journal of Abnormal and Social Psychology, 66, 73-75.

323. and Harmatz, M.G.(1965). Test anxiety and experimental conditions. Journal of Personality and Social Psychology, 1, 499- 505.

324. Sashkin, M., & Maier, N. (1971). Sex effects on delegation. Personnel Psychology, 24, 471-476.

325. Savage, J.E., Jr. Stearns, A.D., and Friedman, p. (1979). Relationship of internal-external locus of control, self-concept, and masculinity-femininity to fear success in Black Freshmen and senior College Women, Sex Roles, 5, 373-383.

326. Schein, V.E. (1973). The relationship between sex-role stereotypes and requisites management characteristics among female managers. Journal of Applied Psychology, 60, 240-344.

327. Schlossberg, N.K., & Goodman, J.A. (1972). A women's place: Children's sex stereotyping of occupation. Vocational Guidance Quarterly, 20, 266-270.

328. Schrank, T.H., & Riley, J.W. (1976). Women in work organizations. In J.M. Kreps (Ed.), Women and the American Economy. englewood Cliffs, N.J.: Prentice-Hall.

329. Schwartz, S.H., & Clausen, G.T. (1970). Responsibility norms and helping in an emergency. Journal of Personality and Social Psychology, 1970, 16, 299-316.

330. Sears, P.S. (1964). Self-concept in the service of educational goals. California Journal of Instructional Improvement, 7, 3-17.

331. Sears, R.R. (1970). Relation of early socialization experiences to self-concepts and gender role in middle childhood, Child Development, 41, 267-289.
332. —, Rau, L., & Alpert,R(1965). Identification and Child rearing. Standord: Stanford University Press.
333. Sen, Amartya and Dreze, Jean (1995); India: Economic Development and Social Opportunity, Delhi, Oxford University Press.
334. Sengupta, P. (1960). Women workers in India, Bombay, Asia Publishing House.
335. Seth, Mira (2001). Women and Development, Sage Publications.
336. Shann, M.H. (1983). Career plans of men and women in gender-dominant professions. Journal of Vocational Behaviour, 22, 343-356.
337. Sharma, Swarna Lata, (2000). Gender Discrimination and Human Rights, K.K. Publications, New Delhi.
338. Shelton, P.B. (1968). Achievement motivation in professional women. Dissertation Abstracts, 28, 427A.
339. Shepard, W.O., & Hess, D.T. (1975). Attitudes in four age groups toward sex role division in adult occupations and activities. Journal of Vocational Behaviour, 6, 27-39.
340. Sherwood, J.J. (1965). Self identity and referent others. Sociometry 28: 66-81.
341. —, (1967). Increased self-evaluation as a function of ambiguous evaluations by referent others. Sociometry 30: 404-409.
342. Shibutani, T. (1961). Society and Personality. Englewood Cliffs, N.J.: Prentice-Hall.
343. Shuval, J.T. (1963). Occupational interests and sex-role congruence. Human Relations, 16, 171-182.
344. Siegel, A.E., & Curtis, E.A. (1963). Familial correlates of orientation toward future employment among college women. Journal of Educational Psychology, 44, 33-37 .
345. Siegel, C. (1973). Sex differences in the occupational choices of second graders. Journal of Vocational Behavior, 3, 15-19.
346. Silber,E. and Tippett, J.S. (1965). Self-esteem: clinical assessment and measurement validation. Psychological Reports 16:1017-1071.
347. Silvera, Rachel (2000). "The Enduring Wage Gap – A Europe-Wide Comparison" – in The Gendering of Inequalities: Women, Men and Work, ed. Jane Jenson, Jacqueline Laufer and Margaret Maruani, , Ashgate publishers.
348. Simmons, R., Rosenberg, F. and Rosenberg, M. (1973). Disturbance in the self-image at adolescence. American Sociological Review 38: 553-568.
349. Simon, J.G., & Feather, N.T. (1973). Causal attributions for success and failure at university examinations. Journal of Personality and Social Psychology, 16, 299-310.
350. Singh, (1974). A comparative study of the attitudes of working and non-working women towards women's education and employment in R. Vohra and A.K. Sen (Eds.) Status, Education and Problems of Indian Women.
351. Singh, P. (1979). Occupational Values and Styles of Indian Managers. Wiley Eastern Limited, New Delhi.
352. Sinha, J.B.P. (1976). Authoritative leadership - A style of effective management, Indian Journal of Industrial Relations, 11(3), 381-389. .

353. Sivaji, K. (1999). 'Sanghamitra's Interface with Gram Panchayats' in Decentralised Government and NGOs, Issues, Strategies and Ways Forward, ed. D. Rajasekhar, Concept Publishing Co., New Delhi .

354. Slocum, W.L., & Bowles, R.T. (1968). Attractiveness of occupations to high school students. Personnel and Guidance Journal, 46 (8), 754-761.

355. Snyder, M., Thanke, E.D. and Bershied, E. (1977). Social perception and interpersonal behaviour on the self-fulfilling nature of social stereotypes. Journal of Personality and Social Psychology, 35, 656-666.

356. Soares, A. and Soares, L. (1966). Self-description and adjustment correlates of occupational choice. Journal of Educational Research 60: 27-31.

357. —, (1969). Self-perceptions of culturally disadvantaged children. American Educational Research Journal, 6: 31-45.

358. Soni, I.M. (1971). Married women and Careers, Femina, 20 August, p.27.

359. Sorrentino, R.M. (1973). An extension of theory of achievement motivation to the study of emergent leadership. Journal of Personality and Social Psychology, 26, 356-368.

360. Spence, J.T., Helmreich, R., & Stapp, J. (1975). Like-ability, sex-role congruence of interest and competence: It all depends on how you ask. Journal of Applied Social Psychology, 5, 93-109.

361. and Helmreich, R.L.(1978). Masculinity and feminity: their psychological dimensions, correlates, and antecedents, Austin, Tx: University of Texas Press.

362. Srivastava, V. (1972). Employment of Educated Married Women, Its Causes and Consequences: With Reference to Chandigarh, Ph.D. Thesis in Sociology, Punjab University, Chandigarh.

363. Staines, G., Gutek, B., Pleck, J., Shepard, L., O'Connor, P., & Allen, H. (1979). A study of occupational sex typing. Final report to Department of Labor, Grant No.91-26-76-51.

364. Stake, J.E. (1983). Situation and Person-centered approaches to promoting leadership behaviour in zero performance self-esteem women. Journal of Personality, 51(1), 62-77.

365. Stein, A.H., Pohly, S.R., & Mueller, E. (1975). The influence of masculine, feminine and neutral tasks on children's achievement behavior, expectances of success and attainment values. Child Development, 42, 195-207.

366. Stogdill, R.M., Goode, O.S., & Day, D.R. (1962). New leader behavior description subscales. Journal of Psychology, 54,259.

367. Strache, K. (1976). Personality characteristics of men and women administrators. Paper presented at the annual APA convention, Washington, D.C.

368. Streeten, P. (1998). The Contribution of Non-Governmental Organisations to Development, Political Economy Journal of India, 6(2), 111-121.

369. Sulliven, H.S. (1953). The Interpersonal Theory of Psychiatry, New York: W.W. Norton.

370. Sundaram, K. (2001). Employment-Unemployment Situation in the Nineties: Some Results from NSS 55th Round Survey, Economic and Political Weekly, 17 March, 2001.

371. Super, D. (1957). The Psychology of Careers, New York: Harper & Row.

372. Supreme Court of India: Visakha and Others vs. State of Rajasthan, 1997(6), SCC.

373. Sutton-Smith, B., Crandall, V.J., & Roberts, J.M. (1964). Achievement and strategic competence. Paper presented at the meeting of the Eastern Psychological Association, In Medrick, et al., (Eds.).Women and Achievement - social and motivational analysis. A Halsted Press Book (1975).

374. Suvarachala, G. (1999). 'Empowerment of Gram Panchayat Members, Experiences of Young India Project, Penukonda, Andhra Pradesh', in Decentralised Government and NGOs, Issues, Strategies and Ways Forward, ed. D. Rajasekhar, Concept Publishing Co., New Delhi.

375. Symonds, P.M. (1951). The Ego and the Self. New York: Appleton-Century-Crofts.

376. Tangri, S. (1972). Determinants of occupational role innovation among college women. Journal of Social Issues, 28, 177-199.

377. Tannenbaum, Robert —, Irving R. Weschler, and Fred Massarik, (1959). Leadership and Organisation: A Behavioural Science Approach, New York: McGraw-Hill Book Company.

378. Tannenbaum, Robert, and Warren H. Schmidt (1958). How to choose a leadership pattern, Harvard Business Review (March-April), 95-102.

379. Taylor, D. (1955). Changes in the self-concept without psychotherapy. Journal of Consulting Psychology 19: 205-209.

380. Taylor, Frederick W. (1911). The Principles of Scientific Management. New York: Harper & Brothers.

381. Terborg, J.R., Peters, I. H. and Ilgen, D.R. (1974). The description and validation of questionnaires on attitudes toward women as managers (Unpublished Paper).

382. —, (1977) Women in management: A resesarch review. Journal of Applied Psychology, 62(6), 647-664.

383. Terry, George R. (1960). Principles of Management (3rd ed.) Homewood, Ill.: Richard D. Irwin, Inc.

384. Throop, W.F. and MacDonald, A.P. (1971). Internal-External Locus of Control: A Bibliography. Psychological Reports Monograph. Supplement 1, vol. 28.

385. Tipton, R.M. (1976). Attitudes toward women's roles in society and vocational interests. Journal of Vocational Behavior, B, 155-165.

386. Touhey, J.C. (1974). Effects of additional women professionals on ratings of occupational prestige and desirability. Journal of Personality and Social Psychology, 29(1), 86-89.

387. Trigg, L., & Perlman, D. (1976). Social influences in women's pursuit of a non-traditional career. Psychology of Women Quarter, 1(2), 180-189.

388. Turner, B.F., & McCaffrey, J.H. (1974). Socialization and career orientation among black and white college women. Journal of Vocational Behavior, 55, 307-319.

389. Turner, R. (1968). The self-conception in social interaction, pp.92-106 in C. Gordon and K. Gergen (eds.) The Self in Social Interaction, Volume I, New York: John Wiley.

390. —, and R. Vanderlippe (1958). Self-ideal congruence as an index of adjustment. Journal of Abnormal and Social Psychology 57: 202-206.

391. Tuscano, Alex (1999). 'PRAXIS's Experience in Gram Panchayat Elections' in Decentralised Government and NGOs, Issues, Strategies and Ways Forward, ed. D. Rajasekhar, Concept Publishing Co., New Delhi .

392. UN, United Nations Statistics Division, National Accounts System of National Accounts.

393. UN, (2002). The World's Women 2000: Trends and Statistics (brought up to date till 2002), United Nations.

394. UN, Beijing Declaration, Platform of Action, Critical Areas of Concern, Strategic Objective A.4, 68 (b).

395. UNDP, Human Development Report, 2002, United Nations Development Programme, Oxford University Press.

396. Unni, Jeemol and Uma Rani: "Informal Sector: Women in the Emerging Labour Market", the Indian Journal of Labour Economics, Vol. 42, No. 4, October – December 1999.

397. Varma, A.P., Rehman, M.M. and Chauhan, Poonam S. (1996). Women Labour in India, V. V. Giri National Labour Institute, NOIDA. .

398. Vasanthakumar, Kamla, (1964). Her Emotional Problems, Social Welfare, Vol. II, No.5, 12.

399. Veiga, J.F., & Yanouza, J.N. (1970). What women in management want: The ideal Vs the real. Academy of Management Journal, 19 (1), 137-143.

400. Verma, M. (1964). The study of the middle class working women in Kanpur. The Indian Journal of Social Work, No. XXI, December, p p .283- 286.

401. Verma, N. (1985). Leadership in Interpersonal Perspective, ICSSR Report, New Delhi.

402. Verma, P.C. and Srivastava, B.K. (1983). A study of attitudes of teacher trainees towards women's participation in social activities and professions. Asian Journal of Psychology and Education, 11(1).

403. Veroff, J. (1969). Social comparison and the development of achievement motivation. In C.P. Smith (Ed.), Achievement related motives in children. New York: Russell Sage.

404. Vogel, S.R., Broverman, I.K., Broverman, D.M., Clarkson, F.E., & Rosenkrantz P.S. (1970). Maternal employment and perception of sex roles among college students. Development Psychology, 3(3), 384-391.

405. Walby, S. (1997). Gender Transformations, Routledge, London.

406. Walter, B.W., Schuerger, J.M., and Schwartz, E.B. (1979). Male and female managers: self-concept, success and failure. The Journal of Psychology, 103, 87-94.

407. Webb, W. (1955). Self-evaluation, group evaluations, and objective measures. Journal of consulting psychology 19: 210-212.

408. Weed, S.E. et al., (1976). Leadership style, subordinate personality, task type as predictors of performance and satisfaction with supervision, Journal of Applied Psychology, 61(1) 58-66.

409. Weller, L., Shlomi, A., & Zimont, G. (1976). Birth order, sex and occupational interest. Journal of Vocational Behaviour, 8, 45-50.

410. Wells, L.E., & Marwell, G. (1976). Self-Esteem, Sage Publications, London.

411. Wertheim, E.G., Widom, C.S. & Wortzel, L.H. (1978). Multivariate analysis of male and female professional career choice correlates. Journal of Aplied Psychology, 6 3(2), 234 - 242.

412. Wolfe, L.K., & Betz, N.E. (1981). Traditionality of choice and sex-role identification as moderators of the congruence of occupational choice in college women. Journal of Vocational Behavior, 18, 43-55.
413. Wolters, R., & Bell, R.R. (1977). Some Relationships Between Managerial Value Profiles and Sex, Age, and Supervisory Experiences. Proceedings of Southeastern American Institution for Decision Sciences, February 23-25, 89-90.
414. World Employment Report. (2001). ILO, Geneva.
415. Wylie, R. (1957). Some Relationships Between Defensiveness and Self-concept Discrepancies. Journal of Personality 25: 600-616.
416. —, The Self Concept. Lincoln: University of Netraska Press.
417. Ziller, R. (1969). The Alienation Syndrome: A Triadic Pattern of Self-other Orientation. Sociometry 32: 287-300.

Index